SWEET FIGHTING MAN

BY
MELANIE LLOYD

SPORTSBOOKS

Published by SportsBooks Limited

Copyright
Melanie Lloyd

Cover design by Kath Northam

Photographs supplied by Les Clark

SportsBooks Limited
PO Box 422
Worcester
WR1 1ZT
United Kingdom
Tel: 08700 713 965
Fax: 08700 750 888
e-mail   randall@sportsbooks.ltd.uk
Website   www.sportsbooks.ltd.uk

ISBN 1-899807-15-2

Printed by Biddles Ltd.

CONTENTS

INTRODUCTION

Boxing. It lives in a world all of its own. No sport is more hated and no sport is more loved. There are no shades of grey in this unique territory of the gloved fist. So what is it that makes this 'game' so compelling? How can a simple sport evoke such extreme emotion in so many people? Maybe it is simply a case of human nature that prevails. And that is what boxing is all about at the end of the day, human nature. The shining hero, the adoring fan, the unconditional sacrifices so willingly made, the naked love, the blood and the sweat and the pain, the respect and the dignity and, on occasions, tragedy. This myriad of thought provoking elements work their poignant thread through the very fabric of boxing to produce the fabulous boys and men who soldier on to keep the sport alive today.

Jimmy Tibbs once said, "It takes a special type of person to climb up in that ring, for the real thing. It takes a special type of courage to do that." But for the massive majority of us who are not blessed with that 'special type of courage' the best that we can do is to focus our adoration on those who are. For they are the chosen few. They are the heroes who stride boldly into a dark and fearsome place where lesser men fear to tread.

Most boxing people that I know can remember the moment when the drug first infiltrated their system, be it a fight or a fighter that forced them to sit up and take notice for the very first time. For me it was a fighter. It was Mike Tyson. It was late November 1986 and the fight was for his first world title. In the other corner was Canadian Trevor Berbick. I was at a party and they were showing the fight in the next room. I cannot remember whether it was live or on video. In the second round Tyson suddenly decked Berbick three times – with the same punch! It was a left hook. They say that the flutter of a butterfly's wing can turn into a force ten gale on the other side of the world. I knew absolutely nothing about boxing in those days but for me that left hook was the flap of the butterfly's wing. The resulting hurricane blows right through my heart every time I see two boxers bravely pushing each other to the limits in that square ring, be they amateur or professional, top guys or domestic battlers. And as for Mike Tyson, these days my feelings for this blazing butterfly of sunnier days are heavily tinged with sadness. I only hope that one day he works out what it is he is looking for, so that he can finally lay down his burden.

But moving swiftly along to the book, and most importantly the men who have contributed to it. Sweet Fighting Man is a series of chapters based on personal interviews with British boxers. Each of my 'victims' as I have fondly christened them, gave me his time and his trust, readily and freely. The result has fused into a veritable cocktail of characters and personalities, as colourful as a rainbow. And I am proud to report that each of my subjects has become a friend of mine in one way or another. However, I hasten to add that this is not a sycophantic work written through rose-coloured glasses. Far from it. While each boxer has obviously been 'on his best behaviour,' they have all spoken honestly and candidly about many aspects of their lives.

I have embarked on each chapter by introducing the boxer and along the way I have tried to guide his story efficiently, in some cases more so than others. But most of Sweet Fighting Man comes to you straight from the horses' mouths. The words that really bring this book to life are not mine, but those of the fine human beings who grace the following pages.

It has taken me four years to put Sweet Fighting Man together. Each chapter has been an entire experience in itself. I have conducted interviews in the electric atmosphere of professional boxing gyms and the smoky haze of crowded pubs, in the convivial comfort of cosy front rooms and even in a Leeds car park in the pouring rain. I have been all over the country and I have made some of the finest friends a girl could ever meet. And, perhaps most importantly, I found my second home with the lads at the Foley ABC, where I proudly occupy the positions of Secretary, Press Secretary and General Mother Hen Type Person.

My oldest 'victim' is Johnny McManus who at the tender age of 15 in his amateur days became one of Benny Lynch's sparring partners. Johnny went on to become Scottish lightweight champion in 1944. He never defended his title because the army seconded him to Burma a few weeks later. My youngest is Spencer Oliver, our very own walking miracle, who managed to keep his footing so adeptly when a horrific accident so brutally dragged the rug from beneath his feet. Spencer has now become a symbol of hope for others in his trade and although he will never box again he remains very much involved in the boxing world.

The wise words of Jimmy Tibbs and the strong philosophies of James Cook are complemented by the mischievous humour of Crawford Ashley and the impish charm of Colin Dunne. And it was my greatest privilege to interview the Welsh Wizard himself, Howard Winstone. None of us knew it at the time but that wonderful Welshman would pass away just three weeks after I met him. God bless you Howard. Your memory will live on for ever.

Every fighter I interviewed gave me a born again insight into his sometimes barbed world. I have had plenty of laughs along the way, and I've shed a few tears also. I have learned so much about the boxer's wisdom. His special ability to throw back his head and laugh in the face of situations that would send most of us howling into the night. His patient kindness for the 'boxing experts' who never laced a glove. His love for his fellow fighter that manifests itself in a warm and tight embrace at the final bell, when the fighting is all over. As Colin Lake once told me over a pint or two in a tiny pub in Islington, "The thing is with boxers, there's always a chance that you might meet a bad one, but you'd have to be very unlucky."

I love boxing and I love boxers and I'm proud to say so. This sport has given a sense of discipline, respect and confidence to millions of youngsters all over the world. It has produced some of the finest athletes in history. Beautiful, beautiful boys who have dedicated their lives to boxing, simply because they love to box. And then, when some of them reach a certain age, they turn over into the professional ranks where they must work even harder at their trade, just so that they can remain fit enough to compete, never mind reach the top. Determined to survive in a world that can cut them to ribbons with the blink of an eye. Pounding the lonely miles away in the dawn hours, whatever the weather. Relentless fighting machines who submit themselves to brutal training regimes and harsh periods of self-denial. And all the while most of them know that their chances of ever really making it big are likely to remain both out of reach and out of sight.

I have included an acknowledgement section at the end of the book but before I sign off from this introduction, I would like to take this opportunity to give thanks. Firstly, a massive thank you to all my 'victims,' who are the very essence of this labour of love. And I must not forget several wives, trainers, families and friends who also contributed to various chapters. I would like to thank everybody that helped me to make this book into a living breathing thing.

Also, I want to thank the families and loved ones of all fighters everywhere. These are the people who have given bravely their unconditional love and support to their beautiful, beautiful boys who have chosen to be a part of this often cruel sport.

And finally, I would like to thank every fighter who ever lived, past and present. Thank you all for lighting up my world so sweetly.

This book is dedicated to my mum and dad.

"This may not be totally original but it's the truth. In all the years I've been involved in boxing, Jimmy Tibbs was one of the most dedicated boxers I've ever come across. He should have got so much further than he did." – Mickey Duff

Jimmy Tibbs is one of the most respected men in British boxing today. He started out as a hot light-heavyweight prospect before becoming involved in gang warfare which resulted in his imprisonment in 1972. He was released in 1976 and picked up the pieces of his life as a boxing trainer, going on to work with several world champions. He has also played the starring role in two boxing films. These days he continues his work in the corner and enjoys a renewed life as a born-again Christian.

I met Jimmy for the first time in February 2000 at the Elephant and Castle Leisure Centre. He is a most imposing character. Tall, dynamic, his features deeply etched into a handsome face that breaks out into the brightest of smiles, but only when he finds something genuinely funny. He has brooding green eyes, knowing eyes that have seen so much in their time. His thick dark hair and excellent physical shape belie his age. But don't get too excited girls, Jimmy only has eyes for one lady, his wife Claudette. These two have been together since they were 14 years old. Anyway, that night at the Elephant Jimmy and I had a brief chat and when I tentatively broached the subject of interviewing him he could not have been kinder. And I have to tell you it took me about five hours to wipe the smug grin off my face.

James Edward Tibbs was born in Canning Town in 1946. He has two brothers and a sister. He and Claudette have two sons, Mark, who used to box professionally and Jimmy junior, who for a while was a semi-professional footballer. Both boys have now established themselves in more durable careers. There are three grandchildren, Georgia, James and Olivia. Jimmy and I met for this interview at his work place, the Lennox Lewis College in Hackney.

Jimmy discovered boxing early. "I was about ten years of age and still at primary school. I liked all sports at the time but it was boxing I showed most interest in. My dad took me along to West Ham Boys Boxing Club and I stayed there until I was about 19."

Jimmy had his first amateur bout when he was 11 years old and went on to have more than 70, losing only six. He was schoolboy champion in 1961 and 1962, and Class B NABC champion in 1963. In April 1965 he boxed in the North East London ABA Divisional Championships at West Ham Baths. His opponent in the quarter-finals was one of his clubmates, West Indian born Mortimer Hackett. In the first round Jimmy did not seem to want to hurt Hackett and the referee had to call both boxers together to give them a stern talking to. Jimmy won it on points. He went on to fight Mark Rowe of Fitzroy Lodge in the semi-finals and the *Boxing News* described their fight as: 'one of the best contests amateur boxing could produce.' The 5,000 sell-out crowd were on their feet from beginning to end. Pig farmer Rowe, blonde and handsome, won the bout on points but it was a close one. Jimmy looks back on these days fondly, unconcerned that Rowe was given the decision. "He was 17, I was about 18. I first boxed him when I was about 14 actually and beat him. Now that was a good fight. I beat him comfortably enough on points the first time. He was a tough nut, a good fighter, very strong. When it came to the ABA championships, I won the North/East Divs, Mark Rowe won his side. I drew Mark for the semis. We had such a hard fight, it was a really ferocious fight. Actually, the referee wanted to stop it but it showed favour to me that he didn't. And I went and got beat. It could have gone either way but I'm glad it went to Mark because I couldn't have gone through with it (because of injuries). And I was satisfied with the verdict. I would say that Mark Rowe was the strongest amateur that I ever boxed."

By this stage in his life Jimmy was working in his father's scrap metal business and was once described in the *Boxing News* as 'West Ham's Real Life Steptoe.' He was a prime candidate for the Olympics but it was not to be. Instead, in early 1966, at the age of 19, he turned professional with legendary duo Terry Lawless and Mickey Duff. Lawless did the managing and Duff the promoting.

On the 22nd February 1996 Jimmy made his professional debut, romping home with a second round stoppage over Wigan's Eddie Lennon. The venue was the Albert Hall. "It was great. Boxing was my life. The bigger the crowd, the better the opponent, the better I performed. That was my first fight, I had a good management team behind me and I felt good."

He went on to win his next fight on points against cagey southpaw Joe Somerville, of Berkhampstead, over six rounds on the 1st March 1966 at Bermondsey. Somerville was a well known character around the London rings, well known for turning up with his boxing boots slung over his shoulder, ready to step in at the last minute. You could say he was the equivalent of the journeymen boxers of today.

A month later Jimmy stopped Billy Thompson of Belfast in two. Three weeks later he demolished Tommy Woods in one minute 55 seconds (including the count) at Shore-ditch Town Hall. Even at this early stage in his career Jimmy remembers regularly giving weight away. "Billy Thompson was a big light-heavyweight! You see, where I only weighed 11st 11lbs, all my family were big people. So my management team thought I was going to grow into a heavyweight, and you can't blame them because I thought it as well. I was a big, big middleweight, I could have been a super-middleweight but they didn't have it in those days. So with me boxing as light-heavyweight around about 11-11 or 12 stone two top whack, I was giving weight away all the time. Tommy Woods was a big strong guy, but I caught him with a nice left hook and stopped the fight. And it made it sensational – I learned this from Terry Lawless and Mickey Duff – as he went over, he done the back flip, flipped up again and everyone went crazy, and then bang! He went over again!"

In May 1966 Jimmy boxed Tom Calderwood at Highbury, on the same bill as Muhammad Ali vs Cooper, that memorable night when Cooper unsuccessfully attempted to wrestle the title from Ali (then Cassius Clay) at the Arsenal Football Ground. During the build up to this fight Mickey Duff arranged for Jimmy to spar with Muhammad Ali. "Well as you know, I was managed by Terry Lawless and he and Mickey Duff worked very closely together. I was up and coming, I wouldn't say I was a superstar, because I never ever proved to be one, but I was a good kid. A prospect. So when Ali came over they thought: 'Get Jimmy down for a bit of publicity.' Obviously he never sparred with me properly, but I chapped him with a good left hook and he hit the deck in the second round. I couldn't believe it!" I asked Jimmy if maybe Ali did it on purpose? "Oh yes! Of course he did, but the old cameras were clicking away and it was all good publicity. It worked out well."

Meeting Muhammad Ali meant everything to young Jimmy Tibbs. "I felt very honoured at the time. I was only a young kid, 20 years of age. Today I feel even more honoured because of the way he's gone on and conducted his life, and the way people think of him. I can say I've met that man and I've sparred with him, and I've got the photos to prove it."

There was an estimated crowd of 46,000 in attendance at Highbury that night, the majority of whom were there to support Henry Cooper, of course. But for young Jimmy Tibbs this was his chance to showcase his abilities before the eyes of the rich and famous. In the audience were Rocky Marciano, Ingmar Johansson, Georges Carpentier, Terry Downes and Billy Walker. "I've never met Rocky Marciano but I've met people who have. But I've met all the others you mentioned. Elizabeth Taylor was there, Richard Burton... They were all there."

Of the fight between Jimmy and Calderwood, the tough Glaswegian almost scored a major upset, putting Jimmy down twice in the first round. But Jimmy turned the tables in the second, flooring Calderwood who retired at the end of the round. "I got knocked down twice in the first round. I half slipped the first time, it was half a slip and half a punch. The second time was a punch. I was in control, I wasn't hurt really. I was watching Johnny Kramer fight Johnny Pritchard before I went on and Pritchard was slipping all over the place because it was a bit damp out there. It was open air. So I got a pair of scissors and cut my boots but it didn't help a lot. Anyway, I got up, I was in control. I came out for the second round and I thought: 'I know exactly how to do this geezer. I'm going to let him attack me,' and I opened up and when I stopped him in the second round, Mickey Duff said: 'That's even better, you going down twice and getting up and doing it.'"

A month later Jimmy was back in the ring against Vern Allen at the Albert Hall. Despite a big weight difference, Jimmy proved too good for the Welshman who retired at the end of the fifth. "Actually, I got married on the Sunday and boxed on the Tuesday. I got married first, Terry Lawless and Mickey Duff and everyone was there, then Claudette went home to her mum and I went home to my mum. Then I boxed on the Tuesday and then Claudette and I went home to our house. We got married in St Margaret's Church in Canning Town and had the reception over Woodford." I asked if it was a big do? "Big, yeah, big enough. I remember being driven along in a Rolls Royce, going to the reception and my mate and his girlfriend were waiting at the bus stop. I made the driver stop to give them a lift."

Before 1966 was over Jimmy had three more fights. A tough points win over Hugh Lynch, another against Ernie Field and a second round stoppage over Chris Cox. 1967 arrived and Jimmy was not wasting time. He was back in the ring in January against Johnny Ould at the Albert Hall. This time he was to suffer his first professional defeat, a points loss over eight. I put it to Jimmy that it might have been a case of experience triumphing over youth. "Yes, I would agree with that. There's no use screaming about the weight now, I boxed as a light- heavyweight and I accept I was a light-heavyweight. He beat me fair and square. His experience told. He done things to me, you know, turned me around a little bit, which I couldn't comprehend."

In March 1967 Jimmy stopped Italian Franco Macchia at the Albert Hall. In danger of being stopped because of cuts, Jimmy dug deep to pull out a sixth round stoppage win. A month later he was back in against crafty Frenchman Daniel Leuillier at the Hilton Hotel. Jimmy came out of it with a bruised left hand, battered nose and cut cheek. After another fight in June, a fourth round stoppage of Mahmoud Le Noir at Wembley, Jimmy got in with rock hard Nigerian Guinea Roger at Shoreditch Town Hall. Roger weighed in four pounds heavier but by the time they faced each other in the ring, it is likely that the difference was closer to a stone. He knocked Jimmy out in the second round. "These things do happen, I got caught. He was much, much bigger than me. But I'm not making any excuses. Guinea Roger, I used to spar with him quite regular. I used to handle him quite well. I was second on the bill at Shoreditch and my original opponent fell through. They said: 'Do you want to fight Guinea Roger?' And I said: 'Yeah, no problem.' And I got caught and that was the end of it. I've got no hang-ups about that. I got caught with a good shot. I ducked his right hand and he hit me with a left hook, a good left hook. And after that he went on to knock many of the top contenders out. He went on to do them all."

Jimmy emerged undeterred by this experience . He began 1968 with a third round stoppage of Clive Tranter, who went down eight times before it was over. "It felt good to get in there and start getting my career back again. You see, today a lot of people in this country, they write you off because you've had one loss, which is absolutely ridiculous. It all depends how you lose and who beats you, and how you cope with it afterwards."

Two weeks later Jimmy stopped Nigerian Joe Nwansi at Shoreditch, referee Bill Williams intervening with only 26 seconds of the fight left. Then he had a two year break from boxing. "I sort of got disillusioned with the game, and with myself really. I was a bit disillusioned with everything. Things didn't go the way I thought they would, not from my management team or anything like that, just myself. So I had a bit of a rest." He came back on the 20th January 1970, dropping down to middleweight to stop Ray Hassan in the fourth at the Albert Hall. The game was back on!

In February 1970 Jimmy stopped Bill Deasy in the second round at the Albert Hall. Deasy felt the canvas five times before referee Sid Nathan intervened. Later that month Jimmy stepped up the opposition and went in against hard Johnny Kramer of Canning Town at York Hall. This fight went the distance and there was no doubting that it was a tough one. Referee Sid Nathan scored the fight in Jimmy's favour by three quarters of a point. The pro-Kramer crowd were not happy with the decision and neither was Kramer. Jimmy was eager to have a re-match but this was never to be. If Jimmy Tibbs had continued on the path he had etched out for himself as a fighter he could certainly have gone on to great things in the ring. But sadly his next fight was to be his last.

On the 24th March Jimmy won a re-match against Ray Hassan, stopping him in five at Wembley. Unbeknown to him, he was in the early stages of shingles when he stepped through the ropes. "That's right. I didn't know it at the time. They told me afterwards. I felt a bit run down. But I thought it was just nerves. Anyway, I carried on and afterwards, when I came out of the ring, I didn't think I boxed too well that night and Terry said: 'Well, it's shingles.'"

Jimmy had been set for a re-match against Kramer whose camp were still making big noises about the previous decision, but the shingles prevented this from happening. In May 1970 Jimmy decided that enough was enough. On the 8th May 1970 the *East London Advertiser* issued a report headlined: 'I Quit – Tibbs.' When Jimmy talks about his decision to finally throw the towel in, the sudden flatness of his voice lends impact to his words. "I was just fed up. It's stupid when I look back now, but I was just fed up with the game. It's the same old thing. When you've got something there in the palm of your hands that can make you have everything you need, and then you just push it away. Then years later, when you can't do it, when I got nicked and I was arrested, then you want it back so much, then you are ready to die for it. You don't know what you've lost until it's gone.

"I look back on my fight career with very fond memories. But also it's very sad. I think I let myself down when I look back at what I could have done. But it's no good saying what I could have done, saying I could have been champion, because it never happened. When I look back at the chance that I had and the people that I had looking after me, I wasted it. But the things that I did achieve anyway, I've got very fond memories of them.

"I looked up to a lot of fighters, a lot of American fighters. Don't get me wrong, there were a lot of good fighters in this country at the time, Terry Downes, Henry Cooper, Joe Erskine, all good fighters. And I was a great admirer of Sugar Ray Robinson, and obviously in later times Muhammad Ali, but my favourite, my first idol was Sugar Ray Robinson. He was a great fighter. And Terry Downes is a great friend of mine. See he's a bit older than me, Terry, but I used to look up to him. I used to go to Wembley to watch him and Terry Spinks fighting. I used to go on my own, that's how much I loved boxing."

Jimmy still holds Mickey Duff in the highest regard. "Well, I've had my ups and downs with Mickey. You see, the older you get, when you step back and look at the other side of the game, like training fighters, the more high regard I've got for the people that looked after me. At the time you think, they are just doing their job, and they were doing a good job, I was very happy with what they did, but you don't realise how many head-aches that go along with that job. I've said it before, there will never ever be another Mickey Duff, not while boxing goes on. When he was in control of boxing in this country he could tell you what your opponent had for last year's breakfast!"

Jimmy was certainly caught in a weight trap during his career, too big to be a middleweight, not quite big enough to be a light-heavyweight. He constantly gave away half-a-stone or more. But if looking across the ring to see so many bigger, heavier opponents every bothered him, nobody could have known it. "No, it never frightened me, it was never a fear factor. I don't believe there is a fear factor with any guy that gets in that ring. Maybe nerves, but being nervous is different from being frightened, that's the difference. I don't blame any fighter that gets a little bit nervy. But once you're in there and that first bell goes. Bomp, you're gone!"

In March 1972 Jimmy decided that one more bite of the cherry was in order. At the age of 25 he felt the time was right to return to the ring and make his mark. He announced his plans to return to boxing and began training in earnest. His comeback fight was planned. The opponent was to be Maurice Thomas of Antigua, the venue London's Hilton Hotel. But a few days before the fight was due to happen, the heavy hammer of the law came crashing down to smash his plans to pieces. In April 1972 Jimmy was arrested for various charges related to gang warfare in the East End of London and remanded in custody. A total of 11 other men were eventually arrested. The headlines screamed blue murder, their reports christening the men "The Tibbs Gang," comparing them to the Krays and the Richardsons.

When I was researching this chapter I had to find out exactly what happened during this stage in my subject's life. Obviously, I was viewing Jimmy in a favourable light because, after all, he had agreed to let me interview him. Therefore, in an effort to gain some objectivity I visited the British Newspaper Library to read up on past events. It was an extremely high profile, gangland oriented case. The 12 involved arrived at Old Street Court escorted by three police vans. Inside the courtroom security was strict. No reporters were allowed in without press cards. More than 30 policemen surrounded the dock as the defendants were led in to appear, three at a time, before the magistrate.

Having gone out of my way to see this story from both sides, one must accept that this is a decision that could have gone either way. And yet, I have to say at this point, that according to the *East London Advertiser*, there was certain evidence presented in court that I found difficult to accept, despite my new found, adamant objectivity. One witness, who shall remain nameless for obvious reasons, declared that he was attacked by at least three members of the Tibbs Gang twice in one afternoon with knives and a gun. Not only did he escape both times but was fit enough to drive his car to the police station. I found myself thinking: 'Who is this guy? The Birdman or what?' I read on through the report to discover that this particular witness was currently serving 30 months for theft at the time of giving evidence.

Collectively, the Tibbs Gang faced a total of 34 charges including possession of firearms and attempted murder.

Jimmy, for his part, was sentenced to ten years. "I was arrested in 1972. Things happened in the East End, got out of control. I finished up getting ten years imprisonment. At the time I thought it was the end of my life, never mind boxing. But I got through it. My wife Claudette stood by me, we had two children. I got parole second time out, built the business up. That's when I got involved with Terry Lawless after a few years working back in the scrap metal business." His voice became quiet and reflective with his next words. "I went to prison because I was protecting my family, not because I wanted to be a gangster."

Jimmy was released from Chelmsford prison in 1976. He and his brother returned to their scrapyard. They made a big success of things and were earning a good living for their family. In 1981 the Greater London Council decided to build a road through the yard. The Tibbs boys were paid a substantial amount of compensation and Jimmy decided it was time to try something new. "When I first came out of prison I used to have dreams about being away in training camp, getting ready for a fight. I used to wake up crying. I never, ever thought in a million years that I would be a boxing trainer. I walked into Terry Lawless' gym one day and just happened to talk to him about the yard being shut down by the council. Terry said he was going to America for a couple of weeks. He asked me if I'd mind helping Frank Black. I said: 'Yeah, if it's alright with Frank,' and that was where it started. That was 20 years ago."

And so the Jimmy Tibbs, Boxing Trainer success story, was to blossom. That gym, the Royal Oak in Canning Town, became one of the most respected in England. Nearly every fighter who trained there fought for one title or another, be it British, Commonwealth, European or world. During his career Jimmy has worked with many fighters who have won championships at all levels. His success story include the likes of Charlie Magri, Mark Kaylor, Lloyd Honeyghan, Frank Bruno, Nigel Benn, Gary Stretch, Terry Marsh, Tony Sibson, and Barry McGuigan, to name but a few. To write about his relationship with every fighter he has trained would take volumes so I have focused on a few specific ones.

One of the most famous boxers to emerge from the Royal Oak stable is Frank Bruno. In his book, published in 1986, Bruno referred to himself, Lawless, Black and Tibbs as the 'A' Team. The 'A' is for 'Appy.' Bruno wrote, "The trainer who works most with me is Jimmy Tibbs... There is 'the Tibbs touch' to nearly everything I do in the ring, and I will always be grateful to him for all the effort he has put in to make me a more formidable fighter." Jimmy and Frank are still good friends today.

The last fight Jimmy worked with Terry Lawless was Frank Bruno's challenge to awesome American Tim Witherspoon in July 1986 at Wembley Stadium. That night Bruno's bravery was never in question but the American was to win the fight in the 11th round. Jimmy was sad to see the fight end as it did. "Well, you get hardened to it. But he done a great job Frank. Up until about the seventh or eighth round he was in front. But then he got a little bit weary and Witherspoon gradually wore him down with body shots. After it was stopped, we all rushed in there. We all tried to cradle him a little bit." After this fight, Jimmy, for purely business reasons, moved on and began working with Frank Warren.

Moving down the line of Tibbs' success stories I have to mention London middleweight Mark Kaylor. Kaylor was one of the most exciting fighters to hail from these shores. British fight fans idolised him. They would clamber close to him at any opportunity to touch him, to smear his sweat on their faces, as if some of his magic would rub off on them. All the boys wanted to be him and all the girls wanted to be with him. Kaylor would never become world champion but his career was still extraordinary. The reason that he is so relevant to this story is that his trainer, and best friend, was one Jimmy Tibbs.

Any boxing trainer, amateur or professional, will tell you that it is radically wrong to have 'favourites' but the relationship between Jimmy Tibbs and Mark Kaylor was something else. "I was very close with Mark. It wasn't any more special in the ring or in the gym than with anyone else. But it was a relationship that went outside of the ring. But once I was in that gym he was no different to anyone else."

My two personal favourite Kaylor fights are the ones against Roy Gumbs and Tony Sibson. Kaylor challenged Gumbs for his British and Commonwealth middleweight titles when he was 23. Gumbs was a massive middleweight, unbeaten over five years and on the verge of a world title shot. He was generally thought to know too much for the relatively inexperienced West Ham hero. Kaylor wanted those titles. Predominantly a fighter, that night Kaylor surprised everybody by completely outboxing Gumbs, but the Tottenham man did not hand his titles over on a plate. These two hard men were at their ferocious best that night. In the fourth, Gumbs caught Kaylor with a right hand to the temple, turning his legs to rubber before shoving him down with his left forearm. Kaylor got up at eight and forced Gumbs back into a corner, fighting on sheer instinct. He came blazing out for the fifth to batter the champion into submission. Jimmy, who worked the corner that night with Terry Lawless and Frank Black, was delighted. "Oh yes. I was over the moon for the kid. Because it was all against him. Roy Gumbs, the bigger man, even though they was both middleweights, he was the bigger man, more mature. I was thinking maybe it's come a little bit too early. But to give Terry Lawless his due, he knew how to pick 'em when they were ripe, and he caught Gumbs on the right night. It was a great win, and everyone in the camp was happy."

A year later Kaylor fought Tony Sibson for the European title. It was a battle of sheer wills that went the 12 round distance. Sibson was rightfully awarded the decision but it was one of those fights when it was a shame there had to be a winner or a loser. In the final round before the climax Kaylor, who was standing and staring at Sibbo, just spat his gum shield out, marched forward and went for it. What a fight! Jimmy agrees that it was an exciting one. "But he got beat fair and square that night though. Tony Sibson was a little bit too experienced for him. But let me tell you something. Kaylor done a marvellous thing that night, even in defeat. He had just come off a knockout by Buster Drayton, and then he has a 12 round defeat by Tony Sibson. And he was a very, very good fighter Tony Sibson. He was experienced. He was one of the best middleweights this country has ever had. He could do everything. He could box, punch, he knew how to kid, good jab, a great fighter. I was at the Albert Hall the night Tony Sibson won the middleweight title when he 21 years of age. A marvellous feat. Out of this world!"

Mark Kaylor's career came to an end in June 1991 when he challenged James Cook for the European super-middleweight title. Back in the eighties, when Kaylor was at his best, Cook had been one of his hired sparring partners. Now the boot was on the other foot. Kaylor, who had once been right up there, was now struggling to make his way back. Cook had reached the highs of European champion. The apprentice was now the master. Jimmy stopped the fight in the sixth round. "Well, it was a chance for Mark to earn a few quid, and at the same time win the European title. I was looking after his affairs then, he wasn't contracted to anyone else so he asked me to do it. We got the European title fight and I always knew it was going to very, very hard for Mark because he wasn't the Kaylor that he used to be, whereas James Cook was still coming up, firing away. I had in my mind to give him three or four rounds, see how he goes, but he lasted longer than that. But in the fifth round I said to Dean Powell: 'I'm going to pull him out in the next round.' But, I didn't want to pull him out in the corner because the fans were all a bit excited. They were all Mark Kaylor fans, and this was in York Hall, a small venue, so I let it go. And then, in the sixth, I done something that I shouldn't have done really. I chucked the towel in and then I got in and stopped it myself. I apologised to the referee afterwards because it was the wrong thing to do, but I wanted it to be stopped. Mark was so sick that I stopped it, he was going off at me. But after a few minutes he came round and he said: 'Thanks Jim, I'm knackered.' And I knew that he was.

"And all the fans were going off and it was turning into a big riot, and I stopped that. I don't know how I stopped it really, it was a miracle! I was just going to do an interview on TV and I saw my two sons getting involved and one thing led to another and I thought: 'This is going to go all off here.' So I jumped up onto some chairs and said 'You stop that' and they all stopped! Then it all calmed down and it all worked out alright." Mark Kaylor still lives in America. He and Jimmy keep in touch by telephone and Jimmy's affection for Kaylor shines through when he speaks about him.

One of the hardest jobs that Jimmy has ever done is train his own son, Mark Tibbs, who was a strong super-featherweight prospect in the late eighties, early nineties. Mark, like his father, turned professional at the age of 19. He made his debut against Mike Chapman of Llanelli in November 1988. Mark was announced the points winner. Jimmy, bursting with pride, tried so hard to play it down in front of the cameras during a post-fight interview but as he stood there alongside his son, he found it hard to maintain a neutral expression. In fact, his face broke out into the broadest of grins which lasted for the last 20 seconds of the interview. However, Jimmy is quick to admit that there were times during Mark's career that he was extremely over critical of him. "Well, I wasn't a Christian then. And you see with Mark, when he turned pro, I wanted him to do so well, not just for himself, but for me as well if I want to be totally honest. I used to ask him to do a certain thing and he used to do it to perfection. And I used to go in and I used to bollock him. Pat Clinton came up to me one day, the world champion I was training at the time, and he said: 'Jim, don't think I'm poking my nose in but you're too hard on that boy.' And I looked across at Mark and I thought: 'I love that boy and I know I'm too hard on him.' And then when I became a Christian I learned to relax a bit, and I changed. I wasn't so hard on him. And it didn't matter if he got beat. I mean obviously, I didn't want him to get beat, but it didn't matter so much any more." Mark finished his boxing career in March 1994. He had a 25 fight record, 22 wins with two losses and one draw.

Seeing Jimmy and his son together, two generations of fighters, prompted me to ask Jimmy if he felt things were harder in his day. "No, there was less medical stuff going for us obviously, and the gloves were a lot lighter, everyone wore 6oz gloves. But I never used to take a lot of stick. I knew lots of fighters who didn't take a lot of stick. Because the game has got a lot stricter safety wise, it doesn't mean the fighters are taking less stick. I tried to take as little as possible, but you know, sometimes you get caught and that's that at the end of the day."

Boxing has moved on and Jimmy Tibbs is a realist who believes that you have to move with the times. "Yes it is a lot different. I wouldn't say it was better but it's different. They've got all this razzamatazz, and you've got to move along with the times whether you like it or not. Years ago when I was boxing it was the fanfare and the genuine fans, but now you've got the likes of your Prince Nazeem fighting, who is a great fighter in my eyes. He's drawn a lot of youngsters to the game, and most of them come just to see his entrance! I was watching the one when he came out on the carpet and it was marvellous to look at. They were all just traumatised, watching him. I believe that those type of kids wouldn't have come years ago when I was boxing. I couldn't have drawn that kind of public. Nazeem has been marvellous for the game. Like Chris Eubank. When he was on ITV when he fought Nigel Benn, sixteen million viewers switched on to watch it. Nazeem is in the same class as Eubank, if not better, but they've bought it down to Sky. Sky have bought up all the rights so there are not as many viewers because not everybody has got Sky TV. But what I'm saying is that the audience that they draw today, there is more show business involved in it with all your entrances."

Another string to the Jimmy Tibbs bow is a talent as an actor. He has played the leading role in two successful films and Jimmy is, in fact, as comfortable as he looks in front of the camera. "I just do it natural, I don't feel under pressure." His first project was *Fighters*, a documentary made for Channel Four in 1993. Written and directed by Ron Peck, this thought provoking film catches the very essence of the electric atmosphere generated in boxing gyms all over the world. Among the principal boys in the film are the late Bradley Stone, Jimmy Flint, Mark Kaylor and Mark Tibbs. Ron Peck captures the boxers' relationship with their trainer beautifully. He describes the boxer as being "a man many find frightening and do not want to know. Jimmy knows that man to be there, has trained him out of the darkness and into the blazing lights of the ring."

A major player in *Fighters* is Jimmy Flint, who fought at lightweight in the seventies. Flint talks to Ron Peck about his fighting days with venom. "If they hit me I like to be hit. Its all a part of the game. I sap the strength out of them when they hit me. And I bash them back." Flint, a professional actor, also played a major role in Jimmy's second film, *Real Money*, a drama filmed in 1996 and another Ron Peck project. All parts were played by boxers and boxing people. Flint plays a drug dealing porn merchant, quite frankly not a very nice chap to know. Tibbs plays an East End boxing trainer. The action mushrooms into a ferocious showdown between the two Jimmys, at the end of which Tibbs' two heavies drag him from a boxing gym before he kills Flint, having already smashed him across the face with the butt of a gun. Jimmy laughs heartily as he remembers, "Yes, that took about ten takes. My mates had a job dragging me out because I was making them work, I kept dragging them back in. They was going: 'Jim! Don't put up such a fight! And I was doing it on purpose. It was good, because I come off of Jim (Flint) there. Because he's a professional actor, Jimmy. If someone's done something more than you and they're pretty good at it, which Jim is, with his experience I was led by him, you know what I mean? Yes, Jimmy Flint did help me a lot."

In the early nineties something major happened to Jimmy Tibbs which changed his life for ever. He became a born-again Christian. It all started when an old school friend told him that one of their friends, Benny Stafford, had become a born-again Christian. Jimmy asked, "what's that then?" and his friend replied, "I dunno". Jimmy declared "Well, if it keeps him off the booze it will do him good!" Later on down the line, Jimmy's and Benny's paths were to cross and with Benny's help, Jimmy found his way to one of the deepest faiths I have encountered. When he talks about God it's as if he's talking about his best mate, somebody he really admires. He speaks about his faith naturally and, at times, with gentle humour. There is nothing false or forced about his quiet confidence that God is always with him. But he is emphatic that he should not be viewed as religious. "Well I'm not religious actually. I follow Jesus and it's nothing to do with religion. It's purely out and out faith in Jesus Christ. In my eyes, religious people are people who have got to do this and have got to do that. I haven't got to do anything. All Jesus has asked me to do is believe in him, and then you'll actually want to do the things that he wants you do. But I don't get the hump with people who say I'm religious because most people don't know any different.

"You have got to make the decision to follow God for yourself, whether you be ten, 20, 30, 40, 60, whatever. And you've got to mean it with your heart. It's a heart thing. I didn't make the commitment straight away, but the feeling wouldn't leave me. And I thought: 'I'm not cracking up, I know what I'm doing.' I was handling people's careers! Since the day I made that commitment it ain't been all roses. I still have to come down the gym, I still have to work, I still have to go up north to the fights... But it's turned my life around in the way that I know there really is a God. And I know that when I die I'm going to be saved, because he died for me. That's why I go around the country to talk to people. I went to the Brecon Valleys one day, to tell them about Jesus. Four hundred miles I drove, there and back, to tell them about Jesus.

"A lot of people think: 'If I become a Christian it will ruin my life, I won't be able to have a drink, I won't be able to do this, I won't be able to do that.' I still have a drink. Of course I do! I love to go out and have a drink with my dad on Thursdays. In fact, sometimes I get so excited I can't sleep Wednesday nights!

"When I first turned to God he didn't go: 'right Jimmy, I've been waiting 44 years for you and I'm going to do you now!' He'll give you a better life, a fuller life. God acts in different ways. You can't work God out. When you try and put God in a box, then he ain't God no more. There is nothing impossible for God. But you mustn't analyse things too much. You have to keep it simple. I don't want to work God out, it will start doing my brain in. I accept him. I've never seen him but I know he's there.

"Don't get me wrong, ever since I made that commitment, don't think I haven't sinned since. Of course I have. I've tried to sin less, but it's hard work so I leave it to the Lord and I don't keep putting myself down. I'm not saying I'm a better person than you, or any of those boys out there, but it's turned my life around. It's made me feel so contented. Before I became born-again I was always worrying about getting more money, more money. Money buys power. Don't get me wrong, money helps. Of course it does. It's common sense. When you start saying 'I'm a born again Christian and I don't need money,' that's when people think you are cracking up.

"I believe in Jesus. He's my mate! When I get in a bit of trouble I think: 'Right, what are we going to do?' Not: 'What am I going to do?' We are in this together. And I do it every day, I talk to him every day. There is not a day goes by...''

And so our brief glimpse into the life of Jimmy Tibbs comes to an end. And I, for one, feel so much richer for the experience. For here is a man who has seen so much and inspired so many. A man who has not only danced and paid the piper, but starred in his own movies. And along the way, he discovered the kind of faith and inner peace that too many people can only dream of. And there is still more to come. What a man!

"Steve Robinson. They are realising now what a great little fighter Steve Robinson is. It takes a good kid to beat John Davidson." – John Davidson

At the age of 24 Steve Robinson was a professional boxer, prepared to travel anywhere and fight anybody, simply to earn a decent purse. Early in his boxing career he had grown to expect no favours. In April 1993, his luck changed dramatically when his manager Dai Gardiner secured him the chance of a lifetime. Two days later Steve Robinson was world featherweight champion. His reign lasted until September 1995. During that time he made seven successful defences, winning four of them inside the distance. Because of the rags to riches nature of his story they called Steve 'The Cinderella Man,' an accolade bestowed decades earlier upon a tough American heavyweight named James J. Braddock.

It had been such a long time since Wales had been able to boast of a boxing hero and when Steve brought home the cherished prize of a world title he became the perfect ambassador, not only for Wales but for boxing. His polite modesty, his diligence and dedication made him a very popular man. I remember the night Steve won his world title. I have lived in England for many years but I was born and bred in Swansea so, being Welsh and all, I was one of the huge army of fans who got right behind him. In those days I was a big boxing fan, but not as deeply involved in the sport as I am now. So I used to go down the pub to watch Steve's fights on the television. He was never a flamboyant superstar who demanded the red carpet treatment, but that was a big part of his charm. His solid, meat and two veg style of boxing appealed to the purists and he came across as one of the good guys. His fairy tale story warmed the hearts of millions and my English counterparts used to describe him as, 'That nice black kid from Cardiff.' They were almost as enthusiastic about Steve's success as I was... almost.

The night Steve lost his world title to Nazeem Hamed I stood in the pub and cried openly while the Sheffield puncher tore my hero apart. My English friends, and some Irish pals also, stood around me and comforted me in my sorrow. Little did I know that woeful night that a few years later I would be sitting alone with Steve interviewing him for this book. A few months after our first meeting, I was given a second bite of the cherry. This time Steve's trainer, manager and friend Dai Gardiner was present. Dai's views and opinions are also included in the following chapter.

I met Steve for the first time in June 1999 in his hometown of Cardiff, where he still lives today with his family. Steve was my very first 'victim' and as I sat waiting in the reception area of Cannons Heath Club in Splott I felt very nervous. He walked in at our designated meeting time of 11 o'clock exactly. He was bigger than I thought he would be, a few inches taller than me in heels, his superbly conditioned body radiated fitness. He has strong black features and massive charcoal eyes that twinkled warmly as he said hello and shook my hand. His characteristically calm manner rapidly put me at ease and we were soon sitting together over a soft drink, having a good old chinwag.

The early years:

"I was born in Cardiff on the 13th December 1968. I've got one brother, three half brothers, one sister and one half-sister. We grew up together. I was about nine years old when I started boxing. My older brother Paul was into it. He's about five years older than me and I started because of him. He took me along to the Ely Star boxing club and I never looked back."

The trainer at Ely Star was Ronnie Rush, a thick set gentleman, bald of head and wide of smile. "He was a big influence in my career, Ronnie was." Rush coached Steve through 14 junior amateur bouts. "Then I went through a stage when I was about 12 or 13 and you know, I was a teenager. I was on the streets. I just lost interest you know. I gave up the game for about five or six years. I got back into it when I was about 18 or 19."

Becoming a professional boxer:

Steve returned to Rush's gym and told him that he wanted to become a professional fighter. Rush insisted that Steve went out and got some more amateur experience and Steve proceeded to fight eight senior bouts in nine weeks. One of the most important things that Rush fanatically instilled into Steve's mind was that fitness came before everything. This fundamental lesson has always remained with him and he has maintained his supreme physical condition to this day. "These days I love running. I run for five or six miles every day. It keeps the legs nice and strong and it really pays off." Mind you, it was not always this way. In the beginning Steve, like many young boxers, was reluctant to get out of his warm bed early in the mornings to put in miles of road work. Rush, however, was not having any of it and regularly dragged him out of bed, deaf to any feeble excuses. "When I first started training I was weak to the body. I wasn't fit then and I used to get hurt with the body punches and I used to double up. Ronnie worked on my body, strengthened it up. It's solid now, six pack!" Steve gestured proudly to his rock hard body region with a big smile.

The winning team:

In 1989 Steve applied for his professional boxing licence. The body was fit. The mind was set. The time had come to bite the bullet. Apart from Rush, Steve's team consisted of trainers Pat Chidgey and Gary Thomas and most importantly, manager and trainer Dai Gardiner.

Dai, an ex-miner born in a small village in the Rhymney Valley in South Wales, has lived in Cefn Hengoed for more than 50 years and he has been involved in boxing all his life. He won the 1962 Welsh ABA lightweight title and won several international vests. He turned professional under Eddie Thomas and trained and sparred with Howard Winstone. One day while sparring with 'The Welsh Wizard' the top rope snapped and Dai fell out of the ring and broke his back. He spent seven weeks in hospital and he never boxed again. Dai told me, "Me and Steve have been together for years now. Ronnie Rush bought him to my gym and I'd been watching him box as an amateur. I remember one time he got disqualified, I was annoyed about that. He had a couple of bad decisions against him. I told him, 'you might as well box for money.' But it was going to take a while because he hadn't had no experience.

We are very close. Steve is a very capable man who takes his responsibilities seriously." Steve told me "Dai really cares. He thinks highly of me and I respect him."

The family man:

1989 was also the year that Steve met his future wife Angela. Their union produced three children, two sons Luke and Jacob and a daughter Ebony. "When you've got kids it gives you more determination. When Luke was born I thought to myself, 'I've got nowhere to go really.' I had no education, no qualifications or anything like that. The only thing I had was my boxing so I worked hard. My wife Angela has been one of the most important influences in my life. She has always given me the strength to keep on going."

Learning the hard way:

Steve had his first professional fight on the St David's Day (1st March) 1989. It was in Cardiff against Alan Roberts and Steve won on points over six rounds. Less than two weeks later he stopped Terry Smith in four at Piccadilly. His first year as a professional was a busy one with six fights, winning four. But as time went by he became more of an opponent than a prospect and he became resigned to that fact. His first prominently controversial loss came in October 1990 when he boxed Drew Docherty at Solihull. Docherty's hand was raised at the end of the fight but there was plenty of room for doubt. One of Britain's top journeymen boxed on that bill. His name is Peter Buckley and he has his own chapter in this book. Peter told me, "He come up the hard way Steve did. I remember watching him box Drew Docherty on a bill I was on at Solihull. I can't remember who I boxed on there, but everybody in the place thought Steve won it. And Drew Docherty got it by half-a-point and nobody could believe it because Steve beat him out of sight. But he's another kid who deserved everything he got, because he done it the hard way."

Dai Gardiner remembers those early days, "To be honest he survived really. For the first 18 months Steve was a good pro and then he changed. He boxed a boy up Canvey Island (Mark Bates, 10th July 1990). I remember he changed in a caravan. It wasn't happening for him that night and he lost on points but he was still there at the final bell. And I knew then that I could do something with him. Because he persevered. And some of the defeats he's had, he's won really, but he's had to accept them. And then he came back to win the world title."

Realising the dream:

On the 18th July 1991, after 15 fights, eight wins, six losses and one draw, and two and a half years and blood, sweat and toil Steve won his first title. He defeated Peter Harris over ten tough rounds in Cardiff to become the Welsh featherweight champion. On the 19th January 1993, after two more losses and three more wins, Steve won his next title, the WBA Penta-Continental featherweight crown against Paul Harvey in Cardiff. This was the beginning of an incredible year.

The big chance:

On the 17th April 1993 Ruben Palacio was due to fight Geordie southpaw John

Davidson for the vacant WBO featherweight title. Two days earlier Dai Gardiner was in a meeting with Barry Hearn at the Waldorf Hotel in London when the phone rang with the news that Palacio had tested HIV positive. Dai told me, "I was actually there to negotiate a world title fight for Robbie Regan. The call came through that Palacio had failed the test. The next thing they're ringing around trying to get a late substitute. They were thinking of a Mexican fighter. I was sitting there and I thought, 'why not let Steve have a go?' I suggested it and that was that."

Steve remembered the big surprise. "That night I had a phone call from Ronnie just after I'd finished pie and chips! I was up my mother-in-law's I was, and I had just finished off pie and chips and a bit of bread like, and the next minute I got a phone call and Ronnie said, 'You've got a big fight coming up.' I said, 'when's that?' He said, 'in two days time. It's a world title fight.' I said, 'two days time? I haven't got time to train for that.' He said, 'oh you're fit enough, you're a naturally fit person anyway. It's a shot. It's a chance for you. You haven't got nothing to do lose.' So I thought, 'alright. Why not?' My wife Angela, I wasn't married to her at the time, she said to me, 'you must be crazy. You're mad, going up there to fight for the world title.' I said, 'well, I've got the chance and I've got nothing to lose.' It was amazing when it happened though."

The big build-up:

So Steve packed his bags and travelled to the North East for the fight of his life. "For the next two days all sorts of things were going through my mind. Because when I knew about the fight I was about six pounds over the weight at the time, so I had to train and sweat it off. The weight came off easy because I'm a natural featherweight anyway. And then, the weigh-in was on the day of the fight as well."

The big fight:

Fight night arrived. On the 17th April 1993 Steve walked down the gangway to the ring in the Northumbria Centre; the crowd were ferocious in their support of Davidson, their deafening roar bouncing off the low ceiling. But Steve had faced many hostile crowds during his early years as a professional fighter. To him this was just another night's work. "I just kept my mind on the fight you know. At the end of the day, it was just me and him." As Steve, Dai and Ronnie stood in their corner staring over at Davidson's corner, the massive noise of the partisan crowd bore down on them from every direction. Dai tore his steely gaze away from the opposition for a few seconds to give Steve a reassuring little smile. "Steve's a professional. A lot of people can say this and say that but they can swallow it when they see that big crowd. Steve would never swallow. He's had so much experience of fighting them in their own back yard, he just goes for it in the first round. And that's very, very unusual." The bell went and from the first round Steve's boxing was clean and sound, his attitude cool and his defence virtually impregnable. As wily Davidson tried to draw the young outsider into a fight, Steve calmly weighed up his style and boxed him perfectly. As Steve fought he had a smile on his face as he often did when he was boxing. There was nothing malicious about this. It was actually a smile of happiness because he was doing exactly what he liked best. By contrast, Davidson appeared to visibly age as the fight progressed. Then suddenly in the eighth round...

"A week before the fight I had been suffering from cramp in my calf muscle. And it was starting to go again in the fight. And see, the first seven rounds I was beating Davidson every single round, easy. But then all of a sudden it went again and my mobility was cut down a bit." Dai told me, "He came back to the corner and said it was gone. We hid it with towels while we worked furiously on it." Steve battled through the pain barrier and the ninth round was spent mainly in a toe-to-toe exchange of hard body punches. At the end of the tenth, Steve looked exhausted as he sat in his corner with his head down. "He was a very strong fighter. So I'd had to more or less box him. Because I wasn't as strong then as I am now. And all of a sudden the cramps came and he was starting to catch up with me. He was throwing his body shots. He was a good infighter and he hurt me a few times to the body. So all of a sudden I just had to dig deep and mix it with him." The bell went for the 12th and final round and the fighters battled through their exhaustion before Steve came on with a ferocious two-handed attack, actually knocking Davidson's gum shield out in the process. Davidson held on and the final bell sounded. They announced a split decision. While the scores were being announced Dai affectionately put a protective arm around Steve's shoulders. Dai remembers the agony of waiting, as if it were yesterday. "Although I knew we had well won the fight, when they announced a split decision I thought it was going to be another home-town verdict. I can't begin to tell you what it was like. That five seconds was the longest of my life." Then they announced that Steve was the winner. Jubilant elation swept through the Robinson corner. Steve could not believe it. "Normally what happens is, I beat the guy in his home town and the next minute I don't get the verdict. So when they said, 'Robinson, champion' it was like a dream come true! And then they put my hand up, and it was brilliant."

Going home:

Steve grinned widely as he remembered, "We went home on the coach that night. It took us about five hours from Newcastle. It was a long trip and I enjoyed every minute of it. I was on a high. I had to pinch myself. I was world champion. Because it come so quick, you know. Two days!"

Defending the throne:

Steve defended his WBO title for the first time on the 10th July 1993 in Cardiff's National Ice Rink. In the other corner was tough, aggressive, hard hitting Sean Murphy. It was a battle of strength and wills and in the ninth round Steve knocked Murphy down and he did not make the count. After this first defence, Steve's hairdresser suggested he have a small stripe etched into his closely cropped hair to mark the occasion. Steve kept the tradition going throughout his championship reign and as the victories piled up people began to wonder if he would end up totally bald.

Next defence was against Colin McMillan in October 1993 at the Cardiff Ice Rink. World champion or not, Steve was still driving around in his second-hand Rover which broke down on the way to the weigh-in ceremony. Despite the fact that Steve was the champion,

McMillan was the favourite to win. But nobody appeared to have told the massive crowd this and they chanted "Stevo, Stevo" and proudly sang the Welsh national anthem. Steve's strength won the day and a unanimous points decision. "I met Colin McMillan a couple of times and he's alright. He's a very nice guy outside the ring. Very respectful."

Next in line was former WBC featherweight champion Paul Hodkinson from Liverpool. Steve defended against him on the 12th March 1994. This was Steve's first fight for Frank Warren. He had already signed a contract to fight three defences of his title for Barry Hearn and Tommy Gilmour, the first reportedly for £35,000, the second £65,000 and the third for £75,000. Having fulfilled the first two options, it was reported that Frank Warren had offered Steve more for the Hodkinson fight. Steve took him up on the offer, a decision that he would later sorely regret.

Steve's fight against Paul Hodkinson was one of the greatest performances of his career. That fight will remain in the memory of all boxing fans who witnessed it. It is one of Steve's personal favourites. "It's got to be hasn't it? It was a classic, boxer against box-fighter more or less. And what it was, I was supposed to be the underdog and I don't know, I was quite frightened really, because it was a big fight for me. That fight raised my standards really, made me fight better. His style suited me as well."

As Steve bounced up and down in his corner awaiting the first bell he seemed concerned only with the fight ahead, oblivious to the deafening roar of a crowd that adored him. For by now he had become a local hero, a people's champion but as chants of "Robbo, Robbo" reverberated around the Cardiff Ice Rink his facial expression was one of quiet determination, his dark eyes reflecting complete focus, no different to that of his earlier, small hall fights. The fight started and continued at a rapid pace, neither man prepared to back down. Hodkinson marched forward while Steve covered up, and then Steve would retaliate with powerful clusters of shots, forcing Hodkinson onto the back foot. The deafening crowd went mad as the fighters stood toe-to-toe in the centre of the ring in the fourth. In the fifth, Steve caught Hodkinson with a peachy right to the head and the Liverpudlian wilted at the knees as Steve unloaded with both hands. Miraculously, Hodkinson came back seconds later to again stand toe-to-toe with Steve in the ring centre once more.

Reg Gutteridge was commentating at ringside and declared, "This is going to be the survival of the fittest, and the bravest." Never a truer word spoken. The battle continued and Hodkinson attacked and Steve replied, each pushing each other back and fore to the ropes, pushing each other to the limits. In the 12th and final round, as Hodkinson marched forward, Steve caught him with a right hand to the head and followed up with a flurry of leather that battered the Liverpool fighter to the canvas. Hodkinson courageously dragged himself up from the floor and there were gasps of disbelief when referee Dave Parris allowed the fight to continue. But seconds later Hodkinson went down again. This time, he sat on the canvas with his back leaning against the ropes, and he remained there looking dazed and bewildered. Hodkinson was marvellously brave that night. He gave it everything he had. Incidentally, this fight won the award for 'Fight of the Year' at the 1994 British Boxing Awards dinner. Steve smiled fondly at the memory. "Yes, that's it yes." I asked if he was pleased to see his old adversary again. "He didn't turn up."

On the 4th June 1994 Steve defended his title for the fourth time, against Freddy Cruz at Cardiff Ice Rink. The 32-year-old veteran from the Dominican Republic had seen his fair share of fights, winning 43 out of 53, and had never been stopped. Meanwhile, word of Steve's talent had travelled across the Atlantic and WBC champion Kevin Kelly had recently declared that he would happily come over to Wales to fight him. Steve won a unanimous points decision against Cruz. At ringside was Nazeem Hamed.

Shortly after this victory, the newly formed Professional Boxers Association held it's first Awards dinner. Steve was voted 'Fighter of the Year.' The competition included Nigel Benn and Lennox Lewis.

Four months later Steve defended against reigning British featherweight champion Duke McKenzie at Cardiff Ice Rink. This was the first time Steve had been ranked the clear favourite but nobody said it was going to be easy. In December 1993 McKenzie, former three-time world champion at two different weights, destroyed John Davidson in four rounds for the British featherweight title, and of course Davidson had gone the distance with Steve, losing their world title fight on a split decision. McKenzie had fought and beaten men such as Charlie Magri and Jesse Benavides, at a time when McKenzie himself was considered the underdog. Taking Steve's title would make him Britain's first four-time world champion and he wanted it, badly. Before the fight Dai Gardiner declared, "we'll be taking nothing for granted, it will just make Steve train harder." At this, Steve's fifth defence of his world title, the atmosphere was electric, the crowd in full force, drowning out Steve's introduction with their roar. The bell went, the fight started and it was not pretty to watch. McKenzie got warned for a low blow in the first and there was a bit of animosity between the two at the end of the round. The fight went on and McKenzie, feeling Steve's superior strength, held on, making the fight look very untidy and drawing loud protests from the crowd. McKenzie kept very much in Steve's face, frustrating the champion by using spoiling tactics. In the eighth, referee Roy Francis deducted a point from McKenzie for holding, to the jubilation of the crowd. Twenty seconds before the end of the ninth round, Steve finished it with a short left hook to the body. Duke floated down to the canvas like a tent with no poles in it. Afterwards the Croydon boxer told the press, 'It was a great punch and there was sweet FA I could do about it." Steve told me, "well, it's always a bonus to knock someone out but my style is pressure and break them up. But I know I can punch harder to the body. I'm a very heavy body puncher because I've knocked a few people out with one punch to the body. That one was a short punch to the ribs. And he made it awkward for me you know." After the fight the two boxers embraced warmly.

As Steve's career soared, awards came in bundles. In November 1994, aside from the award for the Hodkinson fight, he was also named 'Boxer of the Year' at the British

Boxing Awards dinner. The same month he was awarded The Dave Crowley Memorial Belt for 'Best Boxer of the Year' by the London Ex-Boxers Association. As well, in November, Steve was invited to the Rhondda Sports Centre to celebrate Tommy Farr's inauguration to the Rhondda Hall of Fame. Steve accepted a posthumous award on Tommy's behalf. And to round off the year, BBC Wales voted Steve '1994 Sports Personality of the Year.' This award was presented to him by Howard Winstone, who had won it three times himself.

But, as Steve basked in the sunshine of his success, an angry cloud loomed ominously on the horizon in the shape of Nazeem Hamed. The Sheffield boxer was baying at the door, making big noises about taking Steve's title away. By the beginning of 1995 Naz was a regular spectator at Steve's fights, perched hungrily at ringside. "Yes. He seemed to pop up from nowhere."

Steve was by now deeply locked into the legal battle with Barry Hearn and Tommy Gilmour that had arisen from the move to Frank Warren. If things went against him he stood to lose at least £200,000. With these tensions taking their toll, Steve stepped into the ring at the Ice Rink on the 4th February 1995 to defend his title for the sixth time against Argentine tough guy Domingo Damigella. Steve won a clear points decision, but, as they were waiting for it to be announced, he looked right on the edge emotionally, the claws of his troubles digging viciously into his mind. After the fight, he admitted, "I felt sluggish tonight. I wasn't concentrating and I just didn't feel myself... It was my toughest title fight for a long time. I've got a few bruises this time." He made no mention of his money problems.

That spring Barry Hearn and Tommy Gilmour were reportedly awarded approximately £100,000 in damages against Steve at the High Court and on top of that, his legal costs exceeded £60,000. Steve's defence had been built around his claim that the options system contained in his contract with Mr Hearn and Mr Gilmour constituted restraint of trade. But the judge, although appearing sympathetic towards Steve's predicament, did not agree.

On the 7th July 1995 Steve fought Spaniard Pedro Ferradas Couso at Cardiff. Three days before the fight, the court ordered that his assets and bank account be frozen. Yet, as Steve marched into the ring through a crowd whipped up into a frenzy of support for their champion, nobody could have guessed at his mental turmoil. Early in the eighth round Steve knocked Ferradas down with a right hand and in the ninth he nailed him with a left hook and stopped him seconds later with a flurry of shots. The fight was over and Steve looked ecstatic, his face exuding naked relief. At ringside, sitting next to Don King, was the ever present Nazeem Hamed. After the fight, Nazeem was called to the ringside to be interviewed. On his way into the ring he was verbally abused and spat upon.

Two weeks later Steve forgot his troubles for a day when he married Angela. "We got married in Cardiff. A big church up in town and we had a big party in a hotel. It was a good day. I've been with Angela since 1989 so it's been quite a few years. Anyway, we went away on our honeymoon..."

Nazeem Hamed:

"Before I went away they were talking about me fighting him and I told Frank Warren, 'no, I want some more time to fight him.' While I was away on honeymoon I phoned Dai and he said they wanted me to fight Nazeem Hamed on the 30th September. All of a sudden they had made him the new WBO number one contender. I had 48 hours to give them their answer. I thought, 'Where did this guy come from?' So I came back and that only give me about three-and-a-half weeks to prepare. There wasn't much time really and I was a bit overweight. I was over there having a good time. I don't drink but I was eating a lot. It's natural that you put the weight on. I did a couple of runs over there but I didn't do much. And I could be walking around about nine stone, eight or nine. It was hard because there wasn't much time.

"And the money wasn't right, I wasn't happy with the money. It wasn't a bad purse, but to fight someone like him it should have been much bigger. I heard rumours that he got paid a lot more than me, but I don't know if that's true. And I wasn't sharp, my mind wasn't focused. At the time with the legal problems and everything my mind wasn't quite there. They always say you've got to be 100 percent focused. It's amazing what goes through your head.

"They said if I didn't fight him they would strip me of the title and that title meant a lot to me. It was lovely being world champion and I didn't want them to strip the title off me. And I probably underestimated Hamed at the time. I thought, 'He's going up a weight to my weight now, and I'll be alright, even though I won't be 100 per cent fit. I'll be too strong for him.' It wasn't the same Steve Robinson who fought Hamed, it wasn't me." Dai Gardiner was worried. "I wanted Steve to pull out of the fight but he was determined to go ahead so I supported his decision."

The date was set and the pre-fight hype launched into its full assault on the boxing public. Hamed's camp arranged for a van to drive through Cardiff blaring out a recording of his voice declaring "I'm the Prince, I'm going to be King. Steve Robinson, they call you 'The Cinderella Man,' but make sure you're there for the coronation. Steve Robinson, come out and fight me." The van was regularly pelted with missiles from Steve's angry supporters.

Disaster strikes:

The fight took place at Cardiff Rugby Club, an outdoor venue adjacent to Cardiff Arms Park, on the 30th September 1995. Nazeem Hamed made his entrance through a completely pro-Robinson crowd clad in gaudy leopard skin garb, hands on hips, proud and arrogant in his contempt for the sneers and insults from the crowd. In complete contrast, Steve stepped out through the fireworks that preceded his entrance and into the drizzle, covered in a red gown with plastic bags on his feet to protect his boots from the damp, a towel tucked around his neck. As he walked down the gangway it looked for all the world like somebody had just dumped him in the middle of a nightmare and thrown a posh red dressing gown around him for comfort. "At the time, I was in a daze. A lot of people noticed that. I was thinking, 'What's going on?' And Hamed was a good fighter, you've got to admit he is a good puncher.

"When I fought him at the time I didn't throw any body shots, I didn't pressure him enough, I didn't throw enough shots. He's slippery and with him you've got to throw lots of shots and pressure him, rough him up, that kind of fight. I just stood in front of him, just waiting for him to come which I shouldn't have. I was just like a target really."

Steve lost his WBO featherweight title to Nazeem Hamed on that fateful night before a crowd of more than 16,000 loyal supporters. Hamed was on top from beginning to end but his ugly behaviour throughout was unforgivable. Because of his cruel rancour Hamed lost many of his own fans that night, but despite this tirade of verbal insults and childish jibes, Steve remained gallant, determined and stubborn during every second of his ordeal. He was floored in the fifth and many thought the fight would be stopped there and then but Steve insisted on continuing. Hamed finished it in the eighth with a left hook to the temple which reduced Steve to his knees. After almost two-and-a-half years Steve Robinson's world championship reign was over.

Down but not out:

"Oh I was down, you know. The night I lost that fight I just thought to myself, 'I want to give it up now.' I was so cheesed off, the way everything happened, the way they stitched me up. The next day I wanted to give up. Then every day went by and I thought to myself, 'No, I'm not going to give up. I want to give it another shot. I want to carry on and try and regain that world title.'"

A year later, after months of soul searching and hard training, Steve stepped through the ropes once again. He fought an eight rounder with Midlands Area champion Kelton McKenzie of Leicester. He won a clear points decision. "But I was very rusty in that fight. It took me a bit of time to get back to myself after a year out and a shattering defeat against Hamed."

African nights and African fights:

Steve battled on with his career and in March 1997 he stopped Mexican Tomas Serrano in one round for the WBO Inter-Continental title at Brentwood. After three successful defences, he travelled to South Africa to defend against former IBF super-bantamweight champion Welcome Ncita.

On the 3rd October 1998 Steve went the full 12 rounds with Ncita in Sisa Dukashe Stadium in Mdantsane, a sprawling South African township. This trip meant a lot to Steve. "It's my fatherland isn't it? It's very important. I know I'm a Welsh-man born and bred, but it's my roots. It was a long flight, ten hours. We had to see the press when we landed in Johannesburg. Once we got to East London, there was a crowd of people there. They really welcomed me."

Dai Gardiner also has fond memories of South Africa. "I mean, you can walk out there in the big open air venue and you see all the crowd. And they all go shoosh! Oh, it was tremendous. What we did, before the fight, we drove up in this big open truck and Steve jumped out and showed them the belt and they went crazy!" Steve chuckles, "I had it in the ring didn't I?" Dai continues, "And we had to get out from there then and go back to the hotel. But it was a good move. Because Ncita must have thought 'what the hell's going on here like?' We drove right up through the crowd." Steve quietly reflects, "I showed him who's the champion." His face lights up, "And then when we came back to fight there was a line of people one side and a line of people the other side and they were singing African songs and they've got sweet voices. And, I don't know, the songs just go right through me. It felt so nice because my ancestors were from Africa and I just felt really good. It seemed like I was a home boy, you know? It was amazing."

Despite Steve's happy memories of the welcome extended to him by the South African people, unfortunately the same cannot be said of the judges' scoring abilities. Steve had to settle for a controversial draw. The first six rounds were more or less even. Steve knocked Ncita down in the third and Ncita came back to win the fourth. But Steve nearly stopped Ncita in the seventh as he pinned the South African to the ropes and let go with a ravaging assault to the body and head. Referee Eddie Marshall later admitted, "I was seconds away from stopping the fight. Ncita started to punch back just in time." And after that Steve appeared to romp home comfortably on points. When the draw verdict was announced Steve was as philosophical as ever, "I thought I did enough to win. I was the pressure fighter and I was the aggressor and I nearly stopped him. Over here, I suppose you have to knock them out to win." Ncita could not attend the post-fight press conference because he was too bruised. Of Ncita himself, Steve speaks highly. "Before the fight he shook my hand. He got respect from me and I got respect from him. He was six times world champion. He's a good fighter. But that fight, it was so one sided."

European Title:

On the 30th April 1999, three-and-a-half years after his devastating loss to Nazeem Hamed, Steve Robinson put himself back on the map by winning the European featherweight title. In the other corner was Spaniard Manuel Calvo and Steve travelled to Spain to fight him. Calvo's introduction brought the house down. By comparison Steve slipped into the ring virtually unnoticed, his introduction evoking a watery trickle of applause. "Calvo's normally a come forward type of fighter, a rough kind of fighter and I thought, 'Yes, he's going to suit me down to the ground.' But in this fight, he changed his tactics. He was on the move all the time. He's a good natural mover." The fight began just before midnight after ridiculously long and drawn out preliminaries. Steve won on a split decision. "He made it very difficult for me. He didn't seem to want to fight me. He was a slippery sort of guy, running all the time, moving all the time, and holding. It was very close. They gave it to me by one round, but I was surprised when they gave me the decision at all, boxing him out there, in Spain." After the fight Dai told Steve, "It's about time you had a bit of luck."

Steve lost the European title on his third defence, against Hungarian star Istvan

Kovacs. They fought in Budapest and Kovacs won clearly on points. Steve kept on fighting but in April 2002 he decided to hang up his gloves for good. "I don't want to be fighting when I'm an old man. It's a tough old game. You take the shots."

Despite all the highs and lows, Dai Gardiner's feelings about Steve Robinson remain as strong as ever. "When Robbie Regan was world champion, at the top and all the limelight was on him, Steve seen it all. And it never, ever got him down. The cameras would come down the gym and Steve would always be in the background. But I knew from the beginning that Steve Robinson was that little bit different. Seven out of ten fighters, you take them to South Africa or somewhere like that and they would swallow. But Steve would never swallow a fight.

"He's one of the most top professional boxers I've ever known. The only one I had that was like him, and he didn't have a family and he was a lot younger than Steve, was Johnny Owen. But Steve, his dedication, you know to fetch a family up as well. And I've had him up the gym sparring with everybody, middleweights, heavyweights, the lot. And sometimes they've had the better of him because they're fresh and they know they're coming out after two rounds. And I've had Steve turn round and say, 'What's the matter with him?' But he never complains. And he handles bigger boys better than smaller boys. It's unbelievable." Steve cuts in, "That's because I've kept on the move. I've kept on the move a lot!" Dai continues, "With Steve I haven't got to worry about getting the weight off him." Steve agrees, "Dai can just look at me and say, 'You're about nine four.' He just knows. 'Cos I like chips and pie, and the odd curry now and then."

It angers Dai that Steve has had to struggle so hard financially. "Since the Naz fight, I think he had one decent purse, through all the Inter-Continental fights. For purses that were just keeping a bit of bread on the table. And he worked his way back up. And that's the sort of professional he is. And the fights that he's had lined up that have been pulled out. He's lived on the breadline for the past few years, because boxing is the only living he's got. He's had fighters pull out on him when we've been about to go and weigh in. And I've got to go in the gym and I'm like, 'What can I tell him?' It's like working for six months for no pay."

Steve Robinson is a tough man, a dignified man whose strength of mind and faith have remained with him. "I've always believed in God. I don't go to church or anything like that but I'm quite religious within myself. Inside everybody is a church," as he gestures to his heart. Steve has simply focused his mind on the task ahead and done it like a job of work. And that is what boxing has always been for him, simply a job of work. Now that his boxing career is over Steve is embarking on a new career as a fitness instructor. He has also taken his place alongside his mentor and friend Dai Gardiner and looks forward to helping Dai train champions of the future. I am sure that he will make a success of his life whatever he does, but for me, Steve Robinson will always be the Jimmy Braddock of Wales.

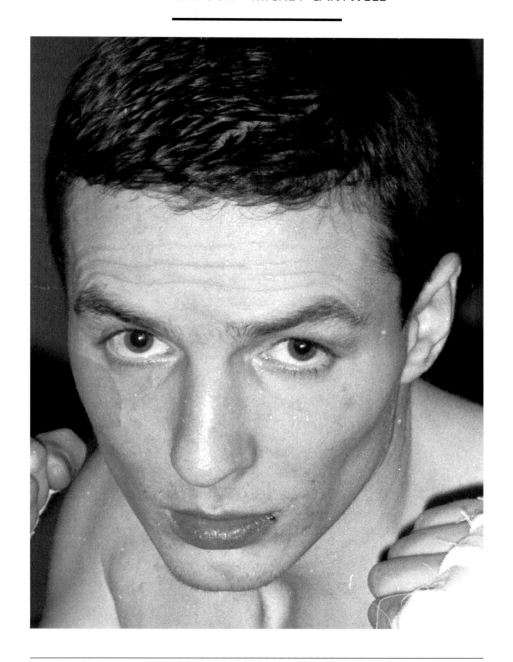

"He's a great kid. One of the nicest kids I've ever met. And he nearly won that fight against Matlala, you know! They all said he didn't have a chance but Mickey went in there and he showed 'em all." – Jimmy Tibbs

London flyweight Mickey Cantwell epitomises boxing's brigade of 'little men.' He is tough, resilient and he simply refuses to give up and go away. Mickey remained in the amateur ranks until he was 26, his biggest dream being to compete in the Olympic Games. But despite winning two consecutive ABA titles and a string of empty promises, his Olympic dream was never to come true. In 1991 he became a professional boxer. He was rewarded for his tenacity in 1996 when he became British flyweight champion.

Michael Cantwell was born near the Elephant and Castle, south-east London, on the 23rd November 1963. He has two younger sisters and his parents are both Irish. However, his accent is that of a real cockney sparrow, or in Mickey's case 'sparrahh'. At 5ft 2ins he is quite tiny in stature and in his own words, "I walk around at seven stone, ten pounds when I'm dripping wet." But his effervescent personality and chirpy sense of humour are enough to fill any room. I spent a beautiful day at the Cantwell home while Mickey and his wife, Tracey told me their story. This pair of love birds have been together since they met at school at the age of 14. Mickey laughingly told me, "She's still hanging around me now. I can't get rid of her!" They have two children, Sam and Amy, and Mickey proudly wears their names on his boxing shorts. I came away that day secure in the knowledge that I captured not only a wonderful story for my book, but the solid friendship of one of the nicest families I have ever met.

A potential footballer, Mickey took his first step into the Robert Browning ABC at the age of 11. "I used to play a lot of football and I went along to my local boxing club with some of my friends to keep fit. By the time I reached 12 everybody else got really big and I never did. Anyway, I really took to boxing. What I liked about it was the one on one. You have to rely on yourself. I have always been very committed. I like to win. I'm a great believer that second is nowhere."

In those days the Robert Browning was run by eminent referee Roy Francis who remained at the helm for nearly 20 years. "Roy was a big noise, he used to get in and spar with everyone, every night. He was always hollering and shouting. If you did something naughty he would ban you for a week or something. But he was a great character and everyone loved him."

When he was 15 Mickey stopped boxing for a year to work nights as a shelf filler for Tesco. A year later he found himself missing the buzz and joined the Lynn ABC. From there he moved to Fisher ABC where he reached two ABA finals. The first was in 1985, the year he and Tracey got married. "I got beat the first time by Mark Epton and I did get beat. He was beating everyone in his way." In 1986 he reached the finals again and once more he lost the decision to Epton. "I thought this time I had definitely won it. I put him down and I got beat on a split decision. I was absolutely heartbroken."

Next came a trip to Athens where Mickey won a gold medal at the Acropolis Cup. "I believe I'm right in saying that I was the last British person to win a gold medal at the Acropolis Cup. It was a hard, open air tournament. I had a tough fight in the semi-finals against a Greek kid. I beat a really hot Canadian in the finals and I won it quite convincingly so I was on a bit of a roll."

Mickey and Tracey had now moved to Kent. Mickey worked in Bermondsey as a plate maker and travelling to the Fisher in the evenings was wearing him out so he joined Eltham ABC. He was trained there by Richard Atkins and Paul Fitzgerald. "I had the greatest time of my life there. They treated me like a superstar, which I wasn't." In 1987 he reached the ABA semis and lost a split decision to Glaswegian Wilson Docherty. "I boxed crap and he won it. He won it fairly."

In 1988 Mickey won his first ABA title. Boxing at light-flyweight he beat Robbie Regan of Wales in the finals. Regan would go on to become WBO bantamweight champion in 1996. "Robbie was hot stuff. I beat him convincingly. It was at Wembley. It was a big occasion for me." Unbeknown to football mad Mickey, Richard Atkins had a special treat in store for him. "I didn't know it but Richard had arranged for me to take a walk out on the Wembley pitch. So all of a sudden I'm walking on Wembley pitch. Unbelievable! I couldn't believe how big it was. Anyway, all of a sudden we hear someone shouting down to us, 'Get off the pitch. Get off the bloody pitch!' There was someone right up in the Gods shouting at us. So we all started waving up at him and having a right laugh."

Mickey's big dream was to fight for his country at the Seoul Olympics. "After I beat Robbie Regan I thought, 'This is it! I'm going to the Olympic Games. I'm going to Seoul.' But they told me that first I had to box in the Canada Cup. It was fine by me. I thought, 'OK, I'll go to Canada and do well there, use it as a warm up for the Olympics.' I got to the finals and lost on a split decision to a Russian. In the third round I suddenly just died. I couldn't understand it. I was really fit but suddenly I was really struggling.

"The night before we came home from Canada they had a farewell dinner for us. One of the referees took me to one side and warned me, 'I've got some bad news. I don't think you're going to the Olympic Games. I've heard a rumour that you're not going.' I couldn't believe what I was hearing. I just started crying." On the way home Mickey noticed that team mate Neville Brown, was wearing dark glasses and looking very down. When Mickey asked what was wrong, Neville told him that he also had his card marked. He was not going to the Olympics either. Mickey arrived home without a Canadian title and with a bad case of chicken pox, the reason for his sudden weakness in the finals.

Mickey had been home for a few days when he received a phone call from Richard Atkins. The British Olympic team had been named in the *London Evening Standard*. Mickey's name was not on the list. "They had picked Mark Epton instead. I couldn't believe it. I mean Mark Epton wasn't even in the ABA's that year! I went upstairs and I just sat on the toilet floor crying. I just could not believe it. I was heartbroken." Mickey was very depressed for a couple of months. Then he picked himself up, dusted himself off and submitted himself to the most stringent training, ready for the following year's ABA championships. "I thought, 'Right! I'll show 'em that they can't treat me like that.' I decided to go into the ABA's again. I mean, when you're beating people like Robbie Regan in the final, you're beating quality boys."

In 1989 Mickey won the ABA's for the second time but making the weight was becoming a struggle and the final fight was a hard one. In the other corner was Liverpudlian Ian Lang. In the first round there was a clash of heads and Mickey's left eye ballooned badly. The injury was so severe that Atkins and Fitzgerald couldn't touch it but Mickey went ahead and won the title anyway.

In January 1990 Mickey travelled to New Zealand for the Commonwealth Games. He lost his first fight which was against Justin Juuko who went on to box the likes of Floyd Mayweather as a professional. "I was really having big weight problems now. I didn't have a drink for 18 hours before that fight and the night before I sat in the sauna for hours. A couple of hours after the fight I collapsed outside. It was dehydration. They took me straight to hospital and kept me there for a day. Then they moved me to the hospital to the Commonwealth Games Village. I stayed there for another three days. I was under observation."

It is no secret that politics are the scourge of amateur boxing and, after winning his second ABA title, Mickey had finally had enough of it. He had heard all the easy talk and he now knew that they were never going to send him to the Olympic Games, no matter what they said. He decided to turn professional. But despite the disappointment he felt at the time he speaks fondly of his amateur days. "I had some great times as an amateur. I would never change what happened because I met some fantastic people. But I felt that my amateur career was a battle from day one until the day it ended."

He turned professional with Frank Maloney who he had known for some years. He had his first paid fight on the 21st January 1991 at Crystal Palace against Eduardo Vallejo. Mickey stopped the Mexican in four rounds. "I was very, very nervous. He was a good opponent. I knew a lot was expected of me, because I had a good amateur career. I boxed well but I remember being very nervous."

Two months later Mickey won a points decision over six rounds against Mario Alberto Cruz. The venue was York Hall, Bethnal Green which would become a symbolic place for our man later down the line.

In September 1991 Mickey won a points decision over Ricky Beard, one of his former stablemates at Eltham ABC. When referee Mickey Vann called them together before the first bell Mickey nodded to Beard affably. "I said, 'Alright Ricky?' He just glared back at me and said, 'You wanker!' Honestly, I was so shocked! I was totally taken aback, especially as we knew each other at Eltham. I went back to my corner thinking, 'What's the matter with him?' Anyway, I came out and threw a jab and he said, 'You wanker!' He continued to abuse me for five rounds. Anyway, I was getting really fed up with it so in the sixth I went out and grabbed hold of him with my glove, right underneath his arm, and I really twisted it, as hard as I could. Beard looked towards Mickey Vann, appealing for help, and Vann said, 'Get on with it Beard. This is a man's game.' I looked at Beard through my gloves and I said, 'Who's a wanker now then?' After eight rounds I won the fight. I went up to him afterwards and shook hands and that was it."

Less than a month later Mickey stopped Carlos Manrigues in five rounds at Bethnal Green. This was Mickey's second and last stoppage win. "I'm a naturally small person. So I ended up boxing these guys who were much bigger than me. If I'm going in to fight ten rounds I will always train for that, like all fighters should. Obviously, if the stoppage comes, that's a bonus. But I wouldn't stop them on sheer power because I simply don't have the power. My way of stopping people is by hitting them correctly."

Mickey continued his unbeaten run with a decision over Leicester's Shaun Norman in December 1991, another over Glaswegian Louis Veitch in May 1992 and a draw in a re-match with Veitch in February 1993. Then he received an offer from Mickey Duff to fight for the Southern Area flyweight title against Darren Fifield. He left Maloney and on the 14th April 1993 he won the title at the Albert Hall. "It was a gruelling fight. I got cut for the first time. It was the last round, a blatant head butt. Me and Darren are the best of friends now but it was a hard fight."

After the fight Mickey's face was left in a hideous mess. Tracey showed me a photograph taken the same night. As I came to terms with the alien looking person staring back at me from that picture, Tracey took me through events directly after the fight. "Up until that fight I had never gone to the changing rooms. But as the Albert Hall emptied out I was thinking, 'He'll be up any minute,' but in the end I realised that something was wrong. I got someone to take me down to the changing rooms and when I got there somebody warned me that he was a bit swollen and to be prepared. But nothing could have prepared me for what I saw. He had never had a cut before, never really had a black eye. Anyway, he come out and I thought, 'Oh my God!'

"That night we got home and I said to his mum, 'Right, he's going to come in and he looks really bad. Don't start crying when you see him because of the kids.' I told the kids that their daddy had fallen over and hurt his face so he doesn't look like daddy at the moment. I didn't want them thinking it was because of boxing, because every time he boxed they'd be thinking...'" (she holds up the photo.) These days, Darren Fifield and his girlfriend visit the Cantwell home regularly.

After winning the title Mickey returned to Frank Maloney. "Frank's a funny character. The good thing about him is that you can have a row with him one day and be best friends the next day. Fair play to him. I think he could see a bit of me in him, because he's small, a bit of a character. He fought for what he's got, and I've fought for what I've got."

Mickey had a rest from boxing for the summer and in September 1993 he dropped down a weight to fight for the vacant WBC International light-flyweight title against flamboyant Mexican southpaw Pablo Tiznado at York Hall. That night, Mickey suffered his first points loss but he gave it everything he had and did his rapidly growing horde of fans proud. "It was a really tough fight. At the weigh-in he looked really scrawny. The next day he looked about five sizes bigger." Six weeks later he won a decision against Anthony Hanna over eight. Hanna came from Nobby Nobbs' notorious stable of journeymen and Mickey holds him in high regard, "He's a naturally good fighter."

In 1994 Mickey was named as mandatory challenger for the European flyweight title against Italian Louigi Camputaro, possessor of a short, chunky body, a pony tail, moustache and a ramrod solid left jab. Camputaro's career defeats had all come at the hands of genuine world class fighters. Those in the know believed that the Italian's natural strength and wider experience would be too much for the little Londoner, and Camputaro would retain his title. The fight was scheduled for the 27th April 1994 but the night before something unthinkably tragic happened.

On the 26th April 1994 Mickey's stablemate Bradley Stone fought Richie Wenton for the inaugural British super-bantamweight title at York Hall. Bradley, a tiny, tough nut with the looks of a street urchin, trained at the Peacock Gym with Mickey. They were regular sparring partners as well as friends. "At the time I was sparring quite a lot with Bradley." Mickey pauses, struggling to find his words. "We helped each other. Bradley had his fight against Richie Wenton and we all know what happened."

Bradley was stopped in the tenth round that night and although he was acting normally directly afterwards, he collapsed a few hours later and was rushed to the Royal Hospital in Whitechapel. This brave young man, an exceptional British talent whose dream had been to fight for a Lonsdale belt was now fighting for his life. As Mickey remembers his voice is flat now, all enthusiasm crushed. "With my European title fight the next night I couldn't go to watch Bradley box. On the day of the weigh-in for my fight everyone kept it secret from me that Bradley was in hospital. I didn't know until afterwards. I knew that he got beat. I was gutted that he got beat. They told me to get on with it because they wanted me to do well that night. They told me not to worry. So I thought I'll give Bradley a call to see how he is. Unbeknown to me, he was in hospital. Then they told me he was in hospital but just for observation." Tracey cuts in, "They were trying to make it all right for Michael." Mickey continues, "So I went back to the hotel, they put me in this hotel up Park Lane. I'm sitting in my hotel room on my own. It's not normally like me to be on my own."

In the meantime Tracey, at home preparing to go to York Hall to support her husband, had received a telephone call to inform her that Bradley was on a life support machine. "They told me that Bradley was not going to come through. So you can imagine the state that I was in all day. I couldn't handle it. All I could think about was Michael."

Mickey, still unaware of his friend's grave injuries, rang Tracey that night at about 6pm. Mickey has a habit of flicking through the TV channels and he was doing this as he asked his wife, "What happened with Bradley, is he alright?" Suddenly Bradley's face flashed onto the screen. Mickey froze. "Tracey, what's Bradley doing on the TV?" Now Tracey had to confirm the worst. She told him, "Michael listen, as soon as your fight is over we will go straight to the hospital to see Bradley. Now you've got to think of you. Because you've got to get in there tonight and that's what Bradley would want. As soon as your fight is over we will go and see him. Look you've got two kids here… You've got to get yourself together." Tracey, brave to the last, travelled to York Hall to be at ringside for her husband, the very same ring that Bradley had fought in the night before.

Mickey arrived at York Hall to fight Luigi Camputaro at about 7pm. He was sick with worry for Bradley. "I'm going to the venue on my own in a taxi, which I've never done before. As I pulled up outside there were loads of press and TV cameras. There were hundreds of people protesting with banners. They all pounced on me, asking me for my opinion. I didn't know what was going on. Then I was ushered into the changing room and I had to start thinking about my fight which was very difficult. But I thought Bradley would want me to go in and win so I think I put in an extra effort for him. Now I knew that he was on a life support machine, I was praying that I could go out and win the belt so that I could go back and show him, maybe turn…" Mickey was unable continue talking for a moment.

As expected Luigi Camputaro retained his European title that night. Mickey lost a points decision over 12 rounds. But what nobody expected was Mickey's staunch resilience as he pushed the Italian to the limits. The decision was so close, so close and yet so far. After the fight as Mickey reached the dressing room, the shock of the whole situation began to set in and he began to vomit. Tracey was petrified, "Now the doctor is around us big time, saying things we've never heard before, telling us, 'If he does this tonight, if he feels ill, rush him straight to hospital. Don't mess about.' I just wanted us to get home and be normal." Mickey told me, "All I was thinking about was going to see Bradley." Mickey and Tracey were travelling home in the car of their friends Mark and Jo Roe when suddenly Mickey started to vomit again. Seconds later our hero found himself on his hands and knees on a hard, cold Bethnal Green pavement, all dignity gone now.

Bradley Stone died at about 8:30pm on Thursday, 28th April 1994. His funeral was held at Ascension Church, Leyes Road on Monday, 9th May. He was buried at the East London Cemetery, Hermit Road, Plaistow. His family invited all to attend. Mickey was still bruised on the outside from his fight with Camputaro, but badly battered on the inside by the death of his friend. "I remember going to the funeral all bruised, but it didn't matter. I just wished we wasn't going there that day. We should have been, you know… It was a tragic day. There were thousands of people there and it was so sad. I just felt that Bradley had so much to live for. Obviously there were people much closer to him than me, his family and his girlfriend, but I just felt that he had so much to live for."

The team at the Peacock paid tribute to Bradley by having a bronze statue of his likeness erected outside the gym. Mickey was asked to model for the sculptor. "It was an honour in my eyes. I had to stand like Bradley. That was hard, but I did it because I know that he would have done it for me. We had the opening at the Peacock Gym. It's great because the Peacock have not forgotten him. Every day you see him so he's not forgotten. Bradley would have loved that."

I asked Mickey if Bradley's death ever made him feel like throwing in the towel himself. His reply was adamant. "People like Bradley Stone wouldn't have wanted you to pack up. I wouldn't want anybody to pack up if it happened to me, God forbid. It's something that you don't think about. Getting hurt is the last thing you think about when you're boxing." Tracey adds, "I think you would find that any boxer would say exactly the same thing."

Less than two months after his fight with Camputaro, Mickey lost an eight rounder on points to Lyndon Kershaw at Southwark, a result that shocked the boxing fraternity. Mickey fights well when the odds are against him, but the chips were through the floor at this time in his life. Having given up his job as a printer to buy Ttitle, the boxing equipment company, things had not gone as planned. Mickey was forced to leave the business, a move that crippled him financially. And more problems were looming on the horizon.

After two more points wins over Anthony Hanna, by the end of 1995 the Cantwell's financial situation reached rock bottom. Twelve days before Christmas their home was repossessed. The family were moved into temporary accommodation. Tracey remembers only too well, "I wouldn't wish that on my worst enemy. But we've come through it. We've come through it strong."

On the 21st March 1996 Mickey, at the age of 32, finally got a shot at the British flyweight title. His opponent was 27-year-old Scot Keith Knox. The venue was the Elephant & Castle Leisure Centre. Mickey's fans packed out the arena on his home turf and he rewarded them by winning the fight on points. He was now British champion. However, his victory was shrouded by controversy. Many, including *Boxing News* editor Claude Abrams, saw Mickey as the winner. But many did not. It was a scrappy fight in many ways but at the bell for the last round, Mickey was up early and marched straight in on the attack. The two fighters gave everything but referee Mickey Vann decided that Mickey had given that little bit more, enough to win the title.

Tracey firmly believes her husband was the true winner. "What nobody knows is that from round one Knox was hitting with an open glove. Mickey Vann was saying to him, 'If you don't punch correctly Knox, I'm going to chuck you out. You're not scoring nothing with this.'"

Mickey was saddened by the doubters who cast a shadow over his British title. "If I say so myself, I was lucky. But I knew that my correct punching had won the fight. It was a massive struggle because he was much bigger than me. He was like a bull. I didn't care. I had the belt. To be honest with you I've always been a great believer that in our sport you've got to take the rough with the smooth. If you're lucky, you hold your hands up and say, 'Yes, I'm lucky' but you call it how you see it."

On the 29th June 1996 Mickey won a six-rounder against former Bulgarian amateur star, Krasimir Tcholakov in Kent. But behind the scenes there was deep unrest in the Cantwell camp. Mickey was angry with those who continued to call his victory over Knox a liberty. And the purses he was receiving were not helping his financial situation. He was paid just £3,000 for the Knox fight. Then he was invited to meet with Frank Warren.

"Frank offered me a brilliant deal that included a world title fight. It was a dream come true for me to box for a world title. Secondly, to earn really good money. Thirdly to box on a big bill with Naseem Hamed and Steve Collins was a massive thing for me." Mickey's task was to fight the WBO light-flyweight champion, Baby Jake Matlala of Soweto. It is worth recording here that this would be Mickey's 17th fight and Matlala's 57th.

Mickey went to see Frank Maloney to explain his situation. He pointed out that if he boxed Keith Knox again and lost, at the age of 31 his career would be over. He knew that it would be hard for him to get a decision against Knox after their first controversial battle, and the likelihood of stopping Knox was remote to say the least. "To be honest with you, I was not going to give them (the Knox camp) the opportunity because they gave me so much grief. What with me winning the title, and them not being men about it. I told Frank Maloney that they could have the British Title. I told him, 'I'm going to box for a world title, with or without your blessing.'" Mickey and Frank Maloney parted on amicable terms and are still friends to this day.

Meanwhile, Mickey was becoming deeply concerned about Tracey, who was getting very upset by certain press reports. Tracey told me, "All we had ever been in the paper for was because we lost our house, and there's more to us than that."

Mickey agreed, "And we were trying to get ourselves back on our feet. All of a sudden there are people in the paper slagging us off again for no valid reason. What people should have remembered about us is that we had no money as such. We had just got this council place and there was nothing done in here. All the people around us, they should have been pleased for us that I was getting this chance."

As if to add insult to injury, boxing's political machine had its way and certain people the Cantwells believed to be close friends let them down badly, deserting them in their hour of need. This depressed Tracey deeply and Mickey became increasingly worried about his wife.

On top of everything, nobody believed that Mickey stood a chance of beating Matlala. With the fight of his life approaching, Mickey decided the time had come to enlist some serious help. In December 1996 he paid a visit to veteran trainer, Jimmy Tibbs. Mickey had always rated Tibbs highly and had dreamed of having him as a trainer since the day he turned professional. Tibbs, well known in the trade for his exceptional motivational powers, told Mickey, "I know what everyone is thinking, but you are going to beat him. We are going in this to win it." He told Mickey to get a tape of Matlala and study it. "I looked at the tape and I thought, 'What have I got myself into here?'" That night Tracey came home and Mickey was watching the tape. She asked him what he thought. He told her that he thought he could beat Matlala but Tracey felt her husband was hiding his true feelings from her. She kept her thoughts to herself.

A pre-fight press conference was held at the Four Seasons Hotel, Park Lane. This kind of high profile exposure was a new experience for Mickey. "In the past I was used to going to press conferences at a pub somewhere with two or three people turning up.

Suddenly, here I am sitting next to Steve Collins with my own name plate in front of me. And I'll never forget the way Naz treated me. I knew Nazeem Hamed like you do when you go to the big shows, but I didn't really know him. But he was so kind to me."

As Mickey settled down into his training for the fight, the media continued to hound him about his financial situation. The 'experts' continued to ridicule his chance of success against the South African. Jimmy Tibbs was a real tower of strength throughout. And of course, the main person in Mickey's life was there for him in a big way. "One day Tracey sat me down and said, 'Look this will come and this will go. In five weeks time you are going to be boxing for the world title, come what may. Whatever happens, whatever they write, you are going to be there. You've always dreamed of becoming world champion. Just go and enjoy yourself. As long as you come home safe, I don't care.' That changed my attitude a bit. The training was going well. I was really looking forward to it. We were finally getting some nice press and all of a sudden people knew who I was. It was really nice. I ended up enjoying it too much." Tracey chimed in, "Yes! I was worried sick and he was having a great time!"

Tracey remains extremely grateful to Jimmy Tibbs for his support during those difficult times. "Because of Jimmy's influence Michael began to love the game again. I had never met Jimmy, I had only spoken to him on the phone but I wanted to thank him for what he had done for my husband. But I didn't want to thank him after the fight so I sent him a card that would arrive on the day of the fight. When he received it Jimmy was really pleased. He was so surprised. He couldn't get over it."

A few days before the fight Mickey watched the Matlala tape again, but this time he saw it through different eyes. That night Tracey came home and asked what he had been doing. He told her, "I've been watching that tape. I can beat him." This time, she believed him.

On the 8th February 1997 Mickey lost on a split decision over 12 rounds against WBO light-flyweight champion Baby Jake Matlala, one of the judges present at Millwall feeling that Mickey had done enough to win. But what a fight he gave that wonderful old Zulu warrior.

Mickey started strongly but his eye was badly damaged in a clash of heads in round three, a moment he remembers vividly. "When he cut me he rode in and done me with his head, because that's the way you do it. He done it clever. He looked at me and said, 'Sorry Mickey' and he laughed! He said it sarcastically, so he knew what he'd done." The fourth round was delayed because a blazing row flared up between Jimmy Tibbs and Puerto Rican referee Roberto Ramirez. Throughout the altercation, Tibbs' hands continued to work deftly on the cut. Mickey went out and boxed well in four and five. Halfway through the fight, Matlala started to turn things around but Mickey came back with some quality boxing to win the ninth. Mickey came out for the last round and fought like a tiger, but Matlala's strength was the deciding factor. Mind you, the tension on the South African side showed when Matlala did a strange little Zulu dance in the last round and South African promoter Cedric Kushner jumped out of his seat in horror, willing Matlala not to take unnecessary chances. Mickey saw the final bell on his feet, something that many said he could never do. *Boxing News* reported, "Cantwell can hold his head high and look back on this as a night when he proved once and for all his pride, skill and fighting heart."

Mickey told me, "I got to round ten and I thought I was winning the fight and then I saw the crowd and all of a sudden I lost my concentration. The last two rounds Jimmy begged me to just box him but by then I thought, I was winning the fight and I fancied just sitting down and having a fight with him. I thought he wasn't particularly strong like everybody said he was. But I proved everyone wrong, that's the good thing about it. So out of defeat came a lot of credit which was good."

Three months later Mickey scored a clear points decision over David Coldwell in Manchester and on the 19th December 1997 he tried once more for a world title. This time his opponent was Filipino Eric Jamili. The prize at stake was the vacant WBO straw-weight title. The fight took place at Millwall. Jamili, the younger man by 12-and-a-half-years, stopped Mickey for the first time in his career. The catastrophe began when, in the first round, Jamili caught Mickey with a shocking right uppercut that split the bridge of his nose wide open. Bravely, Mickey gritted his teeth and fought on, his face a bloody mess. Despite his wounds, Mickey was always in the fight, flooring Jamili in the seventh, but the cut was getting progressively worse and Jimmy Tibbs was watching from the corner, his face a mask of anxiety, towel grasped firmly in hand ready to send it sailing over the ropes.

In the eighth American referee Mark Nelson called a halt to the battle, unhappy with Mickey's facial injuries. One of the three judges had Mickey in the lead when the fight was stopped. Mickey was initially unhappy about the stoppage, "As we all know I got beat on cuts, which was unlucky because after eight rounds, to get stopped with a cut when you got cut in the first round? I thought the referee should have let it go on." However, looking back at the situation he decided that Mr Nelson had done what he had to do. "He did his job well but I just felt that I was getting on top."

On the 1st May 1999 Mickey had a re-match at flyweight with Dave Coldwell. After nearly a year-and-a-half out of the ring, our man stepped back through the ropes with one intention on his mind, he was going to win. And what a sparkling performance he put up for the Crystal Palace crowd. Mickey romped home to a comfortable points decision. Incidentally, Brendan Ingle, working Coldwell's corner that night, suddenly started bleeding from his forehead for no apparent reason!

During the following year Mickey remained on the sidelines boxingwise. He and Tracey characteristically grafted away, taking on a cleaning contract at a local sports club to keep the wolf from the door. In the meantime, Mickey kept chipping away, still desperate for a shot at a world title. Finally, things slotted into place and he was offered a fight against up-and-coming South African Zolani Petelo. It would be a challenge for Petelo's IBF mini-flyweight crown.

The fight would take place on the 2nd June 2000 at Ashford. Jimmy Tibbs' life had moved on also and he was too busy with his other boxers to give Mickey the one-on-one training that Mickey felt he needed. However, Jimmy was present in the corner that night as cuts man. I spoke to Jimmy just before the fight and he told me, "I'm not in charge of that corner tonight, but if it all goes off in there, that will change. Don't you worry about that." Mickey told me, "Well, you've got to have Jimmy in your corner, haven't you?"

As Mickey came walking down the gangway that night, his army of fans were right behind him. The roars and shouts of encouragement nearly took the roof off the Stour Centre and over in the far corner the crowd held up a huge banner that read, "Go Mickey, Go!" Petelo stopped Mickey in the eighth round but for the majority of the fight Mickey gave the South African all the trouble he could handle. "I got beat by the better man, it's as simple as that. He was too young, too youthful and too fresh. I thought I was in the fight for six rounds. But I made mistakes outside, with the training side of things. I wasn't really how I should have been. It was my own fault. I messed up. After the sixth round I felt I could still win it but in the seventh I just fell apart."

Mickey eventually retired from boxing in September 2001 after being stopped by his old rival Baby Jake Matlala. Mickey now works for the British Boxing Association (a union set up for boxers past and present) in the capacity of Director of Organisation.

There is do doubt in Mickey Cantwell's mind as to who he holds in the highest regard of all. "The most important person in my boxing career and my life has been Tracey, without a doubt! I'd swap her for a world title though! Nah, I'm only joking. If it wasn't for her I wouldn't be sitting here talking to you. I owe her the world. The people I idolise most in the world are my two children. I live for them. But the most important person in my life is Tracey." Tracey tells me, "The thing with living with a boxer is that nobody knows what goes on before and after a fight. They just all come along on fight night."

Finally, I asked Mickey if he is religious. He looked me straight in the eyes and said, "Mel, if there was a God, I would be world champion by now!"

CHAPTER FOUR – JAMES COOK

"I wouldn't be here today if it weren't for James. He's like a father. I love him." – Matt Brown

James Cook was born in Jamaica in 1959. He has lived in England since he was nine years old. He became a professional boxer in the early eighties. His career lasted more than 11 years. Success came in the autumn of his boxing life in the shape of British and European super-middleweight titles. But, despite the wide grin as I asked him to take a trip down memory lane, in truth James Cook trod a rocky road as a fighter. However, during those tough early years he never lost sight of his goals. These days he is cutting a dash as a top London trainer. If Steve Robinson is the Jimmy Braddock of Cardiff then James Cook has to be the Hackney version. For the record they used to call Braddock 'The Cinderella Man.'

I interviewed James on a chilly Sunday afternoon. As I waited on the steps of his favourite fight venue of York Hall I felt the cold dampness of the day. James arrived bang on time and took me to his home in Hackney where I met his three stunning daughters, Lisa, Keisha and Jamie, and his lifelong partner Carmen who turned out to be the hostess with the mostest. She cooked me a smashing lunch. As the afternoon began to unfold and James began to unwind on his sofa, his 6ft 2inch frame seemed to grow. He weighs 12st 3lbs these days, just three pounds above his fighting weight. His energy flowed and enthusiasm took over but the strong Jamaican accent remained softly soothing.

James has powerful features, the widest of smiles, enhanced by a twinkle in the intense brown eyes. His answers were easy, relaxed, and regularly punctuated by a deep, full-bodied chuckle. These days he keeps his hair cropped short and his moustache finely trimmed but in his fighting days he was known for his big hair and huge moustache. "Yeah, I used to tell people that the afro hair used to help me keep my balance because I was so skinny. The moustache would never get cut because that was sort of my trademark."

Born on the 17th May, James' parents entrusted him to his grandparents as a baby while they came to England seeking employment. His three brothers and two sisters were all born in London. He did not meet them until he was nine years old. "Jamaica was happy memories. But, you know, at the time people from the West Indies was coming over to England to find work. So I grew up with my granny. I was getting letters and things from my mum, but I had never actually seen her. So when my mum did come I looked at my granny and I said, 'Who is that?' She told me, 'That's your mum.' And I thought, 'Yeah man, but what's she coming for? My granny said, 'She come to take you back to England.' And I thought it was a joke! So I used to chuck stones at my mum because I didn't want to come over to this cold place where it always rains."

James was brought up on a Peckham council estate. "I came over here and the British adopt me. Jamaica is still every part of my roots, I won't forget that. But now I am British. Because obviously I was British champion. People say fighters go into boxing because of hard times. It wasn't like that for me. My dad was a builder and he was earning good wages. At those times Ben Sherman shirts and all these different styles were coming out and we used to get one every week. I just liked competing on a one on one level so I choose boxing. I stayed the same throughout my career. On a one to one, I'm coming out on top. But boxing wasn't my favourite sport. I liked athletics, cricket and rugby. I always thought I was going to be a rugby player. I liked running. Even when the skinheads was down the road shining their boots, I used to run to school and back. I didn't get a lot of that [racism]. It was about but I didn't get a lot of it. In that sense life is lucky for me. I never really feel the pressure. I was always very confident in whatever I did. I liked to be the best, even when we was messing about. I remember at primary school there was this guy. His name was Junior and he was winning everything. And Junior was getting all the girls, you know? We was out on the field one day and I had to beat Junior because I wanted all the girls. Anyway, I beat Junior, but it never work!

"I used to go in the playground and mess about with my friends and say, 'OK, you're Joe Frazier and I'm Muhammad Ali.' Ali was my hero. When he lose against Frazier I cried, because I thought it was impossible. I thought, he couldn't lose, you know? My dad look at me and he said, 'What you crying for. We all have to lose some day.'

"It was my mate, Rupert who got me into boxing. I went to the Lynn boxing club and the bloke says, 'Do you want to box? I says, 'Yeah.' And there was this white guy inside the ring, and he says, 'spar with him.' And I went in there and I sparred with this little fella and I couldn't hit him. In fact he kicked shit out of me. He actually had the better of me. And he was smaller than me. And I thought, 'Well I'm not staying here because I'm coming back for you!' So I moved to East Lane boxing club in Camberwell Green."

James' trainers there were local policeman Ronnie White and Jimmy Redwell who had worked with Jim Wicks, Henry Cooper's manager. He had his first amateur bout when he was 14, going on to have 26, winning 20. He boxed for London against Budapest and reached two London ABA finals. In both he was outscored by Johnny Graham at the Albert Hall. James felt that Graham won the first fight fair and square but the second time... "The second time Jimmy [Redwell] said to me, 'If you're going to be cheated you might as well be paid for it' and that's when I went over. I still phone Jim and Ronnie and invite them to the fights. They was good people."

And while James was growing from a boy into a man he became re-acquainted with Carmen, his childhood sweetheart. Their reunion proved to be a strong one. "We grew up together in Jamaica. When I was leaving to come over here Carmen said I must write her. But when I come to England I forgot to write and I never seen her again until she was 17. And when I seen her that time I thought to myself, 'Wow! I wish I did write to her now.' And we just got it back from there."

James became a professional boxer in 1982. Like most of his contemporaries he always worked another job. "I was going to become a motor mechanic. I went to Wandsworth College for a bit and I was always doing part time work. But the mechanic thing kind of failed and then I was working as a driver, doing office equipment. During that time I also ran a youth club in Dulwich. When Lisa was born I thought I'd give up work for a year, concentrate on boxing. During that year it was very, very hard. What kept us going was Carmen. She was a hairdresser. People used to come round and she would do their hair. I didn't even sign on. The one day I did I felt so embarrassed that I went and got a job straight away."

On the 20th October 1982 James made his professional debut against former European silver medalist, Finchley's Mick Courtney. James won on points over six. He vividly remembers his first time. "Shaky. Me and Mick used to spar up the Wellington. Billy Wynter, my trainer at the time, phoned me up and said, 'I've got a fight for you. It's Mick Courtney.' I really didn't understand the game then. I said, 'I'm not fighting Mick. We spar together.' He said, 'You going to let your sparring partner beat you?'" James did not.

He was back less than two weeks later, appearing in Piccadilly against Gary Gething of Abergavenny. James stopped the Welshman early in the second with a perfect left hook but Gething was no pushover. "In the first round I hit him with everything and it sort of bounced off him." He began 1983 with a comfortable points win over eight against Paul Shell at Birmingham, but a couple of weeks later he suffered his first defeat, on points.

In the other corner was debutant Jimmy Price of Liverpool. Twice ABA champion and Commonwealth gold medalist, Price was brought to London under Frank Warren's wing but James remained unimpressed. "Jimmy Price never meant nothing to me, ABA champion and everything. I think I'm a fair judge of a fight and to be honest with you I don't think I lost it. When the result come I thought I could have got the draw at least." It was a tough night's work. In the third round a left hand lead from southpaw Price put James flat on his back but he was up at eight and remained in the fight to hear the final bell.

In March 1983 James was back on the winning side with an eight round points win over tough journeyman Willie Wright who turned out to be a bit of a chatterbox! "In the first round he was speaking to me. 'That all you got Cook? I nearly get you Cook. This ain't no good Cook.' I went back to my corner and I said, 'He's speaking to me!' Billy Wynter looked at me and said, 'Didn't you know? He's a nutter.' And when the fight was done Willie Wright look at me and say, 'Two more rounds and I would have got to you Cook!' And I think, 'Right. This pro game is not as easy as I think it is,' you know."

A month later James won a points decision over Dudley McKenzie at Basildon. James was a friend of Dudley's amazing brother Duke. "Duke was a good friend, we used to meet up you know? When the fight was made I said, 'Duke, you know I'm fighting Dudley?' He says, 'Look. Boxing is boxing. I won't feel no way no matter what the result.' Dudley was brave but after that fight he didn't box again."

In May James destroyed Eddie Smith in the Mancunian's own back yard. Smith, who had a points win over Tony Sibson on his record, was making a comeback and the fight was top of the bill. "When the fight was made Johnny Barclay (manager of featherweight Clyde Ruan) come in the gym every day for two weeks and tell me, 'Cook, he's a body puncher.' So I started increasing the ground work. If it had not have been for

Johnny I don't think I would have done as much ground work as I did for Eddie Smith. And I don't think I knew what a body punch was until I fought Eddie Smith. By the third round I'm keeping my arms at the side because anytime he can, he will catch you. I stopped him inside of six.

"On the way home from Manchester we stopped in the petrol station. The bloke asked where we had come from. We told him the boxing. I was putting £25 worth of petrol in my Granada. He asked me, 'How did Eddie Smith get on mate?' I says, 'He lost.' He says, 'Who beat him?' I said, 'I did.' He says, 'Take the fucking petrol mate!'"

Having had such a busy start to his career (he had been out six times in seven months) James had a six month break but not through choice. "I just couldn't get any fights. It was very frustrating. When I was fighting it wasn't for big wages. I was getting about three or four hundred pounds. Then your expenses have to come out of that. It was upsetting because I couldn't work out why I wasn't getting no fights. I kept training so that even if a short notice fight came along I would be fit. But no fight came."

Eventually another fight did come – in November 1993. The opponent was Stratford southpaw Vince Gajny. "I thought that after six months out they must give me an easy one to get me back in. No such luck! Gajny was a bit of a hard nut I must admit. But when we fought I thought I would just have to keep going to prove to everybody that I'm still here." At the end of the sixth Gajny turned to referee Paul Thomas and said, "That'll do." But James did not escape from the tough tussle unscathed. He damaged his right hand badly and needed another six months to recover.

In June 1984 James won his first title, the vacant Southern Area middleweight belt, against fellow Londoner and previously unbeaten T. P. Jenkins. This fight was also considered an eliminator for the British middleweight title. James stopped Jenkins in nine. This was his first professional appearance at the Albert Hall. "Now I'm starting to realise what boxing at the Albert Hall is all about, what it means. So I was thinking, 'I can't lose at the Albert Hall.' This was my first ten round fight and I had never been there before." James floored Jenkins in the sixth and twice more in the ninth before Harry Gibbs intervened to save him.

In September James fought and lost to Jimmy Price for the second time. This time James was counted out on one knee by John Coyle in the second round. James left Wembley Arena that night under a cloud of depression. But little was he to know that as he walked the dark London streets he was about to meet a mysterious stranger whose words would change his life. "I was knocking Jimmy Price all over the place. And then I went in for a shot and BANG! He caught me. That was it. I was so annoyed with myself. I couldn't face nobody. I couldn't face myself. I felt ashamed. When you have to come out of the ring and look at those people and it's like, you weren't good enough. So I went driving around the West End. My car ran out of petrol so I got out and started to walk. And I don't know where this old boy come from, I think he was probably one of these old boys who was at the fight. He just stopped me and he say to me, 'Cook, in this game, if you can't take losing with winning, you shouldn't be in it.' And those words have stuck with me. After that, every time I lost a fight I would go back to the gym and I just work harder and harder. Whoever he is this old boy, he's there, as part of my life. Because when I lose a fight I keep going back, you know? If only I could remember what he looks like."

Six months later James won a real bang-up with Lewisham based Conrad Oscar. James beat the man from Dominica on points over ten rounds. "I remember losing to Conrad Oscar as an amateur. After he fought me it said in the *South London Press*, 'After beating Cook, Oscar goes pro' and that stuck in my head. Anybody beat me along the line, I want revenge. So I defended my Southern Area title against him."

In October 1985 James' career took a backward step. He lost his Southern Area title to Tony Burke at the Midlands Sporting Club in Solihull. A menacing looking Burke stopped James in the second round. "I was rocking Tony Burke all over the place in the first round and then I got a bit cocky and I dropped my hands. On my way back to the corner [referee] Harry Gibbs followed me and he said, 'Cook, keep your hands up. This boy can punch.' I went out for the second round and started the flash stuff, and Tony Burke hit me with the hardest right hand you could ever be hit with. I remember Harry Gibbs looking over at me and saying, 'I told you so.' When I got back to the changing room I think to myself, 'I kind of like Harry Gibbs. He's alright,' you know?"

James decided that it was time for a change in his team and on the 1st March 1986 he had his first fight for Darkie Smith. He travelled to Cologne to fight Graciano Rocchigiani (future IBF super-middleweight champion). James lost on points over eight rounds. "When we arrive we meet up with a couple of blokes and they say to us, 'Do you want to come for a lickle drink?' I don't know if they were trying to catch me, knowing I was going to box, trying to entice me to come for a drink. I said no, but anyway they seemed very nice. And then, when we went to the weigh-in Graciano was very flash and stubborn. He was supposed to lose weight because he was over but he refused. He was really big. Anyway, we let it go. I didn't think I lose the fight."

Less than a month later James travelled to Amsterdam to fight Jan Lefeber. The Dutchman won the fight in three but James was not impressed. "That was the next great experience. I remember that fight so well. Lickle show-off, you know? In the fight he was like everybody else, he was rocking all over the place. But my rude awakening came when after knocking him down the referee came and picked him up off the ropes, turn him round. I dropped my hands and went in to shake his hand and he hit me! I went down and the referee looked down at me and say, 'Cook, I did not call the end of the fight.' But my opinion is when the referee pick a man up and turn him round it's got to be the end of the fight. But once again I remember what that old bloke said and I went back to training."

Two months later fortune took another turn. James achieved the win he had been yearning for against hot prospect Michael Watson. It was a points win and a close one and it happened at Wembley. "Tough fight. But I knew for me to get the result I had to do it properly because he was a tough man." Watson went on to establish himself as one of the hottest properties in British boxing before being devastatingly injured in a fight against Chris Eubank in September 1991. After the win James found it even harder to get fights in Britain. He was forced to wait nearly nine months for another pugilistic pay day.

In February 1987 he went to France to meet Mbayo Wa Mbayo. James lost on points over eight. "I remember that fight well. He spent all night running. I didn't catch up to him to be quite honest. So yeah, I lost that one on points." But happier times were around the corner. In October 1987 he had his first win abroad – in Italy. His opponent was strong American Willie Wilson. James left nothing to chance in this one, stopping the Californian in six. "So that's where I start to develop the right uppercut now. I went and I just hit him with it and he went out like a light. He was tough. He was a good fighter." And that right uppercut would become one of James' most potent weapons. "Because when I chuck it, I'm not chucking it for fun. I'm chucking it because I know it's gonna hurt, it's going to do the damage. When I'm fighting, if I see any sort of weakness I'm looking to throw that punch. I knew that even if I didn't catch you with it properly it would take something out of you."

A few weeks later James travelled to Finland only to lose on points against local hero Tarmo Uusivirta. "The fight happened in an ice rink with carpet on the floor. After the tenth round Uusivirta was sweating and I wasn't. This old bloke look up at me from ringside and said, 'Hey Cook, how's the weather?' I didn't think Tarmo won that. And there was a problem with the money. Two policeman come and this policeman was bigger than me. They tell us, 'Go back to your room before we lock you up.' So we have to phone the Boxing Board and they stood behind us. We were told the money would be at the airport when we reached London."

It was April 1988 before James got another fight. He stopped journeyman Cliff Curtis in four at the Festival Hall. *Boxing News* described it as his one easy fight. James laughs raucously. "If you seen the fights I had before! When I fight Cliff Curtis it never seemed as though I had to put up that effort. Everything I was doing, it was what I want to do, how I want to do it. He was giving me the range to do what I want. It was nice work." But the next one was anything but easy.

On the 8th June 1988 James fought Herol 'Bomber' Graham for the vacant British middleweight title. "This was the first time I went away to train. Actually I went up my Auntie's, in Elephant and Castle! I remember running up those escalator stairs. I was so fit." But seriously, whichever way you looked at this fight the odds were loftily stacked in the Bomber's favour. Graham was a hard hitting southpaw and a spectacular boxer. He was at his peak and highly rated in world class. His one loss out of 40 fights in a ten year career stood out in stark contrast to James' 12 wins and seven losses. To put the icing on the cake, the fight would be held at the City Hall, Sheffield, the Bomber's home town. "When we went to Sheffield I took a few people there in a minibus. But it felt like I was in Germany! People were coming up and saying, 'Who are you, coming here to fight Herol 'Bomber' Graham?' That's the first time I've had me twinge about boxing. Because you're walking up the road and people are looking at you with hostility."

Fight night arrived and Graham stopped James in five but it was far from his best performance. In the opening moments he rushed in and threw James to the floor, a move that earned him a stern warning from referee Sid Nathan. But the left hook that floored James moments later was blameless. When the fifth round came Graham marched out, his hands dangling. James caught him with a big right hand. Graham poked his tongue out in reply as he glided away. He wound up a Sugar Ray Leonard style right hand before landing with a pokey left that caught James, whose eye was now damaged and bleeding. Graham forced James back to his own corner and dropped him with another left hook. The roar of the crowd drowned out the bell as Sid Nathan raised his arms to wave it off. "When the fight was stopped when I got put down, I don't think I was actually sweating. At the time I got put down I was actually getting closer and closer to Bomber. It was referee Nathan's last fight, he was retiring. I asked him why he stopped the fight. He said I looked a bit dazed. I didn't feel dazed. At the time when the fight was stopped I was just getting into it. But I must admit, when I saw Bomber Graham do this move, and I thought, 'You can't make a move like that and hit me,' and he hit me. He was a good fighter. It was a hard fight. After the loss I felt bad because people were looking at me like I didn't try, like I wasn't supposed to be there, like he ran rings around me. But once again I could hear that old bloke saying to me, 'If you can't take losing...'"

Before they fought, James and Herol Graham were friends. After it was all over, nothing had changed. James has fond memories of a particular sparring session with Herol. "I remember we was up the gym in Kings Cross with Mickey (Duff). We start sparring and Mickey was standing there shouting his head off. 'No! Stop, you're not getting paid.' Anyway, we touch gloves and I think that time I was champion, then we start again.' Mickey was going mad! I still phone Herol up now and then. He's a nice guy."

Minutes after losing to Graham, James vowed that if he ever got beat by a British boxer again he would retire. This was a tall order considering that fighters like Errol Christie and Mark Kaylor were on the prowl. After a period of self-examination, James reached out to manager and promoter Harry Holland. "I rang Harry to ask his advice if I should retire from boxing for good. He said I had much more mileage in the tank. So I left Darkie and went with Harry Holland."

James moved up to super-middle and on the 31st January 1989 he had the fight that proved to be the catalyst of his career. In the other corner was Coventry hardman Errol Christie. Christie's career had taken a downward slide and he needed to win against James desperately. "Errol Christie was like this Golden Boy. At that time Christie was at Brockley and I was at Peckham, just up the road. When the fight was made, trust me, Christie trained. It was like, 'Who want to be the man of the town? Christie from Brockley or Cook from Peckham?'" On fight night 'Cook from Peckham' did the business. He stopped Christie in five.

While it lasted it was an all-action fight. James knocked Christie down in the first. Christie looked shocked and got up at two and sat back down again, getting up at nine.

Christie weathered the storm and at one stage in the third round both boxers appeared to be recklessly throwing all notions of defence to the wind, trading leather like there was no tomorrow. By the fourth, James was starting to take over and in the fifth he knocked Christie back across the ring to the ropes with a big right cross. James piled in and Christie was slumping to the canvas as referee Richie Davies jumped in. "It was a fight that we was testing each other to the limits. These were the guys who were making all the headlines and along came the bombshell that was me. Mind you, even after beating Christie there were probably still people who never realised that I could fight. But when I was reading the papers if they say something good I'd smile. If they don't say something good I don't take it to heart. I'm a good judge. I know what I can do."

It was eight months before James fought again. He stopped Brian Schumacher in five in a final eliminator for the British super-middleweight title. Incidentally, this was the first time that he ever fought anybody taller than him. "When we went to the weigh-in Schumacher come over and says, 'Have you ever fought anybody taller than you?' I says, 'No.' He says, 'Well you are now!'"

Another year passed before James was allowed to fight for the title. "There was nothing wrong with me. I was inside the gym training, sparring. It really annoyed me in a sense. But then I was matched with (Sam) Storey and I thought, 'Here we go again.'"

Sam Storey, an Irish southpaw, was the first British champion at the super-middleweight limit. He had been defeated only once, by Steve Collins. He had won the title against Tony Burke, the man who had flattened James in two rounds five years earlier. On the 30th October 1990, in Storey's home town of Belfast, James stopped the Irishman in ten. "I was on a high. I just wasn't going to be beaten. In the Storey fight I thought I'd bide my time, and then destroy him with the uppercut. And yes, I unsettled him.

"What an experience Belfast was. We went there in this little plane, you could hear the engine. And my first feeling was people looking down on you with guns. We was walking to the town and the tank was following you and I think it was Barney Eastwood's son says, 'It's alright, they're boxers.' And you kind of feel the man take his hand off the trigger, in a sense. That's how it feel. And then we got into a cab and the cabbie was speaking to us, making jokes, but his laugh was a nervous laugh. We ask about the hotel we're going to, if it had been bombed? He says, 'No, this hotel is new. This one has not been bombed before.' In the morning they wake us all up and get us out. There was a bomb in the hotel. After beating Sammy Storey I didn't celebrate the way I wanted to because I was frightened. I can see why Barry McGuigan was trying to get them into sport, to get everybody to unite that way. The Irish absolutely love their sport. When I was coming home, people at the airport were saying, 'Cor, we saw you on TV. Great fight!' and I must have come home with about three bottles of whisky. I don't really drink whisky."

And so at the age of 31 James Cook was finally British champion. "When I first went pro, I said by the time I was 30 I would come out of boxing, but by 31 things were just beginning to go good for me now. I decided to stick around for a few more years and see what happen. World titles everybody want but for me, the British and European titles, they were like my world titles. Because I felt people did not want me to win them. They did everything they could to stop me getting close to them. So I was happy with those."

On the 10th March 1991 James travelled to Paris to fight for the European super-middleweight title. He stopped Frenchman Frank Winterstein in the 12th round at the Palais Des Congres. Winterstein was a rugged, shady character known as 'King of the French Gypsies.' "Every week in the *Boxing News* I was reading about this bloke Frank Winterstein. I knew he was a world rated fighter. We were on the plane and I picked up a report on one of Winterstein's fights. I see his record (50 wins in 52 fights, 37 by knockout) and I thought, 'Shit!, I'm going to get killed here.' When we arrived I was warned not to eat in the hotel. So we went to find something to eat in a little cafe. My trainer ate in the hotel and he had the runs all night.

"Winterstein knocked me down in the ninth but I wasn't dazed or anything. I don't know if I was saved by the bell. It was at the end of the round when it happen and the bell went. When the tenth round come I just show him that I wasn't going to run and I wasn't hurt, and I think I just broke his heart from there." In the last round James landed the right uppercut, sending Winterstein crashing face to the floor. James was overjoyed. But when Winterstein stayed down for several minutes he immediately ceased the celebration. By the time Winterstein was up, James could only find room in his heart for sheer relief.

Back in the dressing room after the fight James walked straight into the 'real' king of the French gypsies. And it became immediately obvious that the new European champion held no sway with this guy, nor his little helpers. It seemed that the main man had taken a healthy interest in James' shorts. "I'd just had a pair of shorts made by 'Title.' This was the first time I had ever had shorts made the way I want it, with my name on and things. After the fight I was in the changing room and this bloke come up to me. He had all these people standing around him and he say, 'Cook, can we have your shorts? We want them signed.' I say, 'Yeah, you can have my shorts.' I had a spare pair in my bag. He said, 'No I want those shorts' and he point to the ones I am wearing. I say, 'No, you can't have them.' Then I get a whisper in my ear, 'Cook, he's the king of the gypsies.' So I take off the shorts, sign them and say, 'Here mate, you can have the shorts.'"

On the 1st June 1991 James stepped through the ropes to match skill and strength with West Ham hardcase Mark Kaylor. Fittingly enough this East End bash would be staged at York Hall. Popular Kaylor was on a comeback and he was still such a massive draw. James Cook was on top of his game and ready to rock. Harry Holland aptly billed this fight as 'The Battle of The Proud Ones.' The prize on the line was James' European title. Boxing politics being what they are, James had to relinquish his British title to take the fight.

Life had taken a big turnaround for Kaylor. In happier times, when he was British and Commonwealth middleweight champion, he had hired James regularly as one of his sparring partners. The boot was now very much on the other foot. But Kaylor was still a very dangerous opponent. He was on a successful run in a comeback that saw his record rise to 47 fights, 40 wins, one draw over 11 years. He was two years younger than James but he had fought twice as many times. He had made four previous European title challenges at three weight divisions, against Tony Sibson, Herol Graham, Tom Collins and Mauro Galvano. This fight was his last big chance. James stopped him in six.

The night arrived and York Hall was packed to the rafters. Kaylor was announced and his loyal fans raised the roof. James was announced and they booed loudly. "It was like I am a stranger. I knew it would be full of Mark Kaylor's supporters but when they introduce us, I thought, 'Oh my God!' But I try to block out these things you know? I concentrate on the person. I knew Kaylor would have more supporters than me, so I just concentrate on Mark."

The fight was an absolute brawl. Kaylor was as determined as he had ever been, constantly marching forward with his chin tucked in, forcing himself onto James like a bulldozer. James was as cunning as he had ever been, biding his time, catching Kaylor on the counter with his right uppercuts, waiting for the right moment to step up through the gears. "I was expecting him to pressure me, because he could not box me in the sense that I was the better boxer of the two. So I was expecting the pressure, so I trained for the pressure." In the fourth, a right uppercut from James actually lifted one of Kaylor's feet off the floor. Still Kaylor kept coming. At the end of the fifth Kaylor plonked himself down on his stool, his mouth bleeding. He looked shattered, his handsome features swollen and sore. In the opposite corner, James looked cool, sleek and black like mahogany, ready to go another 12 rounds. They came out for the sixth and James was well and truly in charge now, starting to catch Kaylor with frightening ease. Kaylor's defiant refusal to quit kept him coming forward. Suddenly James landed with a huge right uppercut. Mark's eyes glazed over and his legs started to wobble. At that moment, Jimmy Tibbs, Kaylor's devoted trainer and friend, decided that the fight must end. Tibbs threw in the towel and referee Mickey Vann threw it back out again. But Jimmy wasn't having it. He leapt into the ring, his arm outstretched in desperate appeal. Vann furiously attempted to send Jimmy back to his corner but confusion took over and even though Kaylor was still punching at the time, the action rapidly fizzled to a standstill. Tibbs gently removed his fighter's gumshield, signalling to Vann that it was all over. James himself was quick to react to the situation. "I actually stopped punching. Because I see Jimmy in the ring. I hit Kaylor back because he hit me and I wanted to get back in there you know? But when I saw Jimmy, I stopped punching. And Jimmy did a good job, because by this time I was beginning to get loose, starting to come into my own. It's one of the best things that ever I see a trainer do. Because the pressure was slacking now and I was like, 'OK it's my turn now.'"

In the Channel 4 documentary *Fighters* Mark Kaylor declared, "I want to make it or I want to be carried out. And the next time I'm carried out, I'll retire." This class act was saved from being carried out by Jimmy Tibbs and that night he announced his retirement. He never fought again.

James never underestimated Kaylor. "Me and Kaylor was alright with each other you know? We never say nothing nasty about each other. I had done some sparring work with him. To be honest I think if I fought him any earlier he would have beat me. Because I knew he had this strength that I didn't have. Kaylor would be on the floor and he would still want you. He was that type of man."

That summer James signed up with Mickey Duff and Dennie Mancini. "I had a beautiful relationship with Dennie. In fact, I had a beautiful relationship with Mickey Duff too. He was a businessman. He say, 'Cook I am not interested in what I earn from the fighters this month. I am worried about what I can earn years down the line.' And that's where he was different. I got some great advice off him. Mickey rang me up one time and he says, 'James, why won't you give me trouble. You pay me. You must make me work for you. Everybody else does!'"

With his new team in place, James continued his blaze of glory. In October 1991 he defended his European title and settled an old score against Tarmo Uusiverta, stopping the Finn in seven at Wandsworth. "Tarmo was on my turf now and I'm the champion and like I said, I didn't think he win the first one. When he came over here he said he wasn't scared but I knew he was scared. This time I thought, 'That's my title.' There was no way he was going to beat me." It was a dirty old fight with plenty of wrestling involved. Then suddenly, in the seventh, Uusiverta turned his back in a strange act of surrender. "I got to him early. It was a fight where I was hitting harder and every time I hit him, I hurt him."

In April 1982 James travelled to Vitrolles to defend his European title against Frenchman Frank Nicotra. When he arrived in France, his brother telephoned to tell him that his mother had been taken ill. Powerless to help his family, James' mind was not on the job. Nicotra, who was unbeaten in 27 fights, came out like a train, stopping James inside one minute. "I'm going to tell you something now that I have never discussed with anybody. I didn't sleep that night. But the fight was there and I just wanted to hit him and get it out of the way as quick as possible to get back to London. Instead, it sort of backfired. He hit me and get it out of the way and that was that. I must be honest, he chucked the punch first, he got in first. I felt devastated because I thought a world title has gone out the window. But I was with a good manager and Mickey said 'We'll go back for the British title.' But after that fight the edge went off my training. I was coming in late and I wasn't resting. I could not believe that I had to go and prove myself again at the age of 33. I felt tired."

Five months after the loss to Nicotra James won an eight-rounder against Tony Booth at York Hall. A month later he stopped Irishman Terry Magee in five at Wembley. He began 1993 with a January points win over Carlos Christie. In March he stopped Karl Barwise in six. He had to wait until September that year for his next fight but it was worth it. He beat Fidel Castro Smith on points for the vacant British super-middleweight title. "Now, if you want me to be honest, that was the only fight that I actually think I lost, fair and square. I think I needed a favour that night. I'd never seen Smith until he fight Henry Wharton and I'd always pictured him as an Irishman. When I saw him I was shocked. I thought, 'Wait, there's a black man coming out of the corner!'

"Everything Mickey (Duff) could have shouted and told me, he tell me that night. Because Smith shouldn't have been a hard fight at this stage. I think I could have gone on for 15 rounds and it would have made no difference. There was none of the spirit which I used to have." When it was over John Coyle raised James' hand, making him the British super-middleweight champion for the second time.

In November 1993 it was back to basics with another points won over Tony Booth. "Booth was a late substitute and I think it was just like a workout. There was no zap there. My enthusiasm was starting to go." He began 1994 with a points win over previous stoppage victim Karl Barwise.

On the 11th March 1994 James Cook stepped through the ropes at York Hall to fight for the last time. That night he lost his British title to Cornelius Carr on points. "By round seven I looked at Carr and thought, 'A couple of years ago I would have knocked you out!' But I didn't think he won the fight even though he put me down. But the discipline in me is not to argue. Boxing has taken me all over the world and it's not right for people to see James Cook start shouting."

I talked to Cornelius about the way he felt the night he won the British title from James Cook. He responded, "It was a big, big night for me. James Cook was a big name, a great fighter and I was a nobody. The feeling I got that night, beating James Cook for the British title, I've never, ever had that feeling again, not even when I've fought for a world title. He is a gentleman inside and outside the ring." When I told James of Carr's words he gallantly conceded. "OK, I'll let him off then. But after losing to Herol Graham I said I would retire if a British fighter ever beat me again, and I did."

Mickey Duff wisely advised James that there was life after boxing, telling him to invest his money carefully. "It wasn't like I had earned millions of pounds or anything. I knew I could do two things with my money. I could buy a house or I could open a business for my missus. So I gave Carmen the money and she's got a hairdressing salon now which she has been running for ten years. Sometimes that's what feeds us. From day one when I start boxing I was telling people that I would make my money and come out of it but it was not to be. That is life and that's why I say to people you are never jealous of the next person because you don't know what they have to do to earn their bread and butter, you know?

"My hardest two fights was Errol Christie and Mark Kaylor. Because we were in the same era and we was all local and you didn't want one of the local men to beat you. When Errol Christie was gonna fight Mark Kaylor a lot of people thought Christie was gonna win but I was sparring with Kaylor and I know how rough Kaylor is. I was in the video shop and the man says to this other fella, 'I'll bet you a tenner Christie will beat Kaylor.' And I said, 'I'll take that bet.' I know Kaylor was a very hard man.

"The greatest moment for me was beating Sammy Storey for the British title. I don't have any regrets, but my lowest moment was losing to Jimmy Price the second time, the time he stopped me." And his most memorable moment? "Meeting up with that old boy who tell me..."

James' love affair with boxing would never allow him to leave the sport alone. He was determined that the knowledge he painstakingly banked along the way should not go to waste. In December 1994 his Christmas gift to the sport he loves was himself, as a licensed trainer.

"I always like the boxing. I've seen the standard go down. And you know, a lot of good fighters feel they don't want to be in it anymore because the game has treat them with such a bad blow. But when you're a fighter you don't want to give up, you want to keep fighting. I believe everybody in this world should have a fair chance. This is why I am trainer, for the fighters who don't stand a chance. I will give them a chance, I will teach them to cause upset. I love the game so much. It teach me my respect early. It teach me my manners."

James has nurtured many fighters but one that jumped out during our conversation was Matt Brown. "When Matt Brown first started with me I thought, 'You're horrible man! You've got a horrible stance. The way your leg is crooked. Really horrible!' He used to say, 'but I'm willing to learn.' And to be honest, fighters with a heart like Matt Brown... He challenged for the British title twice. He's still a really hard worker, a painter and electrician... He was a good fighter."

These days James' stable includes Spencer Fearon and Ted Bami (Minsende). James has a reputation for being a tough taskmaster. "That's right. It's a competition actually with myself and the fighters. When you retire, and you speak like you had a good career, the competition is fierce. I still run pretty well. I was out running with Spencer (Fearon), over London Bridge and Elephant and Castle. Spencer used to pass this old bloke every morning and give him some money. So, the first morning we went for a run together, the bloke said, 'Good morning Spencer.' The second day the bloke said, 'Good morning Spencer,' and I said, 'No. Spencer's back down there!' And I'm always telling them, 'You guys are very lucky, that you weren't fighting when I was around.' And yes, I do demand the same of them that I did of myself, the same fitness. The same everything. I try and teach them that it's not everybody was born with a golden spoon. Some of us may have to work hard all our lives, that's just the way life is. And I let them know I'm the only one who sees them training and sparring, I'm the only one who see them running. I'm closer to them than their girlfriend or wife. I will let them know when they can have a rest and when they can have a day off. The only excuse I will take is a note from their mothers. It's as simple as that."

Apart from his training duties, James spends his daylight hours as a youth worker in Hackney. "When Jimmy Redwell was doing the amateur club, he used to say some might 'take over the class from me.' And I used to take the class with people older and younger than me. Sometimes kids used to come in there and they was right miserable and I would always do something or say something to get them smiling. Later on I started up a youth club in Dulwich. For 11 years I was a part time youth leader over there working with kids of five to 15. Then I moved to Hackney and now I work with 13 to 19 year olds. The money is less but it means that I'm not sitting about in one place. I'm going out trying to get these kids off the street, get them in to some form of training, some form of education. At least now I get to go out there and tackle them instead of waiting for them to come to me. On my first day out on the job I was walking up the road and I seen this young man. He says to me, 'You're that boxer innit. So what you doing living in Hackney?' I told him, whether you're Frank Bruno or whatever you have to come from somewhere.

"I am religious the sense that I do believe in God. I was brought up a Christian. I do believe there's only one man up there and he put breath in us. Whenever anything happen, the first thing we say is 'Oh God!' Sometimes I pray when I go to bed. Or before a fight, I say a prayer and I'm thinking, 'He's seeing this. He's watching this.' My mum always said, 'He's slow but he's sure.'"

If I had to compare James Cook with any of the fighters that I have studied for this book, it would have to be Crawford Ashley. I think they are similar both as boxers and men. I expressed my observation to Crawford. His response was mischievously adamant and characteristically straight from the hip. "I'm nothing like James Cook! I'm tall and he's a shortie, I've got dreads and he's a baldie, and I'm much younger than he is!" But when I reminded Crawf' that they both loved to upset the apple-cart, both were members of the 'who needs 'em club,' and neither of them ever took any shit from anybody, ever, his voice softened with fond respect. "Well, I'll have to agree with you about that one, Mel." Crawford and James are good friends and as if to prove that the camaraderie between boxers will never die, James wasted no time in retaliating at the first opportunity. "I saw him at Wembley. I went up to him and said 'Hey! Crawford Ashley! I want a word with you. You might have the dreads but I'll always be better looking than you. You remember that!' I'm telling you now Mel, he's lucky that I'm not thinking of making a comeback!"

"He's one of the best challengers I've fought... With hindsight, the stoppage will be better for him and I'm glad, because I didn't have to go another three rounds with him." – Michael Ayers

In November 1997 Colin Dunne became the WBU lightweight champion. Many dyed-in-the-wool boxing fans tend to regard the large number of world boxing titles that are around today with a degree of indifference, and the World Boxing Union is one of the newer organisations on the block. For this reason Colin has not always received the respect he deserves. I know how hard Colin has worked to hold on to his title for the past five years, often when lady luck has not been in his corner. And there have been times when the lack of recognition has left him feeling frustrated. And, quite frankly, I do not blame him. For this hardy little Scouser deserves as much respect as any boxer I have ever come across.

I met Colin for this interview on a sunny Saturday morning in March 2000 at his home in Highbury, North London. At the time Colin lived with his splendid landlady Audrey, who had prepared a veritable mountain of sandwiches for us to munch our way through. Colin has known Audrey for 13 years and for much of that time he has lived under her roof. She told me, "I could never imagine myself watching a boxing match before I met Colin, but now I'm his biggest fan. I'm off down the shops now but just in case you get hungry later there's some chicken in the fridge." As I stared in wide eyed disbelief at the food mountain on the coffee table, I thought to myself, "Hungry! She's having a laugh isn't she?"

Colin and I planted ourselves like bookends on Audrey's comfortable sofa in her pleasant front room. There we settled down for the day, armed with nothing but the sandwiches, a tape recorder and a Jack Russell dog, affectionately known as Patch. They call Colin Dunne 'The Dynamo' and the cap fits. We talked non-stop for five solid hours. And before the day was over we had not only made the sandwiches disappear but we demolished the chicken too.

Colin has quite elfin features. He keeps his thick, dark hair cropped short and there is a neat, clean cut look about him. He has warm, brown eyes that flash with a mischievous twinkle when you are least expecting it. He speaks with one of those wise old Liverpool accents and one of the qualities that Colin holds in the highest regard is honesty. As you are about to read for yourself, he is a shining example of this virtue.

Colin Dunne was born in the West Derby district of Liverpool on the 19th September 1970. He has two brothers and a sister. He left Liverpool when he was 16 to become a stable lad. These days he is often referred to as a 'London based Scouser.' "As far as I'm concerned, no one can say anything wrong about Liverpool. It's a wonderful place. It gets a bad name but so does every city. It doesn't phase me at all being called a 'London based Scouser.' As long as people recognise that I'm a Scouser, that's the main thing. Because that's where my roots are at the end of the day."

Boxing is traditional in the Dunne family. Colin's uncle, Jimmy Dunne, fought in Tokyo in the 1964 Olympics at lightweight. Sadly, Jimmy died shortly before this book went to print and Colin dedicated his next fight to his respected uncle, wearing his name on his shorts. "I originally went into boxing influenced by stories about my Uncle Jimmy, and my Uncle Harold. My Uncle Harold was a good puncher. He boxed at featherweight. He never turned pro but he had some epic amateur fights. He comes to all me fights, my Uncle Harold. And my dad, he hasn't missed one, my dad since my first amateur fight.

"I started boxing when I was 11 at the Bronte ABC in Liverpool which is no longer there, I'm sad to say. It was positioned by quite a famous block of flats in Liverpool called The Bullring. It's all private now. It was quite a rough area. I used to get the bus down there every night. It was at the Bronte that I won my first schoolboy title. But my dad had close connections with Joe Curran who used to run the Everton Red Triangle, and Harry Currie who used to train us. So I think it was inevitable that I was eventually going to end up there."

Colin's first serious ambition was to win a schoolboy title. Having won the minors' section of the competition on his first time out, he travelled to Derby to compete in the National Finals three years later. All National Schoolboy champions get a Union Flag badge to sew on their shorts. This badge was the driving force behind Colin's early success. "I wanted that badge so much, but I knew that I couldn't buy that badge, I knew that I couldn't nick one of them badges. The only way I would have one of them badges on my shorts was through achievement. So I just strived for that, as small as I was. The first year and the second year, I lost it and then when I was 15 I went for it, and I won it. The boy who was meant to be facing me pulled out. His trainer said, 'I can't believe it. He knew he was facing you and he just went on the missing list.' And when I won it, it was no big deal to be honest. But I got the badge!" Colin also won a Junior ABA title, but never boxed in the seniors while he was in Liverpool because he was too light, weighing a mere six-and-a-half stone at the age of 16.

Colin was drawn to the racing game because he thought he was too small to go further as a boxer. "My dad has always loved horse racing. He's followed the jockeys and things. He asked me if I wanted to do it and I said, 'Dad, I would love to do it.' So I wrote a letter to John Candy at Lambourne, and we got a letter back. So I went down there during my last school holidays to work and see if I'd take to it. I made a few mates straight away. They were all Scousers! It was like home from home. I had the most wonderful four weeks of my life. It was the best summer holiday I had ever had, and I was working!"

So, judging from Colin's enthusiastic and immediate affiliation with the equestrian world, one could be excused for thinking that he really likes horses? "No way! I used to count my lucky stars at the end of every day that I never came out with an injury. I wasn't frightened of them at first, but a few things happened to me when I got into the game. I never feared them but I was wary of them, very wary. Because they've got the most unbelievable power.

"Anyway, as soon as Henry Candy had room for me I packed my bags and left. Henry Candy had the reputation of being very good with apprentices. He's a great introduction into the racing world. I was content there, mucking out, riding out, learning to ride, doing everything. The only time that I ever cried was when my mum sent me a five pound note in a birthday card. I cried because I knew that she couldn't afford it. But apart from that one time, I was happy at Henry Candy's.

"I was on the ponies for six months. There was this little pony I used to take out. Justin it's name was. He was a little bugger. He'd chuck you off four or five miles from home after a gallop. Then he would run off all the way home. You had to walk all the way back!

"I was clipping this horse one day, that's when you clip half their coat from the middle of the body down. It was a horse called Dwadme. It was a bugger to ride. I mean this horse would duck, buck, it used to do anything to get you off. And when it got you off, it would want to kick you. It was a nasty bit of work. And it was clever. Anyway, I'm clipping it and I pinched it's skin. It didn't budge, so I started again. Suddenly it picked it's leg up and gave me what they call a cow kick. It went bang! It kicked me right in between me family allowance and me hip. I went about three foot in the air, hit a wall and just collapsed. I was in shock. Anyway the assistant head lad got a grip of it and sorted it out. That sort of brought home to me how dangerous they are.

"And I've been bitten on the lip! That one was called Warm Winter. I'll always remember that name. I thought my bottom lip was hanging off, but it wasn't thank God. She was a bit of a cow, that horse. I thought I had her in the palm of my hand. I had been sweetening her up over a matter of weeks. I didn't normally feel affection for the horses but one day I leaned over to give her a kiss on the nose, and the next thing, crunch. She bit me bottom lip!

"When you are near a horse's head, you feel pretty safe, although they can strike out forwards but that's not very frequent. Anyway, I was standing in front of this horse and it picked it's rear leg up and scratched the back of it's ear! I thought, 'That's it. There is no safe place around a horse. If they can get their hind legs up there, we've got no chance!'

"Eventually I started riding the race horses. I became quite a good little rider. But as time went on I was getting heavier and heavier. Anyway, I won the Stable Lads Boxing Championship, I beat a boy called Michael Carter. It was a great fight. At the same time I was really disillusioned with the racing game. I was eight stone now and an ideal starting weight for jockeys is seven stone. I used that fight with Carter to decide my future. I thought, 'If I can't win the Stable Lads, there's no way I can do well as a professional boxer.'"

Our principal boy beat Carter, won the title and decided to pack his bags and head for London to become a fighter. In most boxing stories there is usually an anchor character involved, somebody who has been crucial to the success of the main man. In Colin's case, the anchor character is his trainer, Colin Lake. Colin Lake's friends call him 'Lakey' and during my first drink with him at a pub in Islington I got it straight from the horse's mouth that I am now qualified to use this name. So for the purpose of avoiding confusion I shall from now on refer to him as such. Also I shall print all Lakey's words in italics.

Lakey himself was a force to be reckoned with in his fighting days. He issued a brave challenge to Jimmy Anderson for the British junior-lightweight title (now super-featherweight) in 1969. This was the second time these two met in the ring, the first time Anderson got disqualified in the seventh round which Lakey still feels was unfair on his opponent. "I don't know why they disqualified him to be honest. Mind you, I was well ahead on points anyway." The second time, with the title at stake, Lakey lost in seven rounds.

Colin has fond memories of his first meeting with Lakey. "I met Colin Lake at Newmarket. He had already seen me box and he told me that he could see that I had the makings of a good pro. He said that he thought that he was the guy to bring me on and take me through. And it's proved true. He told me the highs and lows. But I wasn't listening to the lows. He said he would get me digs in London and get me a job. So six months later I rang him up." Over the years these two have become great pals as much as boxer and trainer. When Colin Dunne goes out running in the cold, dark winter mornings through the driving rain over Hampstead Heath his trusted pal Lakey is right there running alongside him. Even if his charge does leave him behind from time to time. *"If he waited for me, he'd catch bloody pneumonia!"*

Lakey has fond memories of his first meeting with his little Dynamo. *"I'd seen him boxing in the Stable Lads. I looked at him and I thought, 'He's got it there.' It's funny how some people come along and you know, they shine. Anyway, I was having a drink at the bar and Dave Lowrie, a friend of mine from years ago, brought him over. I told him he boxed well but he needed to do a bit of work. He didn't have the experience but you could see he had something you could work on. Anyway, he says, 'Will you take me to London?' I said, 'I could arrange it. I could get you digs and a job and that.' Then he says, 'I want to be a pro.' I said, 'Nah, you won't go pro yet son. That's a different ball game. You've got a lot to learn.' I was training an amateur club in London at the time, Islington ABC. I told him 'You can start off there and in maybe two or three years time, you can turn over. It all depends on your progress.' He says, 'But I want to turn pro now!' He was so impatient. I said, 'We'll see what comes out of it after you've done a bit. We'll see how it goes.' Anyway, about six months later the phone rings. It's Colin. He says, 'I'm coming down.' I says, 'Oh? You're coming down are you?'"* Lakey chuckled at the memory.

Colin told me, "I arrived in London in March 1990. Lakey's friend, Brad, brought me round to Audrey's. Audrey took one look at me and thought I was a runaway. But as soon as she seen me carry the cases up the steps she said she knew I was a man. I mean, I had been away from home for four years by then. I was quite worldly wise."

"Anyway, he turns up on me doorstep. My mate Brad said he could sort him out with good digs, with Audrey. He was right an' all! They hit it off straight away. She took one look at him and said, 'Yeah, you'll do.' He was only young, he looked so angelic. She didn't realise how cheeky he was! We all sat down at Audrey's and had a cup of tea and I told him, 'This is your new home.'" Colin told me that he was so desperate to become a fighter that would not have cared where he slept. "I was so keen to become a professional boxer at that time,

if Colin Lake had told me to sleep on a bench with a sleeping bag I would have happily done it."

Lakey has always been a stickler for discipline, as young Colin Dunne was soon to discover. *"I got him a job on the removals, and that's a hard job that is. So anyway, a couple of months after he had started with me in the amateurs, I'm waiting for him down the Islington club and he phones me up. He says, 'I've been working really hard today.' I says, 'Yeah, so what's the problem?' He says, 'But, I'm really tired.' I says, 'Yeah, so tell me the problem?' He says, 'Alright, I'm on my way now.' Anyway, a few minutes later he rings me back. He says, 'The motor won't start.' So I says, 'So tell me the problem then!' He says 'Well, I'm not going to get ...' I says, 'Well, you'll have to run down here then, won't you?' Oh, did he have the hump. But he got there. And afterwards he says, 'I'm glad I done that.' I had to show him that this game ain't easy. You can't have a day off willy nilly, there are no short cuts."*

For the next few years Lakey worked hard to get Colin the amateur bouts he needed, taking him all over the country. And so Colin Dunne was on his way to becoming the fighter he wanted to be. But in those early days he lived a far from idealistic life. "Two-and-a-half years went by. All this time I was struggling financially. I done bits and bobs but there was no regular income. During this time I trained quite a bit down at Finchley ABC and I used to spar quite regularly with Spencer Oliver. He was very strong, mature for his age. When I used to spar with him I was quite a bit older than him but he was every bit as mature as me, if not more."

During their early days together, Lakey also used slip the gloves on with Colin. *"I remember the first time we sparred. He was looking at me and thinking, 'You ain't going to spar with me.' I was just coming up for 50 then. He was going, 'You're having a laugh aren't you?' I said, 'Oh, you won't hit me, don't you worry about that.' Anyway, we finished and he said, 'I can't handle this!' I says, 'Listen son, you'll be doing things what I'm doing now to other people later on, when you get the experience.' Anyway, he hung in there."*

Colin is managed by Terry Toole, very much a hands on manager. He sorts Colin's medicals, negotiates purse money, organises contracts, chooses the opponents and makes regular trips down the gym to see how Colin is shaping up. Colin says that Toole's matchmaking skills are second to none and that he collaborates with Lakey constantly on Colin's progress. Colin respects Terry hugely. "He's a great guy. He's really come through for me. He's another character. He's an experience on his own, Terry. He's like me and Colin Lake, he boxed and he was in racing. He boxed as a flyweight. Terry has got to be the best matchmaker in this country and one to one, Colin Lake is the best trainer. He can focus on that one fighter and make life safe for that fighter."

And Lakey likes it that way too. *"I prefer it that way, it works for me. I'm so dedicated to that one fighter. I might be in bed and I'll suddenly think, 'He needs to work on this, or that.' And I'll get out of bed to write it down. I'm always thinking about ways to improve him."* Colin has deep respect for his mentor's dedication to his well-being. "Colin

Lake has had his ups and downs in boxing. But boxing is Colin's life. He's thinking about it now. He's in the pub, talking about me, now."

Eventually, Lakey decided that Colin was ready to take that first step into the professional boxing arena. But first, he needed a ring name, something that reflected his identity. "'The Dynamo.' It came to me when he was amateur. I thought, 'That's what he's going to be called.' Because he's like a dynamo, he generates energy. It looks like he's tired but he's got another gear. He's always got another gear."

Colin had his first professional fight on the 7th December 1993 against Mark O'Callaghan at Bethnal Green. He won it in 31 seconds. "It was a bit of an anti-climax really, because it was stopped so early. But it was a bit of a relief as well, to get it out of the way and in that sort of style. It was great all the same. It's quite an occasion, having all your supporters there for the first time." A month later Colin stopped Wayne Jones in three at York Hall in Bethnal Green. Two months after that he stopped Malcolm Thomas in one, flooring the Welshman three times and taking just one minute, 59 seconds to do the job.

Colin quickly established a strong army of fans. "For that I must give great thanks to my trainer Colin Lake. He used to take me round various pubs and introduce me to people, which I used to just hate! But to give him his due, he used to put up with my miserable face and drive me around. He'd make me shake hands and once I get talking, I can bloody talk. But at the same time I used to dread it. We done that for a number of years, in fact we still get about and see people now."

Another person who has worked tirelessly for Colin over the years is a character who is fondly known as Johnny 'Rambo' Stephens. "He's quite notorious up in the Finsbury Park area, very well known, for his fights and street fights. He's an ex-para. He was Johnny Rotten's personal minder when he was with the Sex Pistols. He's such a lovely guy! Anyway, he's met a girl and he's marrying her out in America. It's a bit of a love story as it happens. John used to spar with me down in Islington. He brought me on a great deal. He'd just started back in boxing, he was about 34 then. John was more rugged and I was more smooth if you like. He often tells the story of when it went off in the gym one time and I caught him with what he calls a rhythm punch, I hit him with a left hook. He said afterwards he was seeing little coloured lights flying around and everything. And I get embarrassed because he tells this story in front of people who look at John as a right hard man and I'm going, 'John, shut up!' but he doesn't care. He's proud of it! For all my fights, John must have sold in excess of 800 tickets. And his cousin's the same, Mickey Neagle, he used to train the boys down at Islington as well. He's also been very influential for me, Mickey Neagle and his family. Between them two they've sold the most tickets for us, and they've done it every fight. They've took the tickets off us, took the pressure off us, gone away and come back with the money. And they've been there all the way through." For the record, the ex-Sex Pistol Johnny Rotten (John Lydon) is also one of Colin's biggest fans and a regular face at his fights.

On the 26th April 1994 Colin stopped heavily-tattooed Welshman Steve Burton in two at York Hall. Burton never stood a chance. Colin was on his case right from the first bell. This was Colin's fourth consecutive win as a pro, all inside three rounds. But, on a sad and quiet note, the late Bradley Stone had his last fight on the same bill. "It had a profound effect on me. I was at the funeral but I just couldn't let it sink in if you know what I mean? I was trying so hard not to let it affect me in an overly dramatic way. And then when Spencer Oliver got hurt, I was watching that in the pub and when he went down I couldn't believe it. And then he didn't get up."

Three weeks after stopping Burton, Colin went the distance for the first time to win on points over six against Phil Found in Kettering. Colin is quick to admit that Found was a tough fight. "Terry Toole thought I needed to get a few rounds under my belt. Terry's away all the time and he watches these shows from beginning to end. When he spotted Phil Found he felt that he was the guy to stretch me. He said, 'You can't just keep knocking them all over. You've got to take your time.' And yes, Phil Found was a tough nut and I learned a lot from that fight, which was the whole idea."

On the 23rd September 1994 ,Colin returned to his early night strategy stopping Steve Howden of Sheffield in two minutes 44 seconds at York Hall. "As you get on in boxing it's great to get a few rounds under your belt. But I was classed as a bit of a puncher in my early fights. Not so much now but there again, it's all about stepping up in class." Next time out Colin won on points over six against Jimmy Phelan. *Boxing News* reported that Phelan had been Colin's toughest fight so far. "It was only tough in that I wasn't myself that night. The way I always describe that fight is that I felt like I had a sheet of lycra in front of me. Every time I threw a punch it had to go through the sheet before it got to him. It was like I was fighting a force that was stopping my arms from doing what I wanted them to do. That is the way I felt that night. It wasn't my hardest fight. It's just that I wasn't right that night."

Keeping up his busy schedule, in November 1994 Colin stopped Mark O'Callaghan in two at Millwall. O'Callaghan was Colin's first professional opponent back in December 1993 when he stopped him in the first. The Dynamo rounded off 1994 with a December three round stoppage of Hull's David Thompson. Commentating that night was Steve Holdsworth who has always been a very shrewd judge of boxing. During the fight Holdsworth was quick to spot the remarkable similarity of the styles of Dunne and Lakey remarking, "It's almost like watching Colin Lake all over again."

Colin kicked off 1995 with a fourth round stoppage of Leeds fighter Chris Aston. "He was tough. And it was quite new to me as a fight. He was a switch hitter. I had sparred with a lot of switch hitters and Colin Lake gave me such a good education by putting me in with these boys. So when I got in the ring with Chris Aston, although it was all new, I just had a grin on my face. I though, 'OK we'll have some of this. Come on!' Because for me, it's all just been a learning field. And yes, Chris Aston was tough, I mean, my hands were hurting hitting him."

A month later Colin stopped Marco Fattore of Watford in three at York Hall. Prior to the stoppage, Fattore was badly hurt in the second by a big right cross and although he got up straight away he had to take a few more big right hands before the end of the round. In the third, Colin was all over the Watford man and, after taking one of Colin's blistering combinations, Marco went down again. He got up at six and many thought the fight would be called off, but it was not. However, one more big right hand shook Fattore to his boots and the referee stepped in. The general feeling that night was that the fight could have been stopped when Fattore went down in the third round. Colin agrees. "Without a doubt yes. It should have been stopped there and then. But then they've got a bit of weight on their shoulders, these referees, because they've got a paying public. I don't know what runs through their minds. Every fight is different. There might be half a dozen people in the crowd saying, 'Stop it.' There might be two dozen saying, 'Don't stop it.' It's a very hard decision."

In April 1995 Colin secured a six round points win over Rudy Valentino at York Hall. Valentino had just lost seven in a row, but he was hard, experienced and willing. He had the knowledge to make things tricky for Colin. "Rudy was a good test. To pardon the pun, he was a contender. But he ended up being a journeyman, which sometimes happens in boxing. He was a bit of a Bobby Vanzie type of fighter. Not as flamboyant as Vanzie but you know, slip and move, always looking to sneak in there and catch you." A month later Colin was back in for a re-match with Chris Aston at York Hall. He won it in four. "Just at the finish I caught him with a nice left hook to the body and he said to me straight away after the fight, 'It was that last body shot that did it.' Mind you, I wasn't looking forward to that fight. Because as much as I beat him last time, I knew it wasn't going to be easy."

On the 27th September 1995 Colin had a second fight with Steve Howden and this time he stopped him in four. A month later he won another four round stoppage over Chris Clarkson at the Albert Hall. However, Clarkson caused a major scare when he dropped Colin with a left hook at the end of the first round. Colin got up to force the Hull boxer into submission in the fourth. Boxing at the Albert Hall had a haunting effect on a The Dynamo. "It was very daunting to be honest with you. Because sad to say, that's where Spencer got hurt. And it was the first time I ever got put on me arse by the way. He hit me with a left hook, I'll never forget it, it was on the top of the temple. You know the Fairy Liquid advert when the baby bounces on the towels? Well, that was how I felt. I was sort of floating to the canvas. It was a lovely, euphoric feeling. Then me bum hit the floor and I went, booooyyynngg!! And then I thought, 'That's it, I've had enough of that feeling' and I jumped straight up and I thought, 'I'm going to stop him now.'"

On the 8th December 1995 Colin rounded off the year by producing his best performance to date. At the same time he reached another milestone in his career. He stopped Jonathan Thaxton in five at York Hall to win the vacant Southern Area lightweight title. Colin was quick to remind me that the Southern Area is the largest on the map and therefore in his opinion the most important area title. Thaxton, trained by

Brendan Ingle, was moving down from light-welter to take the fight, a division where he had previously held this title. He had been known to put the cat among the pigeons before with his switch hitting, hands low style. This was a fight in which both fighters gave and took relentlessly. Thaxton decked Colin at the beginning of the second but Colin jumped straight back up to fight back furiously. By the fifth, Colin was on top and knocked Thaxton into his own corner with a right hand. He followed up with a few hard left hooks and referee Roy Francis quickly leapt in to rescue Thaxton. Colin remains adamant that his trip to the canvas in the second round was not a true knock-down. "It was more of a shove than a punch. I was off balance. The power of the shot knocked me over but I was straight up. It didn't hurt. And I must have been on the floor for a split second and *Boxing News*, they've got photos of it in there!

"This one was certainly one of the milestones in my career. Because it was for the Southern Area title, which is a stepping stone to a British title. I thought, 'If I can't win a Southern Area title, where am I going in boxing?' That is what my attitude was like. It was the same thing as I felt about the fight for the Stable Lads Championship. Jonathan Thaxton's name didn't even come into it. But having said that, he was a formidable opponent. And I survived the power and the rawness of him and I stopped him, so it was a great feeling. It was nice being Southern Area champion as well."

Three months later, on 5th March 1996, Colin had a re-match with Rudy Valentino, this time stopping him in four. A month later he stopped Kino Rodriguez in two. A month after that he fought Hungarian Lajos Nagy in five at Brent Town Hall. "Now he was a southpaw. I don't mind fighting southpaws. I just get on with it. The way I look at it, he's got the same problem as I've got. I stopped him in five. I just kept at him. He was very tall, he was a good fighter. But I caught him, and I just kept going."

In July 1996 Colin was back at Brent Town Hall to do battle with Marian Stoica. Marian may be a considered a feminine name in Britain but there was nothing girlie about the Romanian's style of fighting. Colin managed a points win but he was certainly not the fiery aggressor his fans had come to know and love. Lakey, seeing that Colin was not on top form, began berating his fighter between rounds. "Stoica was tough, very tough. And Lakey loses it a bit when I'm not doing what he wants me to do, but a lot of that goes over my head. I'm used to him. Mind you, to be honest, as time goes on I'm taking more notice of him."

After an October eight round points win over Bamana Dibateza of Zaire, the time had come for Colin Dunne to attempt his next stepping stone. He would challenge Tooting's Michael Ayers for the British lightweight title. Ayers was the reigning champion and he was then, and still is, a hugely respected figure in the fight game. It was a massive challenge for The Dynamo. Although many people felt that Ayers was on his way down, at the age of 31 with a failed WBO attempt behind him, the Tooting man's world title defeat against Giovanni Parisi had been his only loss in 22 fights. Also, Ayers was one of those fighters who seemed to defy age. He seemed to mature like a good wine.

In November 1996 Colin stepped through the ropes in Wembley Grand Hall to challenge Ayers for his title. This British championship fight was eagerly anticipated by the boxing public. That night Colin lost a fight for the first time in his professional career when Michael Ayers stopped him in nine rounds. This clash between two brave warriors was all action from start to finish and when Colin was stopped in the ninth he won the respect of everybody, not least Michael Ayers, hence the quote at the top of this chapter.

"We knew it wasn't going to be an easy fight. I'd seen Michael Ayers fight before and Colin Lake had a couple of tapes. As far as I was concerned, I'd seen enough. Because I'm watching them and I'm getting butterflies. I thought, 'He can box, he's strong, he can punch but he's so bloody slow. I'll make him miss. I'll wipe the floor with him.' Colin Lake kept telling me to watch the Ayers vs Parisi tape and I kept saying I'd seen enough.

"Well, I watched the Parisi fight after I'd been beaten, which was the wrong time to watch it. If I had watched that fight before I got into that ring, things might have turned out differently. As I climbed into the ring I had never felt better in my life. I was feeling so fit, so confident. Nobody could tell me he was going to beat me. If I had have owned a house I would have put the house on me beating him. And I went out there and sure enough, I made him miss with ease. I went back after the first round and Colin Lake went a bit wild. 'Calm Down! What are you doing!' I remember him saying it to me but all I could see was a pile of gold and that Lonsdale belt sitting in the middle of it. It was like a mirage. That was all that was in my head. I thought, 'This is it, I've won it. He ain't going to last three rounds.' Now if I'd seen the Parisi fight, I would have realised that he can take it all night! So I've got out there, bang, bang and before I know it, it's the seventh round and I'm on my arse thinking, 'What am I doing here?'

"He hit me right underneath the heart. It was like someone putting a scaffold pole all the way through me. That's how powerful he was. My legs just went. It stopped my heart. I went down. I got up. The fight continued. We come into the eighth and I wanted Michael Ayers to know that I was still there, still in his face. And I done a wrong thing. It was just an antic really, it wasn't meant to do him any damage. I kneed him in the groin. It was me saying to him, 'I'm still here Michael, this ain't all your fight.' Well he went into overdrive then. He said to me afterwards in the dressing room, 'You're a great fighter but the worst thing you ever did was knee me in the groin.' And I can understand that. I mean, you can be all out and somebody can spit in your face and you'll find energy from somewhere. When I done that, it just set fire to him. I threw petrol on the flame there. But I'm not going to cry over spilt milk. I learned a lot from that fight, a hell of a lot. And I've gone on to better things so I'm not going to grumble. We don't learn if we don't make mistakes."

Colin was still the reigning Southern Area champion and in April 1997, he defended his title against Lewis Reynolds. He won it in four. Two months later he stopped Demir Nanev of Bulgaria 59 seconds before the end of their eight rounder at York Hall. After an eighth round stoppage of Alan Bosworth at York Hall another major challenge presented itself.

On the 28th November 1997 Colin won the vacant WBU lightweight title by beating Zoltan Kalocsai of Hungary on points. This was the first time for The Dynamo had gone 12 rounds and there were those who wondered how he might take it. As if to spite his doubters, Colin romped the 12 round distance with comparative ease, securing a comfortable points decision. "It was good to get it under my belt. The main thing that I learned from the Ayers fight was how to pace myself. I had done ten rounds in the gym before, in sparring. It's a mental thing, but I knew I could do that sort of distance. I went nine with Ayers at a blazing pace so I knew that at a sensible place I could go 12. Another thing I learned from the Ayers fight was to watch the bloody tape! So I watched Kalocsai versus George Scott for the WBU title. Scott was quite a good fighter, and I knew what I had in front of me. Anyway I won the WBU title."

Then came six barren months. Fights were being arranged, only to fall through. The pressure was mounting. Colin and Lakey roamed the London gyms, looking for sparring, looking to stay sharp. They could often be found down Fitzroy Lodge. "That's a great atmospheric gym. I sparred with Daniel Day Lewis down there. But it was hard because we were training and training and the fights kept falling through."

On the 23rd May 1998 the drought ended and The Dynamo was back in action, and facing his toughest test yet, against Emmanuel 'Sleek' Clottey. Clottey hails from Bukom in Ghana. This is the land that produced Ike Quartey, Alfred Kotey and the great Azumah Nelson, with whom Clottey had sparred many rounds on the concrete of the spartan Bukom gym. Clottey was unbeaten in 14 fights and was his country's former super-featherweight champion. Colin's first WBU title defence was going to be tough.

The contest started and continued at a very fast pace. Clottey was on the attack early on but Colin remained calm under pressure and threw plenty of his, by now, trademark hooks to the body. Clottey went down in the seventh but he was in the fight all the way. The crowd were on their feet for the last round, which was a blazing finale to a thrilling fight. "I would say this fight was the hardest fight I have had. A lot of people said to me afterwards, 'You'll never have another fight as tough as that,' and I said, 'You're joking aren't you?' I didn't class it as a tough fight at the time, but when I watched the tape afterwards I realised how hard it actually was. Up until this fight I didn't really feel like a valid world champion. I felt like I had sneaked in the back door. Because in my mind to lose the British title and then go in for the WBU just didn't sit right.

"I remember he wound me up at the weigh-in. He says 'Can you fight?' and I said 'You'll find out tomorrow night?' And he went, 'Are you ready to die? Are you prepared to die in the ring?' Well that just struck a chord with me, because of Bradley. And I looked at him and thought, 'Little do you know I would die beating you.' He done me a favour because I knew it was a fight that I had to be really up for. I go into every fight respecting my opponents and I was glad that I had no respect for him. And I didn't have any respect for him until I seen him in the gym about two months ago. He was holding my arms aloft and calling me champion, and I realised that he is a really nice fella."

Colin defended his world title against Affif Djelti of France on the 21st July 1998. They fought at Widnes, very close to Liverpool, and this was Colin's first live performance in front of so many family members and friends. "It was great. But the pressure was right on me because all my relatives from all around Liverpool were there to support me. Djelti was a very evasive, very cute fighter. He had a good left hook and he clipped me in the first round and I thought, 'You're dangerous you are.' So I kept my hands high and I pursued him. I was very stiff in the fight, very tense, and I put that down to the fact that the TV were there, and all the friends and family. I wanted to impress, so once again instead of relaxing and getting on with the job in hand and enjoying it, I was trying to finish him off. He caught me in the last round, but nothing I was worried about. He shook me a little bit, more of a surprise than anything. But he respected me because he was always waiting for a little opening you know. A couple of times in the fight he came at me and I managed to fend him off and he acknowledged me both times, as if to say, 'You ain't silly.' Them couple of moments when an old dog like that respected me meant a lot to me, because he could have caught me if I had been a little bit less cautious or less aware. He was a 38-year-old against 28-year-old, out to take the world title and I wasn't going to let that happen. So I won it on points."

Colin rounded off 1998 with by stopping Sedat Puskullu of Turkey in three rounds in December. "That was a warm up fight for Phillip Holiday. We both had fights on the same bill, and he won his and I won mine." On the 27th February 1999 Colin defended his WBU title against former IBF title holder, Phillip Holiday of South Africa. Holiday had lost just once in 35 fights and that was to the fabulous Shane Mosley who took his IBF crown. No shame there. Even though the South African was arguably past his peak he was still a very dangerous fight. "Holiday was a big pressure fight, a big stepping stone. It was ITV, it was top of the bill, it was a fight I had to win." Colin won the unanimous decision. Despite getting cut, he felt so good afterwards that he even put on a little shadow boxing display for the well-wishers back in the changing room.

But Colin was forced to pay a big price for his victory. "Sadly I got the cut over the right eye. Unfortunately for me I had reaction to the deep stitches. It took ages to heal up and I'm still scarred from it now. In the end I went down Harley Street to see this lovely man, Pat Whitfield. He used to box himself in the amateurs when he was studying to be a doctor. He was such a lovely guy, he didn't want me and Lakey to go. He wanted us to stay and talk boxing." After a short wait to see if things cleared up naturally, Whitfield took Colin to a private hospital. "He done it in less time than it would take to drink a cup of tea. And do you know, he never charged me a penny. I walked out looking like Frankenstein had been after me, but it's healed up fantastic." And Lakey leaves us in no doubt about his feelings for Pat Whitfield. *The man is a genius. He loves boxing. He's done Minter, Bruno, the lot! You make sure you put that in the book. He is a genius.*

While the injury took its time to heal Colin kept up his training under the watchful and caring eye of Lakey. It was not an easy time for either man. They were very much in limbo, awaiting a fight date that was taking far too long to arrive. "I just kept training and training and I've always got to tick over, you see Melanie. That's the regime Colin Lake has me under which is a good thing really, because if you let yourself go for a month or more, it will take you three months to get back. He keeps me ticking over and keeps me focused, you know?"

Eventually, after almost a year-and-a-half out of action, The Dynamo stepped through the ropes to resume his career. After two stoppage wins over Leonti Voronchuk and Rakhim Mingaleev, Colin had the fight that finally seemed to win him the unadulterated respect he had always craved. In the other corner was Luton's Billy Schwer.

This was one of those fights that everybody wanted to see. The fight was made on the 14th October 2000 and the venue was Wembley Conference Centre. And that night these two British boxing war-horses put on an absolute sizzler. The venue was sold out and during the supporting action the fans took their seats, Schwer's lot on one side of the arena and Dunne's on the other. Both boxers are hugely supported and as Colin and Billy warmed up in their dressing rooms their fans warmed up their vocal chords, battling to see who could sing the loudest, desperate to show their loyal support for their fighters. The moment arrived and the atmosphere was charged as Billy Schwer entered the ring, resplendent in a white hooded gown. Then it was the champion's turn to make his entrance. The drums of the Glitter Band filled the air as The Dynamo stepped through the doors and as he made his way down the gangway, Schwer danced around to the pulsating beat of the music as he waited in the ring. Finally in the ring together Billy Schwer was tall, blonde, handsome and Colin Dunne was compact, determined, electric.

The first bell rang and battle commenced. Schwer used his longer reach and extra height to box behind his jab a lot while Colin went for his trademark hooks to the body. Schwer looked much bigger but Dunne was strong and fast. After two very close rounds, Colin took over in the third with some clever combinations to win the session. In the fourth Schwer caught Colin with a left uppercut and Colin's eye opened up. I was sitting at ringside and I remember thinking, 'Oh my God. That bloody cut's opened up again.' But I later learned that it was a completely new injury. The round belonged to Schwer. Colin took the fifth and Schwer looked tired as he walked back to his corner. Schwer looked strong as he came out for the sixth and landed with potent gloves. Colin retaliated with his hooking combinations, many of The Dynamo's punches sinking sickeningly into the ribs of Billy Schwer. By the seventh both fighters were battle scarred. In the eighth Colin's eye bled horribly, impairing his vision badly, forcing him to fight through a red fog. Schwer looked cool as the ninth started when Colin suddenly landed with a powerhouse right that rocked the Luton man to the soles of his boots. The Dynamo was back to throwing punches in bunches, bringing Schwer's arms down with his body assault. The crowd were like two armies by now, doing battle with noise, each side erupting when their man scored. In the tenth Colin's eye was a ghastly mess and blood streamed from Billy's nose. By the 11th they both looked exhausted and yet they fought through their fatigue, both feeling that they were still in with a chance of winning this thrilling fight. And then Schwer suddenly looked more tired, and The Dynamo lived up to his name to take the round with energy left in the tank, somehow. The boxers were welcomed by an ecstatic and electrified crowd as they marched out for the 12th and final round. After emphatically touching gloves, they went for it. The final push. Schwer seemed to defy gravity as he pulled out one last try. Colin fought back defiantly, determined that he would not lose the world title that he held so dear. It was a merciful thing when the final bell sounded. Both of these two warriors had given everything. While the judges' scores were being collected, everybody at ringside had an opinion as to who had won and why. I sat there dazed by the performance that I had witnessed, and I felt that Colin had taken it.

They announced a split decision. You could cut the air with a knife as everybody waited to see who had won. It was Colin. After an brief moment of ecstatic energy, The Dynamo reached out to embrace his fellow gladiator. When Sky Sports came for the post fight interview, Colin Dunne and Billy Schwer sat side by side on the ring apron, in it together to the last, shoulder to shoulder. I spoke to Colin and his trusted pal Lakey a few days after the fight. Colin told me, "There was no way that was a split decision. No way." Lakey told me, "*He's a special little soldier, he really is. Oh Mel, I was so proud of him.*"

And I think this epic fight is a good place to sign off this chapter. Colin Dunne is still fighting, still winning, still WBU lightweight champion. His only loss remains the one to Michael Ayers. These days the two Colins travel about the gyms of London looking for sparring partners. They have treated the constant obstacles presented to them over the years as solutions in disguise. Colin remains characteristically positive in his outlook. "At the end of the day, I'm a young man, a healthy young man. And I'm content with that. As far as I'm concerned I was a young man at 12 years old. I knew right from left, I knew right from wrong, and I knew where I wanted to go. All I've done since then is matured, and filled my head with more knowledge. Just learned through the experiences of life." And Lakey remains as confident as ever. "*He's a crowd pleaser isn't he? He's exciting. He has matured now. I'm so proud of him. And Terry's done a good job of matching him. We've had our ups and downs but he's improving all the time.*"

Colin misses Liverpool and the loved ones he has left behind there. Hopefully one day he will realise his dream and return home, having achieved everything that he is aiming for. "The thing is that the Maggie Thatcher years were very cruel to Liverpool. I remember growing up as a kid and Liverpool had become what I would call a ghost town. Everyone was leaving school. I had to leave and go for my goal in life, to get on and make money and be successful. So that I could come back to Liverpool one day, in my Mercedes Benz with a nice bit of money and say, 'Here I am!' And I'm still striving for that now, believe it or not!

"You see, with fighting, it's in your blood. Because, it ain't just fighting. It's what you are going to gain, what you can lose, how you are going to feel about yourself afterwards. And you can't get it out of your blood. I do understand fighters coming back after they've retired. What do you do after you retire? It's always there. The fighter is always there."

CHAPTER SIX – BILLY WALKER

"Of all the heavyweights out there, Billy Walker was the only one who could pack Wembley out three hundred and sixty five days a year. There was somethin' about him man, there was just something about him." – Freddie Mack

It was 1958 and 19-year-old Billy Walker walked through the doors of West Ham Boxing Club for the first time. He had no intention of becoming a boxer but he needed to get fit for his job. One day he stepped into the sparring ring to give it a go, just to see if he liked it. He liked it... and a star was born. Three years later he became ABA heavyweight champion. And then he had the fight that put him on the map. He fought for Great Britain against giant Philadelphian Cornelius Perry and he knocked out the American in the first round. The fight was televised and pubs everywhere were packed to groaning point with patriotic British fight fans. Every boxing fan of a certain age I know can remember where they were that night, the night they watched that fight. Billy turned professional and generated the kind of box office usually reserved for royalty and film stars. Therefore, it seems almost iniquitous that he never actually won a title as a professional. He was after all 'The Blonde Bomber,' 'The Golden Boy.' He was the handsome one who fought every fight as if his life depended on it. Attack, attack and then attack again. Time after time he thrilled the crowds with his style, throwing so many punches he left them breathless.

I met Billy for this interview at Bertorellis in London's Covent Garden district. When he walked into the restaurant he seemed to fill the room. At 62 he is still a head turner. Dressed in an immaculate suit, his elegant wife Patricia at his side, he still looks every inch the star. His manner immediately put me at ease, he was so relaxed and charming and as we sat over a plate of pasta and a couple of glasses of wine he told me the story of his boxing career, heavily punctuated with big smiles.

Billy Walker was born on the 3rd March 1939 in West Ham. He has two brothers, John and George. He has four children, Daniel, Tom, Claire and Kelly. These days he and Patricia live in Essex. Billy grew up in the east end of London. "I worked as a porter at Billingsgate Fish Market. We bought a car when I was 18. It was a big black Chevrolet, with chrome bumpers. Quite fun. God it was old. And I was paying for it weekly, so to get a bit of extra money I took this job at the Ilford Palais as a doorman. We didn't get much but it paid for the car and what we wanted." To get himself fit for his job at the Palais, Billy became a regular at West Ham boxing club. "Well, a few of us went down to the gym, basically to lose weight because we all drank too much beer actually. We shouldn't have really, but we did. And then they suggested that we should box. My other three friends retired immediately and I didn't, I don't know why. I never thought I would box, never. I think someone suggested that I was scared and you think, 'No. I'm not scared!'"

From the moment Billy first laced a glove, his older brother George was at his side. George was 1951 ABA light-heavyweight champion and became a solid professional. His night came when he challenged Welshman Dennis Powell for the vacant British light-heavyweight title in March 1953. It was the most brutal fight and George retired in round 11. He would remain a driving force throughout Billy's boxing career, amateur and professional, when he became his manager. "In those days George and I were very close, very close. I would put it on a father and son relationship rather than a relationship between brothers. He was only ten years older than me but you must remember, being brought up during the war, when we got evacuated from the East End I was about two. And growing up the only person at home was George, because John and my Dad had gone off to war. So I always looked to George. I slept in the same room as George and all through the war I talked to George. And then we came back to Ilford and my father had come back home. I had a nice relationship with my father but he never took control. It was either my mother or George. So when I got to be about six, he was 16. He was a man then, he was out working. I think boys grew up much earlier in those days than they do today.

"Anyway I had my first fight, won it, and it sort of snowballed really. I was really nervous at the time but I went out there, swung a big right and he went down and he was out. I couldn't believe it." In April 1961 at the age of 22 Billy won his ABA heavyweight title, stopping Len 'Rocky' James in one round. "I've just realised, you're from Wales. That boy I knocked out in the ABA Finals, he was from Wales. I fought him four times as an amateur. The first time I made a terrible mistake. I knocked him over three times in the first round, walked out like an idiot in the second round and he swung and hit me on the chin, knocked me down, I staggered around and they stopped the fight. I knocked him out three times after that. He was a lovely guy Rocky, I liked him. Last time I beat him was in Dublin. And I knocked him out then. Afterwards he came marching over and I thought he was going to carry on, and I said, 'What's wrong with you?' and he said, 'You're too good for me. Let's go and have a pint.' And we were in Dublin and he was a nice guy, he really was a good laugh.

"There were so many more boys about in those days. You could box twice a week as an amateur. All the swimming baths used to get boarded over and they had boxing matches there. I look back and there was Leyton Baths, Ilford Baths, West Ham Baths, they all had boxing shows. And they don't now, it's all dinner shows and things, which is a shame."

Billy's finest hour as an amateur came when he fought Perry at the Empire Pool, Wembley on Thursday, 2nd November 1961. Great Britain whitewashed the Americans ten-nil that night and Billy stole the show by stopping the unstoppable in the first round. "When I knew I was fighting him I was shit scared really. I think it sort of gets to a point when you know that you can't get out of it, and I know the guy's got about five inches on me and about four stone in weight and I thought, 'Christ. There's no way out of this.' I don't know. You've just got to go for it. Get in there. I just went out and started swinging as hard as I could and it happened, thank God."

Billy rounded off 1961 by being voted runner-up to racing driver Stirling Moss for the BBC Sportsview Personality of the year. His big style continued to wow the crowds and his heart was set on going to Perth for the Empire Games. However, in February 1962, he had a meeting with Harry Levene. When Billy explained to the legendary boxing promoter that he really wanted a gold medal, Levene characteristically replied, "gold medal? I'll buy you a sack full of gold medals!" and eventually Levene made Billy an offer he couldn't refuse. "I think being an amateur was my best time actually. I loved it. But then money comes into it and they start talking about turning professional and they offered me big money, £9,000. That was an unbelievable fortune in 1962. When I first started, when I was 19, come on, I was fit and well and enjoying life. I never thought of about careers in boxing, I just thought it a bit of fun. I won this fight, let's go on. But when it came to turning pro it was a serious business. I mean, £9,000. I'd never seen money like that before. You could go and buy a lovely house for £3,000. We went and bought a garage, workshops, two little houses in East London…

"Harry Levene promoted most of my fights. Our relationship was good. We got on very well, a bit like an uncle. He had a girlfriend called Georgina and I got on well with her. Harry always stayed down the south of France for a couple of months in the summer and I used to go down there with my friends and we'd pop in and see him and he would always take us out. Mind, he knew about money and I was his draw card. I sold out Wembley about six times for him. And when you've got someone like that you want to look after them. But I wouldn't say it was purely for the money. I would say it was genuine. And I liked Harry. Because he actually brought me in to dinners with him and his girlfriend, and it was nice."

It was a tough time for a fledgling heavyweight to take his first steps as a professional. The top slots were occupied by British and Empire champion Henry Cooper, European champion Dick Richardson and world champion Floyd Patterson. And across the Atlantic a loud and proud youngster called Cassius Clay was getting himself noticed. While Billy prepared for his professional debut, the publicity he received was phenomenal. He was interviewed on TV and his handsome face splashed across newspapers and magazines. The media followed him to the Essex farm where he was training and to Joe Bloom's West End gym. They speculated over how much money he would receive for his professional debut, they said it would be the highest paid debut ever. And finally, the big night arrived.

On the 27th March 1962 Billy Walker had his first professional fight, against Jose Peyre at Wembley. He stopped the Belgian in five. I asked the golden one how he felt about going in for the first time without a vest. "Well, a bit nervous because it wasn't so much the fight, that never worried me. It was the grandeur of it all. It was my first fight and it was an eight rounder and they had a fanfare, and it was all a big… Oh God! And then when I got in there to fight this guy he wasn't in there to win, he was there to survive. And it's much harder to fight someone who wants to survive, than a guy who wants to win. Because you see, when you both want to win, you exchange blows. But when you've got a guy who's ducking, moving, don't really want to fight. Oh, what a boring fight! All he did was run away. Eventually I hit him up the stomach in the fifth and he went down claiming that I low blowed him. It was all a farce really." Although the fight was down the undercard it was broadcast on television and radio and Billy's face adorned the front of the programme. When it was over the ringside photographers made a mass exodus.

After this first fight talk raged about Billy Walker fighting Johnny Prescott, a Birmingham boxer who figures strongly in Billy's story. Both were 23 years old, both handsome, both had good managers, the similarities were all there. "Ah, good old John, yes. Because we were both young, I was the south, he was the midlands. There was always pictures in the paper of him with a girlfriend and me with a girlfriend. It was all set up. They used to get these models to make out we were going out with them and they used to take pictures. The papers are very devious. That's why I never believe the papers. You've got to think twice about what they say. My brother George used to say, 'Look, if they want to take a picture of you let them take it, as long as it's not detrimental. And just make sure they get the name right.'"

On the 22nd May 1962 Billy had his second fight. He drew against Spanish tough guy Mariano Echevarria over eight at Wembley. Echevarria had been six years in the paid ranks. He had been the full distance with Johnny Prescott, Joe Erskine and Karl Mildenberger, all future opponents for Billy. "Now he was a hard bastard. He wanted to fight." In the third round Echevarria put Billy down with three left hooks, the last one catching him right on the jaw. He got up and although shaken, held on to survive the round. In the last round they both looked exhausted and desperate. Walker threw a punch, missed and fell to the canvas. Mariano ran over and helped him up. Then they slugged out the remaining part of the last round toe to toe. "He was nice man. Tough, but a nice man. And I've gone to hit him and fell over and he's laughed. And I realised then that I got a draw because he was so tough. I wasn't a very good boxer but he was worse than me. But he was so tough." Top of the bill was another British hero Terry Downes, against Don Fullmer. "Oh, he's a great guy. They tell me he's been very ill lately. I haven't seen him for a couple of years. I always liked to see Terry. Mind, you could always hear him first."

In August Billy fought Erwin Hack, a man who had taken Johnny Prescott the ten round distance the previous March, on the same Blackpool bill as Brian London and American Howard King. Billy stopped the German southpaw in one round and he remembers vividly how the skies burst that summer evening. "Now that was a funny night. It hadn't started raining when I came on but when Brian London came in, all of the sudden the heavens open and the ring was like a paddling pool. And they fought in bare feet." On the same bill Johnny Prescott beat another German, Ulli Ritter, in ten rounds. The crowd booed the verdict even though both men put up a really good fight.

A month later Billy stopped Robert 'Archie' Moore in two rounds at Liverpool Stadium. He dropped the Ghanaian in the first round and when the end came in the last minute of the second, the final seconds were thrilling. The enthusiastic Merseyside crowd went crazy. In November 1962 Billy continued his winning streak and stopped Phonse La Saga of Newfoundland in one at Wembley Pool. It was another dramatic win but for all the wrong reasons. The Canadian lumberjack entered the ring by vaulting over the ropes and that was about all he did really. The first potent punch that Billy landed sent him crashing down like a falling tree and he lay flat on his face while Harry Gibbs counted him out. The crowd were initially silent while they waited for the Canadian to rise and when they realised that he was not going to, they started to whistle and jeer. Afterwards La Saga had some of his purse money withheld by the Board of Control and was told not to fight in this country any more.

A week later Billy fought Spaniard Jose Gonzales at the Granby Hall at Leicester. The fight lasted less than three rounds and it was a dirty brawl. Billy was disqualified for low blows by referee Austin O'Connor and the crowd booed as he was sent back to his corner. Johnny Prescott, now undefeated Midlands Area champion, drew with Ray Shiel over ten brutally exciting rounds on the same bill. So while Prescott shone, Billy lost his unbeaten record. Six days later Billy settled the score with Gonzales and beat him on points over eight at Manchester.

At the beginning of 1963 Billy travelled to America to train. "I think going over there was a publicity stunt really, I don't think I learned a lot. I was supposed to have learned how to box but you can learn to box anywhere. But it was interesting. We used to run around the reservoir in New York. I was at Harry Wiley's gym on Forty Second Street and Broadway and it was great. We had a few months there and I enjoyed it. I lived in a nice apartment in Harlem. They used to say there was trouble in Harlem but we never had any trouble. I took a friend with me, and we used to go out down Harlem Broadway and have great fun. We used to go in all the clubs. And I'll tell you who was a good friend of Harry's and Harry used to train him, was Sugar Ray Robinson. He had 'Sugar Ray's Bar' in Harlem and we used to go in there for a drink and everyone knew us. We never had any arguments, any aggravation. Everybody knew Sugar Ray. And he used to say to us, 'Come on boys, let me take you down to a club,' and if anybody used to get funny with us, like 'What are two big white guys doing here?' Sugar Ray would tell them, 'Oh, these are Harry's friends from England.' 'Geez, you're from England?' And it was all happening because it was 1963 and the Beatles had just become a big number one hit everywhere, and English was nice. It was great fun."

But life was not all fun and games. Billy had punched himself into a position where he was now expected to knock everyone out. "Oh yes. Always. And it was impossible to do. Especially as the class got better." On the 29th January 1963 he obliged and stopped Yorkshireman Peter Bates in two at Olympia. Bates had been boxing for ten years and had fought the best. Two months later Billy stopped American Joe Di Grazio in three at Wembley. Billy entered the ring to thunderous applause, and they were growing to love him more and more. "Well it's amazing really. Even to this day I still get invited to dinners and everything. It's fantastic. I mean I've been retired thirty-odd years now. It's unbelievable really." After the fight Billy went to hospital for an x-ray for a suspected fractured rib, caused by Di Grazio's elbow as they fought at close quarters in the first round. "I remember it going. I can still feel it now. I went back to the corner and I said to George, 'My rib's gone.' He said, 'Hold it in there,' and I ended up knocking him out in the next round."

In June 1963 Billy was back in with old foe Mariano Echevarria at the Albert Hall. Johnny Prescott, who was introduced from the ring, had a points win over Echevarria and he watched the contest with interest. After drawing with the Spaniard in the second fight of his career, this time Billy beat him on points over eight. "I beat him the second time because I didn't try and knock him out. I mean you could have hammered him and you wouldn't have knocked him out. I was pleased I won the re-match but even then he was laughing. He was a tough man and he just used to laugh. He never took it serious really. He couldn't beat boxers but he always beat fighters because a fighter would stand toe to toe with him and they couldn't knock him out."

Two weeks later it was off to Carmarthen where Billy stopped Kurt Stroer. The fight was scheduled for eight and ended in second round confusion. Billy knocked Stroer down to take a count of six and he got up looking ready to fight on. But the German, who did not speak a word of English, caught sight of the time keeper still counting for the mandatory eight count and, looking very confused, he took out his gum shield. Referee Ike Powell stopped the fight. "It was none of my doing. He said he didn't know the rules but you do know the rules. And I suppose the referee thought that he's not doing what he should so he's not in his right mind, so he stopped the fight." Johnny Prescott was stopped in a shock defeat in one round by Alex Barrow on the same bill.

British boxing finally got what it wanted on the 10th September 1963. Billy Walker and Johnny Prescott had their first fight. They fought at Wembley Pool and going in Billy had 11 fights behind him while Prescott had 26. It was a real master-blaster, scheduled to go ten. The crowd was deafening as the fighters took their places in the ring. The first bell sounded and Billy dropped Prescott in the opening seconds but Johnny was up at two and straight back into the fight. Billy got excited and went in for a swift stoppage, throwing punches like a man possessed, while Prescott kept counter punching. Billy landed a low left hook in the second and waved a glove of apology. Johnny waved back across the hazy ring. As the fight continued Billy thundered forwards and Prescott danced away from the flying fists, dropping in some lovely counter shots along the way. Occasionally they stood toe to toe to a backdrop of applause that resembled a wall of noise. In the fourth Prescott turned aggressor and after the sixth Billy returned to his corner with blood streaming from a cut between nose and eye. In the seventh, blood streaming down his face, Billy turned up the heat another level. Johnny returned to his corner a very tired fighter having been swept across the ring on a wave of Walker aggression which was stemmed only by the bell. In the eighth the crowd drowned out the night as Billy, despite all the blood, battled to overcome the tiring Prescott. At the end of the ninth Prescott, relieved to hear the bell to end the round, stumbled back to his corner. Prescott went for it one last time in the tenth and final round and paid for it. Billy clubbed him to the floor with a left and right to the jaw. Prescott managed to struggle to his feet at seven but he was all over the place, clinging to the ropes like a drunken man on a Burmese bridge. Billy steamed wildly in to finish the job before referee Tommy Little made a dramatic intervention 84 seconds before the final bell. Prescott was furious when the stoppage came. He paced and stamped around the ring like a man whose lottery numbers had come up and he had just realised that he had forgotten to buy a ticket. The crowd reaction was split, Prescott's fans roared their disapproval while

Walker's fans cheered the house down. Today, Billy believes that Mr Little's intervention was appropriate. "Well, the point was, and I've seen the fight, I've looked at the fight and he was gone, there's no doubt about it. And I was desperate to do him again when the referee stopped the fight. And I could have really hurt him. But when you've just had the hardest fight of your life and someone stops you, you get very annoyed."

One of the evening's highlights had been a performance from world heavyweight champion Sonny Liston who, having been wittily introduced into the ring by Eamonn Andrews, stepped through the ropes in green tights and purple shorts to entertain the enthralled crowd with a round of shadow boxing and three rounds of serious sparring with Fonedo Cox. Liston finished off his act with two rounds of his famous skipping in time with his favourite song 'Night Train.' Liston, so unpopular in his own country, was given the warmest of receptions by the London crowd. After his little show Sonny did not return to his dressing room despite the fact that he had worked up quite a sweat. Instead he remained in his show clothes and took a seat in the press section, adorned in a white gown and yellow hood, where he watched the fight in respectful silence. The following week there was a photograph on the front page of *Boxing News* of Walker and Prescott shaking hands with Liston in the middle. "Yes, I've got it at home yes."

In the same issue there was talk of both Billy and Prescott fighting Liston for his world heavyweight title. I asked Billy if he would he have taken the fight. "Of course I would have. Because it's all money. It's not winning or losing, it's money. I mean, you did all them years of amateur for fun. But as a pro, when it comes down to it, it's all about what you're getting paid." I asked Billy if he liked Sonny Liston. "No. I thought he was a good fighter but I didn't like him. He was quite an arrogant man. He came down to the gym when I was training and he was alright but he used to have this terrible habit. He had big hands and he'd be talking to you and he'd put the hand out and suddenly, bosh! and he'd hit right in the nuts. And of course, anyone hits you like that, you always go forward and he'd say, 'Take a bow.' That was his idea. Because really, people could say, 'Do you want it on the chin?' but I thought, 'No, better not.' He never done it to me but I've seen him do it to other people. He wasn't a nice man."

The shouts were immediately long and loud for a return match between Walker and Prescott. On the 12th November 1963 the night arrived. Billy Walker and Johnny Prescott got it on once more at Wembley Pool. This time referee Harry Gibbs gave Prescott the ten round points verdict. It was one of the most spectacular heavyweight fights I've ever seen, sadly only on video. If there had been such a thing as punchstats in those days the computer might well have blown up. Such was their workrate from the first bell to the last that they put me in mind of middleweights rather than heavyweights. They reminded me of Chris Eubank and Nigel Benn fighting each other at their best, only they were both Nigel Benn. Or turn the clock back 26 years and it could have been Tommy Farr and Joe Louis in there, and both were Tommy Farr. The final round was out of this world, both of them bent from the waist, both throwing so many punches and the crowd were on the ceiling now. Both men were bruised and battered. "Well he was a much tougher boy than I thought, Prescott. He was good. In the first fight, I had him down and I thought, 'I'm losing this.' And I went out in the last round and made a last ditch effort and I stopped him. Now in the second one I thought I'd coasted it. I went up to George at the end and he said, 'You're well in front.' I said, 'I thought I was.' And he got the decision, but that's life.

"We never fought again. We could have had that third fight but when he fought Erskine and I beat Erskine, I don't want him any more. Because now I've got everything to lose and nothing to gain, whereas maybe before we could have had it. He always swore to me later on that he never knew that he was offered ten thousand to fight me again. He said his manager turned it down and never told him. And when he found out he sacked Biddles from his corner because he loved money and I mean ten grand! It sounds nothing now but in 1964 it was a lot of money then. It was unbelievable money. You can't imagine!"

I asked Billy if he and Prescott were friends. "Well, yes, we were friends, like 'Hello' and things like that. I never socialised with him. He did come over to Jersey once. He married a Jersey girl when I lived there. I was in a restaurant and the waiter came over and he said, 'Sorry sir, but there's a gentleman over there and he's told me I've got to tell you that you were lousy, that you couldn't have a fight to save your life,' and I thought, 'God, like I need this idiot in the restaurant.' And I've looked round and it's him! It was well after our careers had finished and we had a good drink and a laugh."

Billy began 1964 with a January appearance against former Empire champion Joe Bygraves at Olympia. Bygraves had been in with Henry Cooper, Ingemar Johansson, Dick Richardson and Joe Erskine. His finest years were behind him but the big Jamaican was still a force to be reckoned with, particularly as he had nearly a stone-and-a-half on Billy. "That's a funny story, that is. Joe Bygraves was a good fighter, a really good champ. A bit older, but still dangerous. I'd sparred with him a few times and I know that he's strong, but he's not that strong. And he came out and he put everything into it for about four rounds. Anyway, he knocked me about a bit, and I was parrying and all of a sudden I started getting on top. I don't know what round it was, and I thought, 'You're getting a bit tired. It's my turn now.' And all of a sudden he hit me in the balls. And the referee said, 'Oi! Stop that! Low blow!' And bang! He hit me in the balls again. And the referee said, 'If you do that again, I'm going to disqualify you.' And he did it again, and he was disqualified. He wanted to be disqualified. Because he knew that he'd give me his best, and it had got to that time when he knew he couldn't do it any more and I thought, 'What a cheating man. He wouldn't even fight and go down properly.' He got out of it. And I came out of it with a big eye and a busted lip and he didn't have a mark on him!" Bygraves was disqualified in the sixth round after being warned several times by referee Harry Gibbs for hitting below the belt.

Billy was stopped in eight by Bill Nielsen at Kensington on the 10th March 1964 because of eye injuries. "I would have definitely got to him in that first fight, because I was just getting to him, and then all of a sudden I had a few marks and they stopped the fight." Two months later Billy boxed Nielsen again, this time at Wembley, and the Golden Boy stopped him in two. After being floored in the second, Nielsen got to his feet and Billy pounced on him, clubbing him to the ropes for the big attack. Referee Harry Gibbs had to jump in to drag Billy away before he put Nielsen out of the ring. But despite the fact that Billy was all over him, Nielsen dropped his hands and invited his aggressor in. Billy pinned him into a neutral corner for another barrage and once more Nielsen beckoned to an outraged Walker in a crazy challenge. Billy punched him to the floor. Nielsen rose without taking a count and Billy put him down a final time. The fight was over. Billy leapt into the air, clearly delighted. "Yes, but I think he swallowed in the second fight, to be honest with you, because he knew the hard fight he had before and he was going to be exactly the same again, only this time I might be stronger. I would have liked to hurt him more because I was getting marked up badly. But he was quite well marked up too, and he must have thought, this is not going to be easy. And I caught him on the chin, but it was a punch that I felt he could have got up from. But, you know, happy days."

Incidentally, the week before this fight a Board rule forbidding blood relatives in the corner had been abolished. George was in Billy's corner for the first time, the Walkers being the first family to go in together. "Hmm. That's right. Before that you couldn't have your family in your corner. Cooper couldn't have his brother in his corner because of that. I think the rule existed because families get too involved. And if you love someone and it's your family, you get more involved than if it's just someone you know. Maybe it could cause problems? I don't really know." Another rule that was scrapped for that fight was the forbidding of white shorts on the boxers. Billy climbed through the ropes that night resplendent in pure white satin shorts. "Yeah. Stupid rule that, no white shorts. I suppose it made the blood show too much?" For the record, top of the bill was Howard Winstone retaining his European crown against Lino Mastellaro.

Wales has produced some great boxers in it's time, one of them is mentioned above. Another lovely Welsh boxer was Joe Erskine, born in the very heart of Cardiff's tough Tiger Bay in 1934. His was a fighting family, going right back to the bare knuckle days, including his great aunt, Ann Moore. She fought both men and women with her bare fists. Joe's grandma, known as Nana, used to run a bath house and a barbers down the road and often looked after the great 'Peerless' Jim Driscoll, who had his training quarters in a pub across the road. Erskine had turned pro a few days after Billy's 15th Birthday. Now, ten years later, he had won 45 out of 53 fights. The race was on to box Henry Cooper for his British and Empire heavyweight crowns, headgear formerly worn by Erskine himself. On the 27th October 1964, Billy Walker and Joe Erskine took part in that race and boxed each other at Wembley. In Erskine's previous two fights he had outpointed Jack Bodell and Johnny Prescott. He was confident that he could also beat Walker, but he was wrong.

That night at the Empire Pool, Billy Walker shocked everybody when he outboxed the master boxer himself. "Well, yes. You see, my brother George, he was a good trainer and manager, he said, 'If you try and stand and box him, you won't do it. If you try and throw one punch and knock him out, he'll avoid it 'cos he's clever. You're young and strong and he's older. Don't let him settle. Keep that left hand out, bang, bang, bang, bang, bang. And every time he sticks his left hand out, dive on him. Dive on him.' And I did. And towards the end, he got tired. See the point was, I had it in my mind that I'm not going to let him go, I'm gonna' keep chasing him and chasing him. So I was on him. I wouldn't let him go. I was following him around the ring all the time. And every time we stopped and started I was on him again and I went ten rounds like that, and I won it."

Time rolled by and in January 1965 Billy stopped Californian Charley Powell in two at Olympia. "He was a big guy, tall. And I used to like 'em tall. I used to love it when a guy was bigger than me, taller. I didn't like small guys. I'm six foot and he was six foot-three and I used to crouch a lot." Powell had been flattened by Floyd Patterson in six rounds in his previous fight. He had once been stopped by Cassius Clay and one of his major wins was over massive Nino Valdes of Cuba. Powell had 11 years experience in American boxing rings and was once rated fifth in the world. The night he fought Billy, when the finish came Powell was on the ropes, and as he fought back with a flurry from two hands he caught Billy on the jaw. Billy jumped straight in to the heat of the battle, bashing Powell with two rights to the chin. Powell took a nose dive to the floor and lay there, face down. He stirred momentarily as referee Harry Gibbs continued to count and managed to get to his knees, before he sank back down again. This time he did not try and get up. His seconds worked over him for a couple of minutes before taking him back to his corner while he sat and listened miserably to the booing of the crowd. But the majority of the audience gave Billy a standing ovation.

George Walker was an astute businessman and by this time he and Billy had used their money to build an empire. They owned a fleet of taxis, garages in West Ham and Corringham and they carried their own petrol in their own tankers. Times were good and for Billy's 26th birthday George presented him with an Aston Martin DB5, just like the one driven by James Bond in 'Goldfinger'. Billy was raking the money in with television commercials, newspaper adverts and pop records. Such was Billy's star status that he even sang on Top of the Pops! "Yes! That's right! Now what was it I used to sing? 'A Little on the Lonely Side' and 'A Certain Girl' [he croons a few lines, making Patricia and I giggle] and all of a sudden we're on Top of the Pops and there's all these girls dancing around. I mean, I'd never sung a song in me life. But it was the money! So we did it. As long as it wasn't detrimental to your career, and it didn't make you look too much of a prat. Apparently the record wasn't too bad, sold a few. My mum bought forty-five thousand!"

It was back to boxing on the 30th March 1965 and Billy had one of the hardest fights of his career. He lost over ten gruelling rounds to Brian London. London, who would go on the following year to challenge Muhammad Ali for his world title, was as much of a fighter as anybody, but he outboxed Billy that night, fair and square. Seven years previously, Brian London had won the British and Empire titles by knocking out Joe Erskine in eight rounds. In January the following year, Henry Cooper had taken his titles away and that night, he knew he had to beat Billy to be back in line for another British title shot with Cooper.

Interest in Walker v London was monumental. Weeks before any tickets or posters were printed the fight was sold out completely. More than 10,000 ardent fans packed out Wembley Pool that night. British fascination with Billy Walker, the magnetic, handsome brawler, had reached fever pitch. Battle commenced and London really rose to the occasion. "He was a hard man. But I went out there and I thought I was gonna do him. And I had him down, I think it was in the first round. And then he got up. And I must admit he could box. He boxed my head off. And he was good. And I couldn't get to him again, and he well beat me after that. After that first round, when I caught him, he got on his bike and I never seen him box so well. I'll give him his due, he well beat me. And after I came out of that I wished I'd known how to box better."

Just over four months later, on the 19th August 1965, Billy had his only fight outside Britain. He travelled to San Remo to do battle with Eduardo Corletti and they drew over ten rounds. "To tell you the truth I went down there and it was supposed to be one of those easy fights. And I had already arranged to meet a girlfriend in Sardinia. I was flying on afterwards to meet her. And it was supposed to be an easy fight so I didn't expect to turn up with two black eyes and a busted nose, which I did! It was quite funny really, I had to wear glasses half way through the holiday. But it was all good fun."

Two months later Billy fought Corletti again at Wembley and this time the man from Argentina stopped Billy in eight. "I was devastated. The funny thing is I thought I would have beaten him the second time. But you all know it can happen to you when you've got big men punching each other. He was a good fighter and he caught me coming off the ropes and I went down and I was staggering around, and they stopped the fight. Because the thing is you see, when big men are fighting, if you get caught on the chin at the right time you're going to go. It's not good saying you'll never go down, if you get caught right, you'll go. So I thought, 'OK, let's go on. Climb up the ladder again.'" On the same bill Johnny Prescott stopped Chip Johnson in five. Henry Cooper lost on points to Amos Johnson. And Jack Bodell stopped Yvan Prebeg in two.

After a four round stoppage of Lars Norling in March 1966 Billy stopped Bowie Adams in three in Manchester the following May. Adams was a blonde Adonis just like Billy. "Big Bowie Adams yeah. He was a big guy, he was massive. And he was about half-a-foot taller than me and much heavier." Going in Adams had won 17 out of 19. None of his victories had gone beyond three rounds. Six of them were over in round one. An interesting point about this giant from Arizona is that he was a major daredevil. He had been a double for Robert Mitchum in the movie *Rampage*, and, while doubling for Jack Hawkins in *Black Zoo*, he had been injured in a fight – with a lion! The big cat mauled his left arm and finished his amateur career in the process. Adams had also worked at Ralph Helfer's Nature Haven in California where he had been a big cat tamer. He certainly had a big cat in front of him the night he fought Billy Walker and this one would not be tamed. Despite his massive height, reach and three stone weight advantage, Bowie was put down three times in the third before it was stopped half way through the round.

German Horst Benedens got the one round stoppage treatment when he fought Billy at Wembley in September 1966. Although it did not last three minutes it was an action packed fight which at one point saw both boxers rolling around on the canvas before Harry Gibbs did the compassionate thing and pounced in to save Benedens from a beating. Top of the bill was Floyd Patterson and Henry Cooper. Patterson knocked Cooper out in the fourth.

A month later Billy stopped Jose Menno in ten. Billy had the Argentinian down in the first round but he was up again before they could start counting. Menno was one of the bravest fighters ever and the audience ended up applauding his courage as he saw the fight through to the final round, when Billy's power took over and referee Bill Williams stopped the fight.

In December 1966 Billy stopped Floyd Patterson's brother Ray in eight. "That was quite a good fight. He wasn't bad. He gave me quite a bit of a pounding for about five rounds. And I got on top about the sixth or seventh, I think, and I stopped him."

Billy and George were the British pioneers of the training camp concept and theirs was at Blue House Farm on the Essex coast. In 1967 an American sparring partner called Freddie Mack came to join them. Billy has only good things to say about Freddie. "I remember sparring with Freddie. He came over here for a few fights and he did well. And then he started sparring with me and he never went home! He married a Scottish girl and he lives in Scotland now. I think he was with me for a couple of years on and off. We were good friends."

Today Freddie Mack is a mahogany mountain of a man. His American accent is full of soul and his personality equals the size of his impressive stature. He has a host of happy memories of his boxing days, and his face lit up when he told me of his time with Billy Walker. "Well, you see when I came over to Britain and I decided to stay here, Billy Walker did a lot for me. And in those days, remember it was the 1960s, it was hard for a foreigner to come over here and live in this country. I had this band, Freddie Mack and the Mack Sound Band. I had to keep myself fit so I stayed at the training camp and I used to spar with Billy and all the other boxers and then I used to go off with the band. I remember the first time that his brother, George took me down there. We were in this barn and there were all these cows and pigs and sheep and things, and the odour! I can't tell you about the odour. Anyway, Billy climbed in and we started sparring and he hit me straight in the mouth. He came piling into me and we were on the ropes and I said, 'Hey, Billy. We can either take this nice and easy or we can make it hard. And hey, this odour's bad enough.' And after that, we had the best workouts ever. We never tried to hurt each other or anything like that. And of all the fighters I ever sparred with, Billy Walker was the fittest, and I've been in with the best. Floyd Patterson, the late Archie Moore, all of them." These days Freddie, now 67, is a radio presenter in Scotland and he goes by the name of 'Mr Superbad.'

Billy's first fight of 1967 came in February when he fought Giulio Rinaldi at Manchester. The Italian was disqualified in the first round for butting. "Well, he was another one. He wanted to get out of it. And it was so obvious. He tried to cut me and he didn't succeed in doing so, and then he just kept doing it. And they paid the money for nothing because the guy got out of the fight, he got disqualified. It was a shame really. Because the crowd want to see a good fight."

A month later Billy got his biggest chance yet when on the 21st March 1967 he challenged huge German southpaw Karl Mildenberger for his European heavyweight title. Wembley was packed to full 11,000 seat capacity. The fight was being shown live in 13 British cinemas and beamed out all over Europe. Six months before this fight Mildenberger had put up an excellent show against Muhammad Ali, the German being stopped in the 12th. Mildenberger had won 50 out of his 56 fights and on the fight night he stopped the Blonde Bomber on cuts in the eighth round. Billy was cut in the opening minutes and by the time the end came Mildenberger had well and truly turned back his earnest challenge. Referee Ben Bril jumped in to stop the fight. "I must be honest about Mildenberger. He was a very, very hard man. And I tried everything. I was banging him, I kept hitting him and he kept hitting me up the stomach. He was the wrong way round, he was a southpaw. I didn't like fighting southpaws. And in the end he hurt me, and even though I was trying hard I thought, 'I don't like this Walker, you're in trouble here.' I don't want to get knocked out, I don't want to get stopped but I keep trying hard with this guy and I'm not getting nowhere. And all of a sudden the referee could see blood and my first thought was, 'Great! I've cut him.' And then I realised it was me, and to be truthful, I was pleased. I was pleased because I didn't think I could beat him. He was a tough man." So Billy did not win the European title but Mildenberger was the first to lead the crowd in applauding Billy's courage and everybody joined in, including the referee. Mildenberger also received a warm ovation as he bowed and blew kisses to the crowd. "Yeah, I could have won that and I would have gone on. Because they were all waiting for me to win a title, because being popular, me and Ali, it would have been fantastic." I asked Billy if he ever met Ali. "Yeah. He was a nice guy. I remember I met him when he fought Cooper, the first time. I met him at the Mayfair Hotel. And he sat me down. 'What's he like, what's he like?' And it sounds funny now but I said, 'Well, the thing to watch is his left hook.' The thing was with Ali, he seemed quite normal. But as soon as the camera's come in, he was like 'Yeah, come on...' It was great. He was such a showman."

It was six months before Billy was ready to fight again and he jumped straight back in at the deep end. On the 7th November 1967 he challenged Henry Cooper for his British and Empire titles at Wembley Pool. Cooper was five years older than Billy and he had been king of the British rings for some time. He had defended his titles against Dick Richardson, Brian London, Johnny Prescott, Jack Bodell and three times against Joe Erkine. He had fought Muhammad Ali, Floyd Patterson and Ingemar Johansson. After a massive signing ceremony in front of television cameras at the Hilton, fight night arrived. By now, all the attention was second nature to Billy and he remained calm, in control of his feelings. "I don't think any of them ever worried me, and he only had one hand for a start! Don't forget we were going 15 rounds in them days and I thought, if I get to seven or eight rounds, I'll win. Because I'm younger and fitter and stronger and I'll do him."

Cooper stopped Billy on a cut right eye in the sixth. "We were coasting along and if you look at the video, I was doing quite well. And all of a sudden he caught me with a left hook, just chipped my eye and that and bested the fight. So what could you do? It's life." Cooper was a natural southpaw which accounted for his famous left hook. In other words, his left hand was really his right hand. He used it to lash out viciously in the first as he thought Billy was getting too close with his head. By the end of the second, Cooper's left eye was bleeding and Billy's nose was crimson. In the fifth Cooper suddenly came in on the attack leaving a horrible gash above Billy's right eye. In the sixth Cooper's left jab never stopped snaking out in constant search of that cut, having success after success until the referee George Smith stepped in to look at Billy's eye. He shook his head and sent Billy back to his corner. The fight was over. "I was gutted, but I was alright. I never was one of those who worried. And if I'd have beat Cooper I'd have got Ali..." The night he fought and stopped Billy, Henry Cooper made history because it was his eighth successful defence of his British title. He now owned three Lonsdale belts outright.

Two hard fights in a row left Billy in the mood for some serious soul searching. "After a fight I always used to dash off on holiday somewhere and have the fun that guys do when they're young. A few gels, a few fights, get pissed and then it was back into training again. As long as you had a little break so you could let yourself go, you were ready to get back into it. But after the Cooper fight I took a year off. I got married and we were settling down, new house, and I think we were deciding whether I should retire or not because it was in our minds. I was starting to ask myself, 'do I need it?' We were doing very well in business."

Billy decided that he wanted it and in November 1968 he stopped world rated American Thad Spencer in six at Wembley. "Thad Spencer was a good fighter. I think he won the first five rounds easy, he gave me a bit of a tanning, and then I came through in the later rounds." Incidentally, about four years previously, Spencer had done a few rounds with another 'Bomber', the 'Brown Bomber', Joe Louis at Main Street Gym in Los Angeles. When Louis came out of the ring, he told reporters, "He's a real good boy. He had me afraid in there. I'm an old man. I got no business in the ring with a young boy like him. But I tell you if I had the chance of being a fighter again I wouldn't mind being this one."

On the 25th March 1969 Billy Walker stepped through the ropes to fight for the last time. In the other corner was brawny Swadlincote farmer Jack Bodell. The fight was an unofficial eliminator for the British heavyweight title and Bodell, a southpaw, had recently outpointed Johnny Prescott and stopped Brian London. Walker versus Bodell was one of the most thrilling fights ever seen in a British ring, an upper and downer extraordinaire. Billy was first to hit the canvas, in the last seconds of the first round. He just made it up at the count of nine, and winded by Bodell's body shots he had a job to reach his corner as the bell saved him. In the second Bodell put Billy down again. He was straight back up and marched forward despite Bodell's southpaw right jab. Then Bodell let go with a blistering combination that had Billy flailing under fire but he remained on his feet to the end of the round. Billy made a massive recovery during the next 60 seconds and came out for the third with a new lease of life. Now it was Bodell's turn to feel the pressure. Billy turned it on as he came storming forward while Bodell picked his shots on the counter, but the Swadlincote farmer took some meaty shots to the body along the way. The deafening crowd went wild with every shot Billy landed. As they ventured into the fifth Billy threw hooks and landed with a shocking body blow to Bodell's ribs that had his corner crying out 'Move! Move!' Billy came rumbling forward and he caught Bodell with a big right on the jaw. Bodell flew backwards through the air, his legs outstretched in front of him. As he landed on his back in the opposite corner he almost did a backwards somersault, like a man caught up in the force of an explosion. He got up at nine and Billy tore after him. With Bodell's back to the ropes they stood and fought toe to toe, trading punch after punch. Walker came out for the sixth in the mood for war. He caught Bodell with every punch in the book, a number of which landed in forbidden territory. How Bodell remained on his feet is a mystery. He was like a man with Velcro on the soles of his boots. The crowd cried out in wonder at Walker's ferocity and Bodell's durability. At the end of the round Billy tapped Bodell's shoulder in respect as they returned to their corners. In the seventh the tables turned again. Billy suddenly ran out of steam. As it dawned on them that their hero was spent, Billy's fans were now silent as Bodell jabbed, and jabbed. The eighth round was all Jack Bodell. He put Billy down on his hands and knees with a left uppercut to the body. Billy got up at eight and referee Harry Gibbs caused many a shocked gasp from the audience when he waved it on, but seconds later Gibbs stopped it.

Billy's last fight ended in defeat. "Well then the fight came up with Bodell. And if I beat Bodell I'd get another big pay day with Cooper. And I went in there and Bodell beat me and I was quite surprised. And I realised that I wasn't the fighter that I was before. Mind, it was a great fight that one. Up and down like yo-yos. I had him down, he had me down, and in the end, somebody suddenly pulled the plug out and I had nothing left. In the past I could always pull it out from somewhere, I could get it back. But this time I just couldn't do that. I remember I had him down in the seventh round and I looked at the corner and I knew I was gone and I thought, 'If he gets up I'm knackered.' And he got up."

I asked Billy how he felt when Gibbs stopped the fight. "I thought at the time we had all our business in place, we were getting lots of money, and I thought... Can I swear?" I told him, of course he can. "I thought, 'What the fuck am I doing getting knocked about in this ring?' It was good when I had nothing, but now? What's the point?" Moments after Billy's last fight was stopped he hugged his brother and congratulated Bodell. Then he turned and waved to the crowd with an apologetic look on his face as if to say 'I'm sorry.' Afterwards, when Harry Carpenter interviewed him in the dressing room he asked Billy if he would now think about retirement. Billy replied, "Retire? You're always asking me about retiring. Why should I? Do you think about turning it in if you give a bad commentary?" Years later Bodell declared on TV that this fight with Billy Walker was his favourite of all his fights. He said that he never fought in such an atmosphere again. After defeating Billy, Jack went on to become the first southpaw to win the British heavyweight title.

In April 1969 Billy announced his retirement. "All I thought was no more getting knocked about. No more getting up at five in the morning to run around the back streets. No more going down the gym every day. I think I'd had enough of fighting. Because you see my career wasn't a long one, it was ten years. But I had a lot of hard fights during those ten years."

The Blonde Bomber's destiny was to have ferocious and savage battles. He always rose to the challenge. He always gave everything he had. And title holder or not Billy Walker could still sell more tickets than all the champions of his era put together. I asked how he feels today that he never felt a title belt strapped around his waist. "Well, a bit disappointed, but that's life. I mean, I had my chances. I tried. To be truthful when I look back on my career, I wish I'd started earlier. Because maybe I'd have learned to box. I couldn't box very well. I was a good fighter and I liked to fight, and I could punch. But I used to take too much punishment. If I had started earlier then I might have learned not to take so many punches and my career may have lasted longer.

"The public can be fickle. But I was very lucky, they stayed pretty loyal to me right through my career. And I'm not blowing my own trumpet 'ere, because I don't do that, but even if I lost it was a bloody good fight. I mean I've watched some of the fights I lost and I've thought, 'God that was a good fight!' They were all good fights. And if someone had told me when I was 19 years old that I'd earn all that money and have all those people watching me on telly I wouldn't have believed it. All I was a porter down the market, a chucker-outer down the Palais in the evenings. You just don't know how life can change, what's round the corner.

"These days all I want now is contentment. Patricia and I have a nice little house down in Burnham and everything I do now is for me and her. I like sitting down and having a little drink in the evenings. We like to pop out somewhere but we don't like to go too far. I remember when we were younger we used to go out at night, I never used to start getting ready until about 11 in the evening. These days we go out one night until about two o'clock in the morning and it takes two days to get over it! But I've had a good life. And it's been fun."

CHAPTER SEVEN – SPENCER OLIVER

"Right from day one I knew that I was involved with something special, really special. I even stuck a thousand pound on him winning the world title, I was that confident. I just could not see anyone beating him." – Jess Harding

Spencer Oliver was a genuine British boxing success story. He became European super-bantamweight champion in his 11th fight and he was moving at a hundred miles an hour. Everything he did, he did with the Midas touch. He was young, fresh, brave and handsome. He loved to talk, and he talked a lot of sense, endearing himself to the public with his positive attitude and charming disposition. On the 2nd May 1998, at the age of 23, Spencer fought Sergei Devakov in what was considered to be a routine defence of his European title. That spring evening he was fulfilling a major dream, fighting at the Royal Albert Hall. But in the tenth round a horrific accident left Spencer fighting for his life on the canvas, his dream of becoming world champion shattered for ever.

I interviewed Spencer in a pub in Potters Bar in the autumn of 1999. He stands 5 foot, 4 inches tall. He has an impish smile and laughing brown eyes. There is something thoroughly disarming about a man who listens attentively to your every word and then bursts into life with interesting answers, a man who is so obviously very much in love with life. When he finds something amusing, his whole face lights up and I soon found myself battling a most powerful urge to reach out and give him a big cuddle.

Spencer was born in Barnet on the 27th March 1975. The Olivers are a traditional boxing family. Spencer's grandfather Charlie began his professional career in the fairground booths. His father Jim boxed as an amateur. His uncle John also boxed as a professional and he told me, "to see Spencer getting through was great for us, for all the family. We all boxed but Spencer was the one that got through, made a real name for himself. We all lived through him." Some of Spencer's earliest memories are of he and his brother Danny sparring in the front room. "I was only seven years old and he was ten. So obviously he used to beat me up a bit." He laughs, "I think it sort of toughened me up." Danny went on to box professionally in America.

In 1994 Spencer met his future wife Louise. In January 1996 their son Kane was born. Kane is the image of his proud father. "He looks exactly like me. He's my little double." Spencer says he would let Kane box if that is what he wants to do but he would not actively encourage his son to follow in his father's footsteps career-wise. "Boxing is a tough business. There has got to be easier ways of earning money out there. There is only a minority of people that earn good money out of it."

But going back to the beginning when Spencer was seven he and Danny started training at Finchley ABC. Their father Jim boxed for Finchley from the age of 13. "I finished boxing when I got married. Then Spencer and Danny started boxing, they used to go down there on their own. I used to go down there, just to watch them training." The spark between Jim and Finchley ABC was re-ignited and he is now the club's head trainer.

Spencer always believed that his destiny was to become a professional boxer. His boyhood idol was Marvin Hagler. "I remember watching him and thinking 'I want to be champion of the world like he is.' He inspired me as a kid without a doubt. I always said to myself, even through my school days, that boxing is what I am going to do. My teacher would tell me not to put all my eggs in one basket because boxing may never come off. I used to think, 'Yes it will.'"

In England amateur boxers are allowed to compete from the age of 11. Spencer was not hanging around. He had his first bout on his 11th birthday, in Harrow. In the audience was a man named Jack Lee. A short time down the line Jack would become Spencer's trainer and he has fond first memories of his protégé. "I saw this little kid walking in with a mop of hair. He had a huge grin on his face from beginning to end. His dad had his arm around him the whole time, before and after. As I watched him I thoughtl, 'that boy's got something.' I joined Finchley ABC a year later and I met up with Spencer again. He stood out immediately, a jewel in the crown as far as I'm concerned. Then Jim asked me if I wanted to be his trainer. I went round for him at six o'clock the first morning and we went up to Hampstead Heath. We used to go up there and break the ice on the pond before he had a swim. That first morning I came away feeling so alive, and that was it, we were off! That was the beginning of a 12-year relationship. He is the most intelligent boy I have ever come across."

During those Highgate Pond days Jack used to tell Spencer stories about fighters such as John Conteh and how his trainer, the late George Francis, used to take Conteh up to that pond and make him break the ice before many a refreshing dip. Spencer remembers Jack's tender training methods with a smile. "He used to sling me in there. Jack was my trainer and if he said 'jump,' I'd say, 'how high?' If he said to me, 'go and run in front of that bus' I would have done it. So he'd say to me, 'go and jump in the pond' and I was gullible enough to jump in there. He's even had me in there with ice in it. He used to go in there as well. But now I look at it and I think, 'dirty, filthy water. Why did I do that!'" But it all paid off because under Jack's guidance Spencer won an array of amateur titles, including two Junior ABA titles, one schoolboy title and in 1994 the senior ABA title. He also won a bronze medal at the Multi-Nations and a silver in the Commonwealth Games.

In May 1994, the first Multi-Nations championship to be held in England for 14 years took place in St George's Hall, Liverpool. Spencer boxed Italian Giuseppe Tengattini in the first heat on the 23rd and his dazzling performance against the taller Italian won him the unanimous decision. These two made history by becoming the first boxers in Britain to be judged under the computer scoring system, which involves three judges having to press a button within one second to register a scoring punch. "I think it's bad for boxing because any boxer who has a good long rangy jab will always nick it. Whereas any kid who throws three or four punches, the judges can only score one punch. I think it's destroying the sport." Spencer reached the semi-finals to get beaten on points in a close fight with German Rico Kubat and returned home with a bronze medal.

In August the same year Spencer, his trainer Jack, and several members of the Oliver family travelled to British Columbia for the Commonwealth Games. Indicative of Spencer's rapid progress throughout his entire career, in that one season he had progressed from club to Young England to senior international level. He lost a points decision in the final to tough Australian Robert Peden. "Obviously it was a big buzz for me. I was only a 19-year-old kid and I was going out there to box for my country in the Commonwealth Games. At the time I thought that if I could come back with a medal that would be unbelievable for me. It was like just one more fight and I've done it. And then all of a sudden I found myself in the finals. Normally as the fight goes on I get better but with him as the fight went on I was just getting worse. I just didn't have it in the tank. Some days you just haven't got it there, so he won the fight." Spencer won the silver medal to receive a royal welcome back at home. "It was a big surprise for me. They had even arranged a street party!"

Spencer knew that the powers-that-be held high hopes for him to enter the Olympic Games but he had other ideas. Although he has precious memories of his amateur days he had become disillusioned with the British amateur scene. "In America they all work together (amateurs and pros). I think that's what they've got to do over here, they've got to bond and start mixing together because these kids know in the back of their minds that they want to become world champions. When it comes to turning over they are never going to adjust because the styles of amateur and professional are totally different. These boys want to earn some money, that's why they do it. It's lovely winning medals but they don't pay the bills at the end of the day.

"When I was in the Multi-Nations a guy called Mike Jacobs kept putting slips under my door. He was with an outfit called KOPRO. Then, before I boxed in the Commonwealth Games, they were making all these offers and when I came back, mainly because of the computer scoring, I thought, 'yes, I'll go for it.' Jack rang me up and said, 'What do you reckon, shall we turn pro?' and I said, 'Yeah, sure.' I was only 19. KOPRO were offering me £800 a month. I was on the dole at the time. I thought, '£800 a month, I've hit the lottery here!'"

KOPRO took Spencer to Ghana in September 1994. While he was there he met the great African boxer Azumah Nelson (WBC super-featherweight champion 1996-1997). "When I met Azumah it was a big privilege for me because in the boxing world he's a legend. I was bowing to him and saying, 'Azumah, it's a pleasure to meet you' and he was saying, 'No, it's a pleasure to meet you son.' We went round his house and we stayed round there and trained round there and stuff like that. His house is lovely, he's got a great big place with a boxing glove shaped swimming pool and a big gym." But Spencer was not blind to the other side of Africa. "Ghana is so poverty stricken. There are people on the street corners just dying, just wasting away." The formidable spirit and resilience of the African race made a big impression on the 19-year-old from Barnet. "We used to get up at seven o'clock in the morning and go down the beach, and there would be little kids running down there with sand tied up in the bottom of their trousers. It was so tough.

That's why I used to think anyone who boxed a kid from Ghana had a tough one, because they are all tough. It's just the way they're bred out there. If you're not tough you're not going to survive."

Spencer made his professional debut in Cumbernauld on the 17th February 1995 against Manchester journeyman Des Gargano and won a frustrating points decision over four rounds. He was left feeling demoralised in his victory, but he was quick to develop great respect for the journeymen fighters of this world. "They come up and speak to you afterwards. Des Gargano had boxed a hundred and three and I thought, 'Fuck!' He was running around for four rounds and got me really frustrated. Afterwards he came up to me, sat next to me and told me I was doing really well. Then he got his tobacco out and started making roll-ups. I was just new to the pro game and I'm looking at him and thinking, 'What's going on here? I'm talking it all really seriously and he's sitting there smoking roll-ups!' He is a great character."

In April 1995 Spencer stopped awkward southpaw Marty Chestnut on cuts in four rounds at Bloomsbury. The following month he notched up another points win against cunning Birmingham journeyman Peter Buckley over four at Potters Bar. Spencer took Peter right off his feet with a chopping right hand in the third round, and very few fighters have ever managed to put Peter Buckley down. In November 1992 Buckley had become the first boxer to go the distance with Nazeem Hamed. In January 1994 Buckley had been stopped by Hamed in the fourth round, although it is generally agreed that the referee was extremely premature in his action. However, the fact remained that everybody was trying to better Hamed's fourth round stoppage of the wily Buckley and Spencer was no exception. "I watched Peter box and I knew he was a defensive sort of cross arms fighter. I watched loads of tapes of him and the shot that we were working on was a chopping right hand and it worked in the third round. I let it go and it surprised me because Peter's obviously been the business with Naz and I felt that people would gauge my performance against that." Spencer's followers were rapidly swelling in numbers and a large crowd stayed behind to support their man who boxed after the main event. After the fight Peter Buckley himself was quick to applaud his young opponent.

Spencer left KOPRO after this and went with manager and promoter Jess Harding, a former heavyweight contender who once challenged Gary Mason for the British heavyweight title. Spencer's business relationship with Harding was just beginning but their friendship went back to the days of his youth. "Jess used to knock about the gym, we'd known each other for years. I used to follow his boxing career. Obviously he had heard I was with KOPRO and that it all went pear shaped. Jack approached him and asked if he wanted to manage me and he said yes."

Harding, an astute business man, once described Spencer as 'An eight stone, ten pound walking, talking piggy bank.' He immediately came up with the ring name 'The Omen.' He dreamed up showcase entrances complete with crane lifts, and all the trimmings. Harding's idea was a winner, just like his fighter.

Spencer continued to perform to orders. In September 1995 he stopped Karl Morling in five at Potters Bar. A month later he stopped Scottish southpaw Shaun Anderson in three at Dagenham. But to achieve the win Spencer had to overcome his biggest test yet, a first round knock down. "It was a nightmare. I was sort of climbing all over him, jumping on top of him, and he was sitting on the ropes and I threw a right hand and as I was throwing it I was sort of jumping in and he's a southpaw and he stuck out his left hand, and I just jumped straight on to it. And I was down. I got up and I'm sort of trotting across the ring and the referee, fair play to him, because I was only a young kid, he could have stopped it, and my career would have been over, totally different to what it was. But he let me carry on and then I got myself back together. It was like an alarm call, like a wake up. But it's that feeling of getting knocked down, it's like bang! And the next thing you know, everything goes dizzy and you're on the floor. It was like a message. Welcome to the pro game, this is what it's all about."

Spencer started 1996 with a January three round stoppage against former Southern Area flyweight champion Ricky Beard at Bethnal Green. The following April he won on points in six against Gary Hickman in Stevenage. In June he stopped Lyndon Kershaw in three at Stevenage. Three months later Spencer scored another three round stoppage at Stevenage, against Rowan Williams. Williams made a valiant play of contempt for his rapidly rising young opponent by sitting on his stool with his legs crossed, reading a newspaper during Spencer's entrance. Spencer clearly remembers Williams' impression of a library reading room. "I was coming in and I looked up to his corner and saw him sitting there, reading a newspaper and I thought, 'This kid's up for it.' Then as soon as the bell went he just ran for three rounds and pulled out with a bad hand." In truth, Spencer had caught Williams with a shocking right hand to the chin that turned his legs to jelly. Williams retired on his stool seconds after he reached his corner.

All the while Spencer's following, now proudly known as 'Oliver's Army,' were growing in their numbers. "My dad was a big part of that. He used to sell all the tickets from his furniture shop. He used to work twenty four-seven trying to get me as much publicity as he could and sell as many tickets as possible. I never had to worry about any of that. He used to do it all. When it started off I was selling 150 and then it grew to 300, 400, 500 and it just grew and grew and grew." And along with his boxer's popularity, Jess Harding saw to it that the entrances grew bigger too.

On the 18th February 1997 Spencer faced his biggest test yet. The match was made with Harrow southpaw Patrick Mullings. Both fighters were undefeated and the prize was the Southern Area super-bantamweight title which was vacant at the time. However, the title seemed insignificant to a boxing public who just wanted to see these two classy young Londoners get together in the ring and battle it out, to see who was really the best. The show was sold out solid two weeks before the fight. Jess Harding was typically confident about Spencer's ability to win. "The Mullings fight was the catalyst because I knew that Spencer would win it. A lot of people were saying it could go this way or it could go that way, but we were 100 percent confident."

Before his battalion of fans Spencer put up the fight of his life and deafening applause filled the Grundy Park Leisure Centre at Cheshunt from start to finish. On the first bell Mullings came charging out of his corner and rushed Spencer to the ropes. Spencer covered up and by the end of the round he had turned it around, branding his own mark on the round with ferocious fire. As the fight went on the boxers seemed to step up their pace rather than tire. In the third Spencer caught Mullings with a big left hook early and the Harrow man bravely fought back. The fourth was a good round for Mullings as he swarmed all over the Barnet boxer. Spencer was back in control for the fifth and as he steamed in with a two-handed attack it looked like he might stop the Harrow man, but Mullings' chin was made of granite. They battled on into the sixth and Spencer was ahead on points when suddenly, with about 15 seconds before the end of the round, Mullings caught him with two right hooks that unsteadied his legs. Spencer held on and saw the end of the round. In the tenth and final round Spencer got cut badly over the left eye. Mullings went for the stoppage but Spencer had other plans and turned back the attack with a blistering assault of punches. This time brave Mullings was sent out between the ropes. Referee Richie Davies stepped in between them to save Mullings. Spencer, his white shorts splattered with blood, was ecstatic. When it was over Davies declared that he had never before been involved in a fight to rival the excitement and workrate of these two brave young boxers who had scorned clinches and displayed nothing but genuine sportsmanship. At the age of 21 Spencer Oliver had the world at his feet.

After the excitement was over there was some controversy about the stoppage and Mullings was reported to be unhappy about the referee's decision to stop the fight. Personally I feel that Mullings could have been allowed to continue but the only person who can make that decision is the referee. And in my opinion Richie Davies is an excellent referee. Spencer said of Mullings, "We used to get on really well. We used to see each other out clubbing and stuff like that, we used to spar together, we used to be mates. But I think Patrick's problem was that he's about four years older than me and we used to spar when I was a junior ABA champion and he was a senior ABA champion and he used to knock me about a bit because he was physically that much stronger. He probably thought, 'I'm going to knock this kid about,' because that's what he remembered from when we boxed before. What he can't live with is that we were from the same area and it was like a local derby. I won the fight fair and square and there was no complaints from him at the time. If you watch the tape he had nothing to say at all. He didn't seem to complain to the referee, he just walked back to the corner. Apparently it still hurts him to this day that he's never been able to have that chance to reverse the decision and put things right. But you don't need to go back and fight somebody who is dangerous, for what? I beat him once. I think it hurts him to think that people remember him from the fight we had." Personally I will always remember Mullings for his courage and bravery during that fight. Spencer agrees. "Exactly! It takes two to make a good fight and he was playing his part all the time. It was definitely my biggest test to date. It was the fight that I got the most pleasure from, the one that means the most to me."

Spencer and Jess decided that the time had come to step up another level. Spencer was lined up to fight Bulgarian Martin Krastev for the European super-bantamweight title. Krastev became the first Bulgarian ever to win the European title with a first round knockout of Salim Medjkoune in the Frenchman's home town. *Boxing News* forecast a hard fight that Krastev would win on points. Some felt that Harding was taking a big gamble moving Spencer up in class so rapidly. Harding told me, "There are fighters that you can take at a certain pace and there are those that you can take straight to room one. Spencer was a room one fighter. Spencer's time was ready, and consequently he done the business on the night."

On the 20th May 1997 Spencer stopped Martin Krastev in four rounds at Picketts Lock Leisure Centre, Edmonton to become European super-bantamweight champion. He entered the ring adorned in a rather snazzy pair of silver sequinned shorts and he remembers the occasion well. "It was a good entrance. I was up quite high, I came up on a crane and then I walked off and came down some steps. I remember when I came out I could see everybody and they were all screaming for me. I thought to myself, 'There's no way I can lose in front of this lot!' I knew it was my big chance. The first round was alright, it was quite even. He caught me straight on which was a bit worrying, but it was quite even. In the second round I floored him and then I knew I was hurting him. Every time I was hitting him I saw it shaking him and I knew it was just a matter of time. Every time I went back to my corner Jack was saying, 'Don't rush things, take your time.'" Spencer chopped Krastev down with a shocking right with five seconds left of the fourth. The Bulgarian went down on all fours and although he managed to scramble to his feet by the count of seven, it was all over.

Directly after the fight the new European super-bantamweight champion went back to a party at the Queens Pub in Barnet, held in his honour. "We got pissed on champagne. Then me and Jess went back to Louise's mum and dad's and we sat there and watched the fight. I remember it so clearly. Louise's mum was making us egg sandwiches because we were both drunk. We were rubbing the belt, just looking at the belt and Jess was saying, 'Look at this, it's such a lovely thing.'"

On the 12th July 1997 Spencer made his first defence of his European title against French southpaw Serge Poilblan at Olympia's National Hall in Earls Court. Spencer wore a flashy pair of white shorts, flamboyantly decorated with coloured sequins but there was nothing elaborate about the fight. It was a tough fight and a hard night. Spencer had bruised his right hand badly while sparring the week before. He also had a poisoned toe and he was walking with a limp. The toe thing bothered Spencer throughout his career. "I think it's just where you get run down. Some people get boils and stuff, I used to get poisoned toe all the time. I think it was just from the constant training." Although Poilblan was not what you would call a clever boxer, by the third round Spencer knew that the man in front of him had turned up to make a real fight of it. But Spencer's superior technique kept him out of trouble and his cleaner punching won him the fight, although he did take a few chances, which you might call the exuberance of youth. But call it what you like, Spencer paid for it more than once during 12 hard rounds. At the end of the fight, Poilblan raised his arms as if he believed that he had won, but it was wishful thinking. Spencer, for his part, had learned a valuable lesson. He was fighting in a different league now. "He was in my face all the time. I remember sitting in my corner in round nine and thinking, 'Fuck me, I've got another three rounds to go.' I just wanted it to be over and be out of there, but then I started to enjoy it later on, when I got a second wind if you like. In the party afterwards I had to use my left hand to shake hands will everybody. My right hand was too bruised."

Three months later Spencer faced another gruelling defence of his title. This time the challenger was cagey old pro Vincenzo Belcastro. They fought at London's Alexandra Palace. This was the 36-year-old Italian's 18th European championship fight. By contrast it was Spencer's 13th professional fight and he was in far from peak condition. "The week before the fight I was on crutches with this poison in my toe, with my arm in a sling. I had to go to hospital before the fight for a pain killing injection in my hand." The first bell went and Spencer quickly realised that he was in for another hard night's work. He often found himself having to dodge Belcastro's head as well as his punches, the Italian using his experience to frustrate Spencer, often making him miss. In the eighth round, Spencer was cut near the right eye and in the ninth referee Meronen stopped the action briefly to look at the cut. Belcastro worked away at the cut in the 11th and again Meronen stopped the action briefly to have the blood wiped away. Spencer managed a win on a split decision but he knew that it was not a great performance. "It was a tough, awkward fight. One that I just scraped through really which was due to the condition I was in. He was the only bloke to go 12 rounds with Naz at the time and *Boxing News* were asking if I was going to do a better job on him than Naz. They were comparing us again."

The New Year arrived and 31 days into it Spencer defended his title against Spanish born Frenchman Fabrice Benichou at Picketts Lock. Benichou was 32 years old and had fought 63 times during a 13-and-a-half year career. Before the fight the Frenchman's trainer remarked that this was one of the rare occasions when Benichou had bothered to prepare properly. Spencer was 22, this was his 15th fight and he was on top of his game. He strode down to the ring in glittering gold sequinned shorts to stop Benichou in four. Benichou, who stood up between rounds, went down three times during the fight before Italian referee Massimo Barrovecchio looked the challenger in the eye and decided enough was enough. Spencer had gone out that night to prove something, and he had succeeded. "I knew that everyone was starting to say, 'perhaps this kid's not what he's been made out to be.' And then I went out and done that to Benichou, a former two-time world champion. I went out there and blasted him away and that sort of rectified what happened in the Belcastro fight. Because people only remember you for your last fight. That was probably one of my best performances, yes. Everything went well. The training went well, I didn't get poison in my toe, my hand was good, everything was good."

In April 1998 The Boxing Writers Club named Spencer their 1997 Young Fighter of the Year. Seventeen previous winners of this award had graduated to world champion status. Spencer was elated. "That was massive for me. It was a real big night at the Savoy Hotel. That was only ten days before my last fight."

On the 2nd May 1998 Spencer fulfilled a major dream of his to fight at the Albert Hall but the night would end in horror. In the opposite corner was Ukranian Sergei Devakov, a man considered to be a routine defence for the young champion. Looking back at Spencer's spectacular entrance, to me it feels quite eerie now that he was elevated on a platform while, behind him, 80 choirboys filled the air with their chilling rendition of part of Carmina Burana. This heavenly spectacle proceeded what was shortly to become a nightmare. "To tell you the truth I don't remember the entrance at all. I knew, obviously that it was planned. All I remember is travelling to the Royal Albert Hall. It was a big thing for me because I was topping the bill at the Albert Hall which is a Mecca for boxing. Jess always wanted to do bigger things and maybe he got a bit carried away with it all, some of the entrances, but I just took it in my stride because I thought, if I was going to be a champion, this is what I've got to deal with. So I grew off them as opposed to freezing if you like."

The first bell went and things began to go wrong very quickly. Spencer was floored in the first round, landing on his hands and knees. He appeared shaken as he took the mandatory eight count on his feet to be saved by the bell. As the fight continued it appeared that Devakov was better than anybody had realised and by the fourth round he appeared to be catching Spencer relatively easily. Spencer was hurt again in the sixth when Devakov caught him with a hard right, sending him flying backwards to the ropes. But as Spencer sat in his corner waiting for round ten he appeared clear headed and attentive. He came out for the round, moving around without showing any warning signs of what was to come. Suddenly Devakov caught him cleanly, knocking him to the floor. As French referee Alfred Asaro counted over him Spencer bravely tried to rise, seemingly in a daze, but seconds later his legs gave way and he was lowered to the floor by his corner men. Still conscious and sitting upright, he was given oxygen and then he relapsed and was lowered on to his back where he was given an adrenaline injection. An anxious crowd looked on while Spencer was treated in the ring, and then he was lifted on to a stretcher. As Spencer was carried out of the Albert Hall that night the shocked audience respectfully applauded, but Spencer could not hear them.

Spencer believes his life was saved by one man in particular and that man is Eddie Carter. Throughout Spencer's career Eddie, a male nurse whose interest in the safety of boxers has always been paramount, had worked in his corner. Thank God Eddie was there that night. "Eddie was the man that saved my life. He worked in my corner on my cuts. Obviously he had read up on things like this, what to do, and he saved my life. When I passed out, Eddie said that he saw me fitting a little bit and he said to the anaesthetist, 'right put the line in' and they knocked me out in the ring. The anaesthetists knew what to do but they had never been in that situation before. Eddie took charge. He said, 'right, you do this and you do that'. So they put the line in me and sedated me quickly and luckily, there was no damage at all because they had done that. Fortunately for me I don't remember any of it. One minute I remember going to the Albert Hall and the next thing I remember was waking up in the hospital bed with Jess standing over me saying, 'Don't worry Spence you're going to be alright.'"

Spencer was taken to Charing Cross Hospital but the surgeons there already had their hands full. "There were no beds for me there but I was sedated all the time you see so the swelling on the brain wasn't getting any worse. If I hadn't been sedated in the ring I would have been severely brain damaged now or dead." Spencer was then taken to the National Hospital for Neurology and Neuro-surgery where he was given an MRI scan. In the early hours of Sunday morning he underwent a three hour operation to remove a blood clot from his brain. He regained consciousness the following Tuesday. Jess Harding was the first person that Spencer saw when he woke up.

Of his feelings during those diabolical days Jess told me, "I think your mind shuts down. That's what I honestly believe now, your mind just shuts down. You just hope and pray that everything is going to be OK. You don't really go into the consequences of it not being OK. Once he woke up, as soon as he opened his eyes and tried to get up, I knew that he would be OK. You learn a lot about yourself when you see a guy like that."

In the meantime, Spencer's terrified father and brother were desperately trying to make their way home across the Atlantic. For while his son had been defending his European title, Jim was in Las Vegas with Finchley ABC, a trip they make every year. The whole team had been waiting to celebrate Spencer's victory, a bottle of champagne on ice, when they got the news. Before Jim and Danny left the hotel for the airport Jim rang home to find out how things were and he was told they were just about to operate. Jim told me, "It was the most horrible experience you could ever imagine. We didn't look at the newspapers on the way or anything because we didn't know what we were going to find. We didn't know if he was dead or alive. We flew home via Chicago and had to wait there for about eight hours. When we arrived in England they sent a limousine to collect us. The driver asked us if we were anything to do with Spencer. I told him that we didn't want to talk about it. Until we reached the hospital we didn't know if he was dead or alive. I just spent hours praying."

When Jim walked into the hospital room and saw his son lying there he fell apart. Spencer solemnly told me, "Jess said that it's the worst thing he's ever seen. My dad is quite a big strong guy, covered in tattoos. He just collapsed on the floor and burst into tears like a little baby, and that's just not part of his make-up. It must have been terrible for him because my dad, he's a boxing junkie, he was egging his sons on all the time. He was just proud to tell people, 'Spencer Oliver is my son.' He still is, even today. So it was heartbreaking for him to see one of his sons in that state and obviously, the boxing career was over. I remember the first time I saw my dad after I woke up. They took this thing out of my mouth. I remember seeing everyone. They said, 'do you know who this is?' and I said, 'yes, it's Jess.' They said, 'do you know who this is?' and I said, 'yes, it's Louise.' And then they said, 'do you know who this is?' And I said, 'yes, that's my dad' and he burst out crying. He was saying, 'He knows me! He knows who I am!'"

Somebody had to hold the fort with Finchley ABC in Las Vegas and this was left to Spencer's uncle John. John still finds it impossible to talk about this torturous experience without shedding tears. "When I got home I went straight round to see him and he was lying there with this awful scar. I thought, 'Oh my God what have they done to you?' and then he opened his eyes and winked at me."

It was Jess Harding who broke the news to Spencer that his boxing career was over. At first Spencer did not believe it. "I couldn't speak because I had this thing down my throat but I was thinking, 'what's he talking about, I'm not going to fight?' I thought, 'I've been knocked out. I'll have a year off and then come back.' It was only about three days afterwards that they had got me up to start walking. I asked my wife to take me to the toilet and I wanted to look in the mirror. She tried to stop me but I looked in the mirror and I saw these 60 staples going from one side of my head, right round, tennis ball shape, and half my hair was shaved off. That was the first time that I realised, 'Spencer, perhaps you ain't going to box any more. This is a lot more serious than you thought.'" The following week it was announced that Spencer Oliver would make a complete recovery but he would never box again.

As the reality of the whole situation began to dawn on Spencer he began to panic. The one thing that he believed had made him special had been ripped away from him. He became depressed, afraid of his future. "At first I thought my world had ended. I thought, 'If I can't box, what else am I going to do?'" But with the help of those around him he managed to keep his life together, and he was soon looking bravely forward.

These days Spencer is a regular boxing commentator for Sky Sports. He has also become a boxing trainer and he insists that every fighter he trains has Eddie Carter in the corner, the man who saved his life. "That's boxing. As long as the kids realise what's involved. This is what we get paid good money for. I thought I was Superman until that happened, but obviously not. This is what can happen and as long as people appreciate that it can happen to them, then good luck to them. I don't feel any differently about the sport now than I did a week before the fight. All I remember is being the young boxer of the year, going out for a routine defence of my European title.

"I was always a very confident person. Even when I went in with Mullings and I knew he used to knock me about, I thought, 'no, this is my time, this is when I've got to make it.' Even when I boxed for the European title and everyone was saying this is too much too soon. I'd seen tapes of Krastev and I thought, 'This kid's not going to live with me.' That's why me and Jess had a bet on it. We bet two grand and we won six grand, so we got eight grand back. That's how confident we were."

Spencer says he is not religious as such, "But I definitely believe that somebody was with me that night, otherwise I wouldn't be sitting here the way I am now. I'm a great believer in fate and I think if He's brought me back and brought me back the way I am now, surely there is a next chapter for Spencer Oliver."

In 1999 Spencer ran the London Marathon in aid of the National Hospital for Neurology and Neuro-surgery and the Brain Research Trust. He made excellent time and as he came running along the Embankment, his eyes filled with tears of emotion as he thought about everything he had been through.

"It's just nice to be able to sit here and have a beer and a talk, do you know what I mean? The first time I walked to the toilet after my accident it was 20 meters away and I thought, 'How lucky am I to be able to walk to the toilet and back again?' The whole thing has made me take life and enjoy life much more. And I think to myself, 'Yes, it wasn't a bad career, and I'm still here.'"

"Oh, now there's a lovely lad, and he's a good fighter too. What a great left hand!" – Reg Gutteridge

Crawford Ashley is one of the toughest men I've ever met. During his career this magnificent Rastafarian won the British and European light-heavyweight titles twice. He also made three brave challenges for world titles, the third of which turned out to be his last fight. In many ways Crawford had to fight the system as hard as any opponent he ever boxed. Long periods of time spent in the boxing wilderness, through no fault of his own, left him struggling to pay the bills and support his family. However, he never turned his back on boxing, the sport he loved. He retired in December 2001 after a final challenge for that ever elusive world title ended when he was stopped in the eighth round at the age of 37. One thing is certain. Crawford Ashley owes boxing nothing. He always gave everything he had and he never ducked anybody.

The first time I spoke to Crawford I got a big surprise. I was at the Croydon Ex-Boxer's Association Summer 2000 buffet when I was introduced to his trainer Bob Paget. I explained to Bob that I really wanted to interview Crawford for this book and Mr Paget told me he would see what he could do. A few minutes later I felt Bob's arm on my shoulder. He passed me his mobile phone and said, "Go on! Talk to him."

To catch the full impact of this little anecdote, you need to know two things. Firstly, Crawford Ashley is one of my all-time heroes. Secondly, the moment the penny dropped was the moment that Bob actually placed the phone in my hand! I have to confess that, at this point, my excitement effortlessly overtook me. What I can remember of that first conversation does not make a lot of sense, on my part anyway. Thankfully, a couple of days later I managed to calm down sufficiently to call Crawford back and arrange this interview. The venue was to be his home town of Leeds.

I got off the train and there he was, standing head and shoulders above everybody else. We jumped into his motor, a Shogun he proudly called 'The Baby Carrier', from where Crawford Ashley gave me a guided tour of his home town and his life. "I was born smack in the middle of that park, there were houses there at the time... This is where I grew up. I went to that school over there... That's me local, the Fforde Grene. I'll show you where my first amateur gym was..."

Almost immediately I found myself wondering how on earth this giant of a man ever made light-heavyweight, let alone super-middle. His legs go on for ever, nearly up to my armpits, and his shoulders are enormous. "The last time I got measured was in a police station. I was about 18. I was six foot three and a bit, bordering on six, four." Crawford is a Rastafarian. He wears his dreadlocks in a thick ponytail that hangs halfway down his broad back. In the ring, he wore it plaited and tied but somehow, the odd dread always managed to escape. When he was fighting he often reminded me of a cross between a lion and a gazelle. Out of the ring he has warm brown eyes and a smile that comes straight from the heart. Inside it the eyes became shrewd and calculating and the smile was full of menace.

He has a few tattoos of the Indian ink variety but nothing too over the top. "I've got a bull on my left arm because I'm a Taurean, and two dragons on my left shoulder blade because I was born in the year of the dragon. And I've got a Chinese symbol which says 'Imperial Dragon.'"

Crawford boxed in the orthodox stance even though he is left handed. "I used to throw the javelin for the school. So I throw with my right hand." And to match his 'javelin' right he has one of the best jabs in the business. He is known in the 'game' for his forthright manner and, as you are about to discover, he pulls no punches outside the ring, just as he did inside it. However, there are so many facets to this Northern warrior. When you take away the fire and the aggression, when you peel back the muscle and you look beyond the fighter, only then will you find the real Crawford Ashley. A man who is intelligent and articulate with a massive heart, and a sometimes mischievous sense of humour. And perhaps most importantly, you will find the family man. He speaks proudly and openly of his devotion to his daughter Asia, his baby son Theo and his girlfriend Hayley, as only a real man can. They are everything to him. They keep him going in a world that has dealt him more than his fair share of hard knocks. Incidentally Asia was born on Boxing Day!

Crawford was born in the Harehills area of Leeds on the 20th May 1964, christened Gary William Crawford. He started boxing when he was seven years old at Montague Burtons ABC. His heroes at the time were Muhammad Ali and John Conteh. "I used to walk up there three nights a week, Monday, Wednesday and Friday. My brother Glen went there." For the record, Glen was ABA light-heavyweight champion in 1982. "Burton's closed down and we moved to the Compton Arms underneath Rockys. And then we found Burmantofts." Crawford did Burmantofts ABC proud, winning two National Schools titles and two Junior ABA titles in 1980 and 1981. He was twice a Northern Counties ABA finalist.

Crawford left school aged 16 and began a bricklaying apprenticeship. But for a few years he chose to follow a far more dangerous path than boxing could ever offer. His favourite hobbies were pubs, clubs and violence, not necessarily in that order. As far as the latter is concerned, many of his 'opponents' were local National Front members who busied themselves by handing out leaflets in the town centre. But Crawford is not a man to harbour grudges. "They were alright actually. They were a good fight. There was this one guy, I remember chinning him on one of their marches. A few years later I saw him again in the Fforde Grene. We got talking and he told me, 'I used to be all with them NF and then one day I found out I was half-Irish, and then they used to beat me up.' I was in stitches man!" Crawford laughed heartily as he remembered.

"Everything you wasn't supposed to do I did. And I got into a lot of trouble. I used to go to the Fforde, then over to Streets where I did a lot of my fighting. That were a blood bath in there, every night. Streets used to close about four or five, and then I used to go down to Blues. For about two years I never even saw daylight unless I were coming home. It was like I was looking for something. There was this big hole in my life and I tried all sorts. I could never fill this hole that were there. One night, I was about 19 or 20, I got arrested for armed robbery or something. I never did it. Violence, yes. Robbery, no. They had me in a cell for 23-and-a-half hours. It was in them days when it was 24 hours, charge or release. They let me out. So I'm walking home and a cop car pulled up straight in front of me. I thought, 'Here we go! I'm going back again.' And this copper went, 'Look Gary, I'm gonna' tell you now, straight! They are gonna get you, one way or another, believe me.' And I just decided there and then to stay in the house and go back to the gym." And so Crawford returned to the ring, as an amateur.

Somehow, amid all the mayhem he managed to discover Ras Tafari. "I went over to Jamaica when I was about 18 and there was an old Rasta man who sort of collared me when I was walking around Kingston. I was with me uncles and me mam and dad and he just started speaking to me. And I'd talk to anybody. I had a right attitude when I was younger, you know? You think you're invincible, nobody can touch you. I was always in and out of fights. Everybody said, 'You can't walk around on your own in Kingston, they'll rob you.' But I used to go out all the time, I wasn't bothered. And I used to wear rings on every finger. Anyway, the old man was talking to me for about ten minutes and then my uncle told him to go away. But something he said struck a chord in me. And it made me keep thinking. Anyway, I tried to find out who I was and what I was and I've basically got an affinity with Rastafarians. I've got say that is what I am. It's just my conscience, how I live my life. There's a lot of things I won't do and there's a lot of things I will do. I'm a great believer in letting people live their life how they want to live as long as they don't hurt anyone. I'm not religious, I'm spiritual. I've got very strong beliefs. I'm a great believer in speaking my mind and telling people what I think."

Getting back to his boxing, Crawford was quickly to be come disillusioned with the amateurs. "I was the only kid to escape from the England training camp. The years I won the schoolboys and the junior ABA's I stopped everybody except two people. And I'm down in the England training camp and this trainer told me, 'You're not in this game to knock people out, you're in it to pick up points.' I says, 'Send me home, please!'

"I boxed Michael Gale in the ABA's. In the first round I'm trying to get me distance, trying go get things right and I'm hurting him. I won the first round. In the second round I'm thinking, 'I can't be arsed chasing this guy. I'll try something else.' So I let him hit me and I'm sliding back onto the ropes and let him come in and the referee gave me a standing eight count and stopped the fight. I said, 'I'm supposed to get hit. This is boxing you know, not ballet dancing!' I were fuming. And I thought, 'I can't be doing with this, they're destroying it all.'

"After that I turned pro. A friend of mine called John Durkin took me to the pro gym. He does boxing in America now. He's already brought a team over to box Burmantofts amateurs. He's a right good kid." Crawford's first manager was Tommy Miller from Leeds whom he stayed with for three years.

On the 26th March 1987 our man had his first professional outing. He stopped Steve Ward in two at Merton. "I remember walking down to the ring and Gary Mason was in the audience. I remember thinking, 'He's short for a heavyweight.' And I don't remember much after that. I just remember going in the ring and coming out and thinking, 'I should have done this a long time ago.' I started fighting for a £150 a time. But it just felt like being at home. It were great. I loved it."

After a three round stoppage over Lee Woolis, Crawford tasted his first defeat against Brockley's Glazz Campbell in September 1987. This was a score that he would later go on to settle. But of their first encounter, Crawford remembers, "I thought I won that. I had a big argument with Larry O'Connell about three weeks before and he were refereeing it. He raised Glazz's hand and he came over smiling. I went 'Fuck off!' So I keep referees on me side as well!"

Over the next three months Crawford scored three more stoppage wins. Joe Frater in four, Ray Thomas in one and, in December 1987, Jonjo Greene in seven. Incidentally the Greene fight was the only time Crawford ever fought in his home town of Leeds. Crawford lost his first fight of 1988 on points to Johnny Nelson. But six months later he was back with a three round stoppage over Richard Bustin. A week later he won another three round stoppage over Cordwell Hylton at Basildon.

He began 1989 with a four round stoppage over John Foreman at Kings Heath. "I hit him with a right hand and I heard his jaw going. He was in the corner and I was stood behind him and I looked for the referee. I wanted him to stop the fight but the referee said to carry on. I stood back and then the referee seen him slumped in the corner, and he jumped in then. And my trainer gave me the biggest bollocking going because I never finished him off. He says, 'They'll do it to you.' I says, 'Yeah but I'm not an animal.' He was gone. He was finished."

Next came a one round stoppage win over Lavell Stanley, a stoppage loss to Blaine Logston in two and a seven round victory over Serge Fame. In October 1989 Crawford won the vacant Central Area light-heavyweight title against Carl Thompson, stopping him in six at his hometown of Manchester. Crawford remembers or rather does not remember that fight all too clearly. "Carl Thompson hit me so hard, I've never been hit so hard in my life. And I've been in with some fighters. He hit me in the first round and I remember going down and thinking, 'It's going to get harder than this, but I'm going to win it.' I got up I put him down and then he hit me again. I've gone back to the corner and I've sat down and I've said, 'That were a long first round.' The corner man said, 'You silly bastard, you're coming out for the sixth!' I said, 'Am I winning?' He said, 'No.' Well I went back out there and, believe me, I was boxing on instinct because I was gone! Then I hit him. I remember doing it. And I broke his heart. He gave up in that fight, in the ring. But when he hit me in that first round..."

Crawford kicked off the new year with his first defence of his Central Area title, stopping Brian Schumacher in three rounds. Three months later he stopped Dwain Muniz in one. His last fight of 1990 was another one round stoppage over John Williams at Mayfair. This was his first outing for Barney Eastwood's Belfast stable. He never moved to Belfast but he spent a lot of time there. "I was absolutely crapping myself the first time I went, what with all their troubles in the news and everything. But after two days I felt so comfortable. I really enjoyed it. The people were so nice. I got the shock of my life actually.

Maybe there were troubles among themselves but they knew that outsiders had nothing to do with it. They treated me totally nice."

He began 1991 with a first round stoppage of Melvin Ricks at Belfast. In March that year he travelled to Dusseldorf, stepping in as a late substitute to challenge former IBF super-middleweight champion Graciano Rocchigiani for the vacant European light-heavyweight title. Despite injuring his hand early in the fight, Crawford gave Rocchigiani one of the hardest fights of his career but lost on a split decision. The British Boxing Board of Control representative at the fight was Ray Clarke. He told the judges who voted against Crawford, "I've been in boxing for 50 years, and that's the worst decision I've ever seen."

Crawford remains philosophical. "Bad decisions don't bother me. It's like, I've won fights and boxed crap and felt terrible. I'm a very temperamental sort of person. If I don't perform to me best, or somewhere near it, if I don't put on a good show for the crowd, it hurts me. I never, ever want to have easy fights because I don't think it's fair on the crowd. Mind you, if I go in there and I knock someone down in the first round and it's brilliant, then that's fine. Anyway, I lost. I thought I won it. I broke my finger in the third round. It was the first time I'd ever gone 12 rounds. Afterwards this German came in and he said, 'I'm so sorry. I think they robbed you.' And he gave me a 1,000 Deutschmarks. Well I didn't know what a 1,000 Deutschmarks was. I thought it was a tenner so I said, 'Oh thanks.' I came back to England and went to change the money and it came to £375! I said, 'That'll do!' So I went out and bought this chain (worn around his neck). So now this chain always reminds me of that fight."

On the 25th July 1991 Crawford won the vacant British light-heavyweight title by stopping Roy Skeldon in seven at Dudley. "Titles don't matter to me. It was just a fight. I just want to be the best and that means to be in with the best." Six months later he defended his title, taking just 55 seconds to destroy Southern Area champion Jimmy Peters. This vintage Crawford Ashley performance was staged in Peters' home town of Southampton, at the Guildhall. The venue was packed with Peters' supporters but they were instantly silenced as Crawford caught the home man with a few jabs before opening up with both hands. Peters was swept back by the blizzard of shots and he never stood a chance and referee Roy Francis rapidly stepped in to save him.

Crawford has nothing but happy memories of that fight, "Oh that were brilliant that was. That whole day was just magical for me. Barney Eastwood has got his own pilot and all that. So we've gone to this private airport and we've pushed this light aircraft out of it's hangar. We've flown over and I'm sitting next to the pilot. It were great because I always wanted to be a pilot at school, but the teachers totally destroyed that. So I'm sitting there watching the pilot fly the plane and there's Eastwood behind me and there's Bernado Checa (trainer) at the back. The pilot was in the army and he was telling us stories about just after World War II and jumping out over a mountain in Cyprus. Well Bernado shouts from the back, 'Did you survive?' Now I'm just laughing my head off. I just couldn't stop.

"We've landed and there was this guy who told us 'Peters is my friend's son.' I said,

'Well I'm sorry but I'm going to have to knock him out.' He said, 'You're confident aren't you.' I said, 'No just truthful.' It wasn't bragging or anything, I just seemed to know. At the weigh-in Jimmy Peters thanked me for coming. I said, 'Thank me after the fight.' We're going in for the fight and I've gone upstairs to get changed and I've gone into my little ritual. I go right quiet and I start walking up and down and talking to myself. As we were walking to the ring the crowd was booing and hissing and I just sort of smiled to myself and I thought, 'Yeah just wait, just wait!' I thrive on that. I love it.

"I was in the corner and they announced Jimmy Peters and the roof went up. Then they announced Crawford Ashley and it was like, 'Boo!' and stamping their feet and I just thought, 'That's OK.' Well normally I throw shots and I don't realise I've thrown them. In that fight everything was in slow motion and I knew where every single one was going. I moved to the centre of the ring and I hit him with about five shots and he was gone. Then Roy Francis stopped it.

"Afterwards I've gone back to a pub and it was full of his supporters and his family. This guy goes, 'I'm Peters' cousin. Give us your autograph.' He says, 'Put 'This is from the guy who beat the tosser' I says, 'No way man, I'm going to tell you now. He's a very dangerous fighter. I performed the way I did because I was scared. It were the fear that took over.' He didn't know whether to believe me or not. I says, 'Believe me I knew how dangerous he was so I couldn't allow him to hit me. I had to get him out of the way as quickly as possible.' Because this guy was slagging off his own cousin and I thought, 'No man you can't do that.'" As Crawford recounted that conversation he was so convincing that I had to ask him if Peters really did scare him in any way. He smiled slowly, "I've never been scared in me life."

Next up was a defence of his British title in a re-match against former conqueror Glazz Campbell in April 1992. This was the night that Crawford won a Lonsdale belt to keep. "That meant everything to me. My main ambition was to win a Lonsdale belt and everything else after that has been a bonus. I wanted two but they changed the rules before I got there." Campbell was no shortie at six foot but Crawford looked so much bigger. It was by no means one of Crawford's best performances in fact, there were times when he looked like he was sleep walking in there. Then towards the end of the seventh the dragon suddenly awoke in his lair. He nailed Campbell with a left hook and a right cross sent the Brockley man sliding down Crawford's long legs, seemingly bereft of a place to hide. Crawford jogged back to the corner eager for referee Adrian Morgan to begin the count. Campbell was badly dazed by the assault but somehow managed to get up for the count of nine. And the lion and the gazelle came flying across the ring ready to land that 'javelin' right hand as the bell went. Always the professional, Crawford stopped and smiled almost playfully with his right fist poised in mid-air, turned obediently and walked back to his corner. "I want to win the fight, that's all I want to do. I don't want to hurt nobody, I just want to win the fight. It's all about how good I can be."

Crawford failed to immediately capitalise on his round seven success. Eight was a quietish affair until the opening came and the dragon unleashed his fire once again, this time with the 'javelin' straight on the jaw. Campbell went down, flat on his face. Miraculously he dragged himself up from the floor. Surprisingly Morgan allowed the fight to go on. A few seconds later it was all over, a mere formality. Immediately after Morgan waved it off, Crawford was across the ring, supporting Campbell as he plodded to his corner. All the while he spoke compassionate words to the man he had, moments earlier, battered to submission.

The European title was vacant once again and in September 1992 Crawford made his second attempt at it. His opponent was Italian based Ugandan Yawe Davis and Crawford fought him in Italy. The result was a glaringly controversial draw. This was Crawford's last fight for Barney Eastwood and the split was not an amicable one. Hard words were spoken and the following day Crawford flew home, never to fight for Eastwood again.

He agreed to sign with Frank Warren and at this point in his life an extremely important figure was to make his big entrance. His name was Bob Paget. Bob is a wise and knowledgeable Eastender, quietly spoken and mature in years. He has a kind and intelligent face, he is broad of build and he stands about five foot nine. These two make an unlikely pair from a visual point of view but personality-wise, they are peas in a pod. Tony Breen, who was to join the team later on once told me, "They're both lovely guys, they really are. But let's face it. Neither of them are ever going to make it into the Diplomatic Corps!"

The first time Bob Paget met Crawford things did not get off to a promising start, as Bob well remembers. "I was working for Frank Warren at the time as his general manager, organising the shows. I'm walking out of the office and there's Crawford and his brother waiting there to go in and see Frank. Anyway, I knew he was going to America to fight Michael Nunn for the world title so I said, 'How are you champ,' shook his hand and said to him, 'Look after your money.' As if I need to tell Crawford that, but I didn't know him in them days. And it was either him or his brother that said something a bit saucy. It was the way he said it rather than what he said. When I got home there was a message to phone Frank (Warren) back. He said, 'I want you to look after Crawford Ashley.' I said 'No thanks Frank, I don't want that.' He said, 'Why not, there's a few quid in it for you.' I said, 'They can't pay me enough! All I'm short of is being stuck in America with a six foot four inch Rastafarian and a miserable bastard to boot!' In the end I said I'd give it a try for a week and if we got on alright, we'd see. Well, we got on very well after that. He's treated me well, Crawford." And Crawford's face is one big smile at the mention of his trainer's name. "He's brilliant is Bob. I like Bob. I like Bob a lot."

I would like to note at this point that after Bob Paget had a look at the first draft of this chapter he approached me one Sunday morning at the London Ex-Boxers Association and asked that I give Jamie Brindle a mention. "He should definitely be mentioned. He's been my right hand man with Crawford all the way." So hello Jamie, this is your mention.

In April 1993 Crawford and Bob travelled to Memphis to challenge Michael Nunn for the WBA super-middleweight title. The venue was a 32-storey pyramid sheathed in stainless steel named the Pyramid Arena – only in America! Confusion reigned from the outset. At the weigh-in it was announced that Crawford weighed 11 stone nine pounds (two pounds below the middleweight limit.) Murmurs of disbelief rustled around the room like dry autumn leaves. Then Nunn stepped on the scales and they announced it as a half-a-pound inside super-middleweight. Bob Paget has no doubts that the scales had been tampered with. "Michael Nunn never made that weight again. I said to Frank Warren, 'Do you think I could get Crawford down to middleweight? He's six foot four! I wish I could get him down to middleweight. Then he'd definitely be champion of the world.' I don't care what they say, they rigged those scales for Michael Nunn. What you've got to remember about the Nunn fight is that Crawford had about four weeks notice and it was a weight division below what he was fighting at."

Nunn won the fight in the sixth round and Crawford took a horrible beating along the way, going down five times in all. The American southpaw targeted most of his attacks to the right side of Crawford's body. The sixth round arrived and Crawford went down three times in that round, losing on the WBA three knockdown rule. Crawford had started the sixth so strongly, backing Nunn into a corner early on. But Nunn came back and a left to the body had Crawford on the canvas. He got up and returned to the fight with a vengeance but he was soon down again. With only a second left, Crawford got caught with a final, brutal left hook to the ribcage that sent him down on all fours in his own corner. The fight was automatically ruled as over.

Crawford remembers, "I just didn't have no power. I never ever thought I were going to lose that fight ever! When I went down in the fourth round, that's when he broke the rib, and I blanked out for a split second. And then I fought back but every time he hit me there I went down. But as soon as I were down I just wanted to get back up and get in there. And then he hit me when I was on the floor and I thought, 'You bastard!'" Crawford chuckled darkly at the memory of that. "He put me down and I went down on one knee and he hit me again. And I got up and I still didn't think I were going to lose the fight. In that last round I was down on the floor and I looked into the front row and there was Carl King shouting, 'Go on Michael! Kill him!' So I just winked at him. The look on his face was a picture! Then I got up again and I could see it in Nunn's eyes. He was thinking, 'What do I have to do to put him down?'"

One thing that Crawford's gallant performance did earn him was the respect of the Americans. "On the way down to the ring they were saying, 'We're going to kill you nigger if you win this fight.' On the way out I was getting patted on the back like I was the best thing since sliced bread, after I'd lost! And at the airport there was people giving me hugs and all that and I was thinking 'wait a minute, I lost!' And there was this one woman, I'll never forget it. She came over and gave me a kiss on both cheeks and she told me, 'I was in bed watching it with my husband and I beat him up, because I wanted you to win so bad. I'm so glad you're all right.' I said, 'I'm fine, but I lost!'"

In January 1994 Crawford suffered another crushing defeat, this time a fourth round stoppage against Dennis Andries at the National Ice Rink, Cardiff. Guyana born Londoner Andries, was three time WBC light-heavyweight champion. Having lost his title to a 'top of his game' Thomas Hearns in 1987, he served his time at the Kronk Gym in

Detroit where under the guidance of Emanuel Steward, he regained, lost and won back the WBC title. Crawford had not even started boxing when this veteran Andries contested his first professional title.

Battle commenced and in the second round things started to look good for Crawford when he decked Andries with a big left hook. But the Londoner dug deep, as was his forte, and with nearly a stone weight advantage he started to wear Crawford down. The third round was Andries' as he worked hard on Crawford's body and caught him in a corner towards the end. Crawford tried to box on the back foot in the fourth and final round but he looked exhausted and the trip back to his corner was to be his last that night. He retired on his stool. I asked Bob Paget why they took such a hard fight directly after the loss to Nunn. "Well I must take the best part of the blame there. We took it at very short notice and I said, 'OK if it's Dennis Andries or nobody we'll have him.' Because I thought Crawford would handle him because I didn't think he'd get involved with him. Because when Crawford caught him with that terrific left hook and put him on the floor, and then Andries didn't even look as if he'd been hit when he got up."

Ten months later Crawford was back in business. His opponent was Cardiff's Nicky Piper. The prize at stake was the vacant British light-heavyweight crown. This was Crawford's third ferociously hard fight in a row and this time he emerged victorious, winning on points. *Boxing News* forecast Piper to win in eight rounds. They got it wrong. In fact, it was almost the other way around. Piper was floored in the eighth and the Welshman looked so out of it that Crawford appealed to referee John Coyle to stop the fight. "They should have stopped it when I hit him at the end of the eighth round and he just went limp on me. I went to the referee, 'He's gone!' And I walked back to the corner and I was shocked he actually got up. I thought, 'You're braver than your boxing ability mate and you're definitely going to get hurt.'" Piper saw the fight through and in the final round Crawford suddenly seemed to wilt. The Welsh crowd went wild, sensing that their man might take the victory. This was not to be. Crawford remained on his feet and was announced the winner. He was once again British light-heavyweight champion. "I hadn't fought for nine-and-a-half-months before that. I'd been getting ready for Maurice Core, and not fighting him. Six times I got ready for him and six times he pulled out. I wasn't fighting fit. I was fit to box but the more fights you have the more you become fight fit.

"When they announced the decision I was shocked! I was absolutely shocked! I thought, 'Oh I've lost this!' In the end I was absolutely totally and utterly knackered. I thought I'll dance away and start trouble instead of planting me feet and fighting the way I was before. And my legs said, 'hey you've got no chance mate!' But I knew that there was no way he was going to beat me. He never ever hurt me once in the fight, ever!"

It was an epic performance from both of the fighters. Piper was bruised and battered and he took the decision well, afterwards declaring, "I must admit I thought Crawford Ashley just nicked it... I feel like the elephant man here." But the victorious decision never seemed to satisfy Crawford. He felt that his victory over Piper was never really seen as conclusive. He felt that if they wanted it again, that was fine by him, so he began a single-handed re-match campaign, hijacking many of his post-fight interviews to further his cause. And as time went on, he wanted it more and more, especially when Piper was world rated ahead of him. It never happened.

In February 1995 Crawford was back to early nights when he stopped African Hunter Clay in three at the London Arena. It seemed that Clay did not want to play and when Crawford started to unload in the third the African did not want to know. Referee Phil Cowsill asked Clay if he wanted to continue and stopped the fight. Crawford told me, "I boxed Hunter Clay on the same show as Nigel Benn versus Gerald McClellan. I was really up for the fight. I really wanted to win and produce. I didn't know what had happened to Gerald at the time. I watched the fight and I knew he had been hurt but I didn't realise how badly. The atmosphere was buzzing and I was really up for it. Anyway I hit Clay in the belly and he grabbed his eye! I were just gutted. I was so disappointed. I was disappointed for my fans who had come down."

A month later Crawford headed back across the Atlantic, this time to challenge Virgil Hill for his WBA light-heavyweight title. The venue was Buffalo Bill's Resort, Nevada. This one might have taken place on the 1st April but there were no fools inside those ropes. Hill had lost only once in 40 fights, to Thomas Hearns back in June 1991. The action started slowly, both men showing healthy respect. But by the ninth round their faces told a different story, bruised and swollen and bleeding. When it was over both men knew they had been in a fight. Crawford lost on points and he does not have fond memories of this trip across the water. "They pulled a scam on me in that one. I was all psyched up to go on. There was three minutes to go. I was gloved up. Right, I'm ready now. One minute to go. Next time the door opens and I'm out. They said, 'Oh, we're just going to put a fight on, it won't go that long.' It was a fucking 12 round fight! They said, 'We can't take the gloves off you because you're going on.' I just went flat." Bob Paget insisted that they remove the gloves but the damage had already been done. "I went to sleep for six rounds and then woke up. He were that much of a man that he gave me three weeks notice and then pulled a scam on me."

In July 1995 Crawford was back in action at Kensington with an eight round points win against tough American Lenzie Morgan, a journeyman who has seen it all. Crawford floored Morgan in the fifth and totally outboxed him behind his jab although in the second, Morgan caught Crawford with a good left hook that rocked him just a little bit. Morgan remained in the fight to the end but Crawford had more than enough left in the tank to finish in style. However, Bob Paget was a little less than impressed with his charge's performance in the final minutes. "It was the last round. I told him, 'You've well won it. Now don't do nothing silly, just go out and enjoy yourself and don't get involved.' Anyway, he went out and he was doing the Ali shuffle and all that. He come back and I said, 'You fucking idiot! What's the matter with you?' He said, 'I promised my wife I'd do it.' I said, 'Well do it in the fucking bedroom, not in the ring!'"

In November 1995 Crawford travelled to Manchester to stop Mexican Jesus 'Monje' Castaneda in three. "They said he was an easy fighter, Jesus Castaneda. It took us ages to find his record. I think he'd lost three fights and he'd been stopped in each one. But he'd knocked out about 22 good quality opponents. And this was supposed to be an easy fight for me!" Bob Paget was over the moon with Crawford that night. "That was a tremendous performance. You know, every time he threw something, he hit."

On the 10th February 1996 Crawford stopped Frank Minton in one in Germany. A month later he stopped undefeated Ray Kane in two in Newcastle. It was during this time that Tony Breen arrived on the scene in the role of advisor. Crawford was a little wary of Breen at first. "Basically he got me back boxing. I were the British champion. I had nobody to fight, no manager and no promoter. I couldn't talk to the Board. So I met with Tony and he asked if he could get us some fights. I said, 'Go on then but you're not getting a contract with me. We'll have a handshake.' And he's done what he said he were going to do. Tony's not my manager. I can walk away from him any time I want. But the thing is he's looking after me so why should I walk away from him?"

But finding the way forward was not an easy task for Crawford and his team. A European title bid against Eddy Smulders was arranged. It never happened. And just to add insult to injury he found himself rated number two in the WBO listings behind Nicky Piper. But Crawford did not let the injustice cloud his vision. In December 1996 he stopped Tony Booth in 173 seconds at Southwark, flooring the Hull man four times before the fight was stopped. A month later he dealt out the same treatment to Ukrainian Peter Kamarenko at Bethnal Green. This time he took 109 seconds. Bob proudly remembers, "I mean, Crawford hit him with a left hook there and he had his feet off the floor which nobody should do. You can't get power unless you're pushing forward but he whips it up and because of his timing and his speed... That was a terrific performance. As Jim Watt said on the night, 'This kid's not as bad as Crawford's made him look.'"

On the 1st March 1997 Crawford finally became European champion, stopping Roberto Dominguez in three for the vacant title. Dominguez, reputed to be a big puncher, was nicknamed 'fogonazo' which means 'hot flash.' But if Dominguez was a 'hot flash' then Crawford was 'hot stuff' that night. His performance against the powerful Spaniard at the Everton Park Sports Centre was faultless. He cut him up in the first round and finished the job with a massive right uppercut in the third. It was a nasty knockout and referee Andreasen was quick enough to cradle the victim's head as it bounced off the canvas. As he was preparing for Dominguez, Crawford had a spooky premonition of the outcome. "I walked into Tony's (Breen) office and I said, 'I'm going to knock him out in the third round with a right upper-cut.'"

In May 1997 Crawford defended his European crown against Frenchman Pascal Warusfel at the Palais Des Sports, Paris. He won it on points. Fighting in his opponent's back yard didn't seem to bother him, which was just as well. So far he had fought a top German in Germany, two top Americans in America, a Welshman in Cardiff and now a Frenchman in Paris. Warusfel had nothing to lose and everything to gain. For the man from Leeds, defeat would spell disaster.

The French audience respected Crawford as he walked to the ring. Then the fight started and the crowd lodged themselves firmly behind their man, chants of "Pascal, Pascal," bouncing around the arena. By the end of round two Pascal proved that he could be a bit of a handful, managing to land a few solid punches. Every time he did so the audience cried in wonder, as if they were watching a firework display. In the fourth Crawford put his dancing feet on and forced Pascal to come forward, rewarding him with the feel of the leather in his face. The lights above the ring blazed mercilessly down on the combatants inside and tempers began to heat up. At the end of the sixth they gave each other the eye as they returned to their corners. In the ninth Crawford pounced straight away opening a horrendous gash over Pascal's left eye. He started the tenth looking fresh and then Pascal caught him with a right hand that brought the crowd to their feet. Another right cross had Crawford looking suddenly very tired and the crowd went wild. Crawford survived the round but as he plodded back to his corner he looked like a man with the weight of the world on his shoulders. The final round arrived and the French crowd were once again on their feet urging their man to victory but Crawford single handedly sat them down again with a final breath of fire. When it was over both fighters raised their hands as they embraced. Crawford was awarded the majority decision. Afterwards it was discovered that in the fourth round Crawford had cracked a bone in his wrist and torn several ligaments around his knuckle. "As I came back to the corner after the fifth, I felt sick."

On the 4th October 1997 Crawford walked into the brick wall that was Norwegian Ole Klemetsen. That night at London's Alexandra Palace, the 'Blond Viking' plundered Crawford's European title with a shocking second round knockout. From the start Klemetsen looked strong and determined, like a man who believed in himself. In contrast Crawford seemed blurred around the edges. Bob Paget was worried sick about his man. "He had a lot on his mind that night. In the dressing room, he couldn't get his mind on the job. I told him, 'Crawford, get buzzing!' He said, 'I can't' and I said, 'At least look as thought you mean it! Everybody can see the way you are now. You're not with it!' But he just couldn't get his mind right. He shouldn't have gone in there really but he told me, 'I've been let down so many times. I know what it feels like.'"

The bad blood started flowing at the first bell. Klemetsen was free as the wind with his elbows and about half way through he landed a blow that looked suspiciously low. He continued to dictate the pace of the round and in the last minute he caught Crawford with a massive left hook that put him down. Crawford got up and then Klemetsen hit out after the bell. Crawford retaliated with a glove in Klemetsen's face. Before Mickey Vann could get between them Klemetsen turned and hit Crawford in the chest. On the bell to end the second round the final blow came. Crawford's feet left the floor and his head bounced as it crashed to the canvas. He started shaking as he lay there and Mickey Vann rushed over, waving the fight off as he urgently tended to the beaten fighter lying before him. As they rolled Crawford over into the recovery position, Bob Paget was silently praying. "I was thinking, 'Here we go!' Because he shouldn't have had the fight really, you know? Then you start blaming yourself for not talking him out of it.

But I don't think I could have." Five minutes later Crawford was on his feet. The crowd cheered, relieved.

Crawford remains indifferent about the knockout. "I wasn't bothered. There were some problems and I just didn't want to be there. But I'm glad I was there and not somewhere else. Because if I had been anywhere else I would have probably been dead now. If I'd have been driving a car I'd have probably wrote it off or something. My mind just wasn't there. I wanted to be away. I didn't want to be on this planet, do you know what I mean? I had just had enough, totally enough. John Morris. Everything. Life just seemed to cave in on me, so I just went in the ring and got knocked out." But Crawford is adamant that the knockout was not as bad as it looked. "Nah. People say it was a terrible knockout but it wasn't. I got hit, so what? I got careless. I got caught. I got hit. Boom! That's my job!" I brought it to his attention that he was lying there, twitching. He laughed playfully, "Yeah? Well I were trying out a new break dancing move. What do you want me to say?

"Listen, I'm a fighter and I know all the risks. Don't tell me boxing is safe because it's not. I think that what does boxing more harm is saying that it's safe when we know that it's not. We go in that ring to win and if that means beating your opponent to a pulp and knocking him out, you do it. It's my choice. Fighters are not hurting anybody else but themselves. We are not climbing up mountains and putting everybody else at risk trying to rescue us because we're idiots! Anyway, I got up and walked to the dressing room. The doctor came and checked me over. I didn't even remember the fight. But that was because I wasn't there. My mind wasn't there. I could have won the fight and I would have felt the same. They said I was concussed so I went and got a brain scan. The brain scan said everything was alright. But the Board of Control said I had to have six months off. I was furious. They said it was on advice from the doctors. I asked them which doctors. They told me they were doing it for my own good. They just hate me."

While Crawford was losing to Klemetsen, Nicky Piper was losing a challenge for the WBO title against Dariusz Michalczewski. Piper's corner pulled him out at the end of the seventh. He announced his retirement from boxing that night.

Six months later, on the 14th March 1998, Crawford came back with all guns blazing. He blasted out Stevenage's Monty Wright in two rounds at Bethnal Green in an act of defiance for all those who had said that he was finished after Klemetsen. This was Crawford's first defence of the British title. "Three-and-a-half-years as British champion without one defence of the title! I kept asking, 'Why can't I defend?' They kept telling me there was nobody good enough. They said there were no challengers." Wright, who came from a fairground family, was determined to put up a good show. Before the fight he announced that it was his dream to win the British title. But dreams were not enough against Crawford Ashley at his best. That night York Hall was packed with Wright's supporters. They screamed abuse at Crawford as he strolled down to the ring but their anger only fuelled his cause. He rapidly silenced their hostility to a murmur as he crushed Wright in two rounds. Wright went down in the second and then turned away, confused

129

and once again under fire before referee Terry O'Connor was able to intervene. One of Wright's supporters threw a bottle at the ring. Thankfully nobody followed suit. Crawford, however, does not rate this particular performance. "I were crap. That was the first fight that Hayley went to and I was just playing to the crowd. I've never ever done the things that I did in that fight. I've never stood at the side of the ring and put my hands up and just nodded to him as if to say, 'Wait and see.'"

On the 9th June 1998 Crawford made another defence of his British title, picking up the vacant Commonwealth crown in the process with a six round defeat of former first round victim Tony Booth. But this time Booth was an entirely different kettle of fish. He had pulled off a points victory over Bruce Scott at the Alexandra Palace the night that Crawford had lost to Klemetsen. It was a result that few had foretold, Booth having lost to the Hackney man twice before. Booth was seven years younger than Crawford but this was his 79th professional fight. Having spent much of his career as a journeyman he had won his last five fights in a row. He was brimming with confidence. There was plenty of friction before the fight at the weigh-in. Crawford still gets angry when he thinks about it. "I know my weight. Basically I can get it down to just under twelve-seven. We're supposed to be there at six and I'm there at half-five. Six o'clock comes and no scales have turned up. I'm starting to get a bit annoyed because I just want to get on and get off. The scales turn up and they carry them up two flights of stairs. They plonked them down, and then they didn't want them there, they wanted them over there. They picked them up and plonked them down again. Then they said they couldn't have them on carpet because they had to go on board. They got some board, shoved the board underneath and plonked them down again. So now it's time to get on the scales. I weighed in at 12 stone eight pounds. All I can hear is little whispers, 'He's overweight, he's overweight.' And I know I'm not overweight. And Tony Booth's camp didn't realise. They said, 'He's overweight, he's got to do 12-seven.' The Board official says to me, 'You've got to take it off.' I says, 'I know my job now you just do your job.' Then Tony Booth gets on the scales and it's, 'Tony Booth, 12 stone nine!' Booth says, 'Them scales are wrong.' I said, 'I know they're wrong!' So everybody gets weighed in and everybody's overweight. They're all going, 'These scales are wrong.'"

Half-an-hour later, another fighter walked in to be weighed. It was Scarborough featherweight Paul Ingle. "Paul jumps on the scales for a check weight and says, 'Fucking hell, are them scales right?' I says, 'No they're not, they're wrong.' Paul says, 'Thank God for that!' So they've had another weigh-in. I said, 'I'm not getting on those scales until I see them calibrated.' Paul gets on and he's half-a-pound over. The official is still saying, 'The scales are right. You'll have to take the weight off.' I says, 'You can go fuck yourself!' He says, 'I have got a calibration certificate here.' I says, 'You fucking idiot! How can you say they're calibrated when you've brought them up two flights of stairs, bunged them down over there, picked them up and bunged them down over there, picked them up again and put board underneath them... And you're telling me them scales are calibrated!' I says, 'You're a fucking twat, you!' All the other fighters are just sat there, watching me."

Eventually Crawford and Tony Booth went across the road to a Leisure Centre and weighed themselves again. Crawford weighed 12stone six-and-three-quarters. Tony weighed 12, seven. "Afterwards, we were going back in and all the other fighters were coming out. They were all saying, 'Oh, it's great that you told him, he needs telling.' But they won't say anything. I will, and I get carpeted for it." The horrific side to this story is that Paul Ingle, who had no manager present to state his case, actually went away and skipped the weight off.

Crawford was furious. "Frank Maloney wasn't there. There were nobody there to back him up, only me screaming the odds. Because it was just after Spencer Oliver had been injured and they were all going on about it being down to weight loss. I says, 'If anything happens to him (Ingle) I'm holding you personally responsible. I'm going to tell everybody what you've done.'" This story has a chilling edge to it. In December 2000, Paul Ingle defended his IBF featherweight title against South African Mbulelo Botile in Sheffield. In the 12th and final round, Paul was knocked out. He was rushed to hospital and underwent an operation to remove a blood clot from his brain. Today, Paul is making slow but steady progress, thank God.

When Crawford eventually climbed through the ropes to fight Booth the Hull journeyman nearly caused a major upset. Booth got caught and decked in the second and in the fourth, but both times he came back with a strangely determined look in his eye, like a man possessed. He took some of Crawford's best shots and still he came back for more. But in the sixth Crawford's right uppercut did the job and referee Mickey Vann stopped the fight. After the fight Crawford told reporters, "Every fighter who boxes for the Lonsdale belt gives 120 per cent. When I caught him in the second I thought he wouldn't get up. Certain fighters run and hide from me, but he didn't. He did catch me, but you get caught in the boxing game. If he fought all his fights like that, then his record would be much, much better."

On the 26th September 1998 Crawford once again fought for the European title which had been vacated by Klemetsen. His opponent was Jo Siluvangi, an African based in France who had also mixed it with Klemetsen, outpointing the Norwegian over 12 to win the WBC International title back in April 1996. *Boxing News* had Crawford down to lose late in the fight. Crawford won it on points but when they announced a split decision he shook his head in disgust. "When they said it was split I thought, 'Oh yeah here we go again!" Nevertheless, Crawford was announced British, Commonwealth and European champion.

On the last day of December 1998 Crawford's baby daughter Asia was born. He made sure he was there for the big event. "Words can't describe how I felt. She's gorgeous. She's absolutely fantastic! She is the love of my life, totally and utterly. And my girlfriend Hayley is not only beautiful on the outside, she's a really nice person. (he shows me a photograph of Hayley) Boxing used to be everything to me. Now Hayley and Asia are everything to me."

Three months later, on the 13th March 1999, Crawford had his last fight for nearly two years. It ended a stoppage defeat. Crawford lost his three titles to outsider Clinton Woods at Manchester. Crawford's real battle was with his own weight that night and the towel came in during round eight. Bob Paget has sad memories, "We're in the corner and you could see he was gone, the boy. As he went out for the eighth I told him, 'You've got one minute. If you can do it in a minute all well and good, if you don't that's the end of it. I don't think it even went a minute. Woods caught him with a couple of good punches and Crawford went back. When the left hook caught him, I threw the towel in."

After this defeat Crawford spent two years out of the ring. Today he remains philosophical about that time, "It was all just promises." However, during that time there was one particular instance when he was lined up to fight faded legend Tommy 'Hit Man' Hearns. "That was the one that really, really annoyed me out of all my career of boxing. What made me angry was they said I pulled out because of a rotary cuff injury, and I'd never even heard of it until that day. I went over to Detroit for the press conference. I really didn't want to go over there, but they said the promoters wanted it so I've gone for one day. I've flown out on the Tuesday, done the press conference on the Wednesday and flew back that night. Then we went to Tenerife to do the training and on the last day there was a message to phone Tony (Breen). He said fight had been called off due to management problems and they had to re-schedule it. Then somebody's phoned me up and said look at Ceefax and they said the fight was off because of the rotary cuff thing. There's no justice! That were one of the biggest lows of my career. I've never ducked anybody and right towards the back end of my career for somebody to turn it around and make out it was down to me. I think they saw the size of me and the way I was talking as well. I always give 100 per cent and I always get a buzz for fighting legends. I give him all the respect he deserves but I was going there to win. When they realised that I wasn't in awe of him they suddenly got very short." For the record Crawford footed the bill for the trip to Detroit himself.

Crawford went on to have three more fights. On the 5th February 2001 he stepped in at heavyweight against vastly overweight Shane Woollas. Mind you, Crawford was no skinny-minny that night, at 15 stone 1lbs. He stopped Shane two seconds before the end of the fight which had been scheduled at four three minute rounds. The following March he beat Lee Swaby of Lincoln over eight rounds. This time it was at cruiser and Crawford looked much better at 13 stone 12lbs. Swaby, who had won a shock stoppage victory over Welsh hope Enzo Maccarinelli the previous May had lost one and won one since.

In August 2001 Crawford and Hayley's family was made complete when their son Theo was born. Once again the proud father was at his lady's side during the birth. And Crawford is so proud of his family. "All three of them are magical. Theo's great, he just smiles all the time. And do you know, Hayley went in to hospital to have him on the Saturday night, she had him at one minute past four on Sunday morning and we was all home having Sunday dinner, which I cooked, at two o'clock."

Then, on the 8th December 2001, Crawford Ashley made his final ring entrance. The venue was the Goresbrook Leisure Centre at Dagenham. In the other corner was WBU cruiserweight champion Sebastian Rothmann of South Africa. The fight was for Rothmann's title. Shaven-headed Rothmann was a rough house and I thought he looked like a thug, although I have been reliably informed that he is the most charming man you could meet out of the ropes. His version of the world title is not considered a serious one by many, but he was a hard fight for Crawford. Rothmann (born in Tel Aviv) had been storming his way along since his trainer Harold Volbrecht had taken over and seemed to develop a taste for beating up British fighters. He won his title by stopping Rob Norton in September 1999 in Wales. He had defended successfully four times by the time he faced Crawford, two of those defences against British fighters. But the fact is that five years ago the result could well have been very different. But this fight came five years later on and Rothmann, ten years younger than Crawford, flattened our man at the very end of the eighth round. Crawford had been boxing well, but he started to run out of steam as early as the third round. Rothmann caught him with a massive right hand over the top at the very end of the eighth and Crawford went crashing to the canvas in a shockingly conclusive manner. As he lay there, motionless, he was immediately surrounded by paramedics and members of the Board of Control and, of course, the ever loyal Bob Paget. As Crawford tried to push the oxygen mask away from his face, Bob who was kneeling at his side, told him to calm down. Crawford looked up and said, "I'm never going to be world champion now." Bob replied, "That makes two of us champ. Let's go on the piss!"

Twenty minutes later, Bob Paget took me to Crawford's dressing room and I felt a massive wave of relief sweep over me as I walked through the door and saw him standing there, conscious, upright, strong. I said, "Thank God you're alright." He said, "I'm not alright, I lost!" But there was no anger in his voice, just grim resignation. I said, "You were doing so well." He said, "I was fucked." But he was grinning now, his beautiful girlfriend Hayley at his side, brave for her man. As I looked up at Crawford I found it hard to equate this fantastic physical specimen with the crumpled form on the canvas 20 minutes ago. He had somehow blossomed back into this fine man standing before me. I mean, how tough is that? Some months later Crawford told me, "I could have got up before ten you know. It were only half past eight, so I know I could have got up before ten!"

Throughout his career Crawford always retained his membership of the 'Who Needs 'Em' club. Of all the fighters that I have studied Crawford is the one who has had the most opponents pull out on him. The list of names is endless. "This is the love of the game. When you know you've got a fight coming up it's like having the winning lottery ticket and it's roll-over week. Then they'd pull out on you and it's like, you go to get your ticket and the dog's ate it. I'd get really gutted and really down and depression would set in. And then I'd get the offer of another fight and I think, 'Great I'm fighting again!' And it's brilliant."

During my initial interview with Crawford on that rainy day in Leeds he told me, "I see fighters now who have retired and they've got fortunes but they're not happy. Because they haven't fought the best. I've fought the best in the world. When I retire from boxing I'll be one of the happiest fighters out there. Because I've done everything I've wanted to do."

And so that time has come. Crawford Ashley will never fight again. But despite his earnest attempts to convince me otherwise he will always be a hero in my eyes not only as a boxer, but as a human being. As a boy his hero was Muhammad Ali and his ambition was to become a pilot. He steered his own chartered flight through the sunshine and clouds of his thrilling career, and now that flight has finally landed.

These days Crawford is adjusting to life outside the ropes. Adjusting to the fact that when he wakes up every morning, he is no longer a boxer. And for my part, I am now proud to say that Crawford Ashley is my friend. I could never call him Gary Crawford because to me, he will always be Crawford Ashley. And in many years to come, when I am old and grey, my memories of that wonderful day I spent with him in Leeds will always make me smile.

"Bob used to meet champions on level terms and you had the feeling that secretly he believed he could beat you." – Sammy McCarthy

Bob Paget is one of the most dedicated individuals I have ever met. A quietly spoken Londoner, he just goes about his business without any fuss or nonsense. In fact, Bob Paget cannot abide fuss or nonsense. His motto is, "Do somebody a good turn and don't tell anybody about it." And over the years Bob has done more good turns for more people than you could shake a stick at. But going back to the beginning…

"I was born right bang opposite Blackfriars Boxing ring. It was on the 24th April 1933 – so don't tell too many people that. When I was about 13, me and Johnny Lewis, who was Dick Richardson's trainer, was at the same boxing club as the Kray twins. The Krays came from Bethnal Green and everybody assumed that they went to Repton, but they never. They went to the Robert Browning, which is in South London. In 1947, I won the London Federation of Boys Clubs and then I went into the Army, where I was a PT Instructor."

Bob has worked for many years as a boxing trainer, his most recent success story being Crawford Ashley. But during the 'Fifties and 'Sixties he was a boxing legend in his own lifetime, not as a fighter but as a sparring partner. In fact Bob Paget sparred with everybody, from Terry Spinks and Sammy McCarthy to Terry Downes, Dave Charnley and Henry Cooper. "I was a mechanic's mate. A labourer for the want of a better word but it sounds nicer. It was my job to maintain the vehicles. You only had an hour for dinner and they were strict. You had to clock in and clock out. So before I clocked out I went and put me boxing gear on under me overalls and then I was on starters orders. As soon as 12 o'clock came I'd jump on me bike, cycle down to the Thomas A 'Beckett, do me three or four rounds of sparring with who ever it was and then cycle back to work before my lunch hour was up. I think it was about 30 bob a round in them times so it was six quid a day for four rounds and me wages was five and a half quid a week. So in a day I was earning a week's wages."

Henry Cooper once said of Bob Paget, "I didn't have to worry too much about pulling my punches either. He was tough and I don't imagine anyone every frightened him." I asked Bob if indeed anybody ever did frighten him? He replied, "Yeah Henry Cooper! All of them, I mean they were all big names. Terry Downes, I only sparred with him for his first three fights and I remember when he got stopped by Dick Tiger which, by the way, was on cut eyes, nothing else. I went in the dressing room to see him after and he said, 'Bob, I can't use you any more. You're too light. I'm sorry.' I said, 'Don't say sorry to me. It's a pleasant relief that I haven't got to face you again.'

"See, there wasn't no point in me turning pro because I would never have made it to the top as a pro. But I was earning more money than if I had been boxing six or eight rounds a month. And remember all the money was mine. There was no trainer. There was no manager. There was no expenses. So I lived the good life. I really enjoyed life.

"I remember once I was taking my wife out on a Sunday. We was going to get a train down to Epsom, somewhere like that. All of a sudden I get a phone call. They wanted me to spar on Sunday morning. Anyway I hired a car, run me wife down there, drove all the way back, sparred, got me money that paid for the car and for the day and went back down there to join my wife.

"Mind, it wasn't all pleasant. Sometimes you'd get bruised or something. Charnley was the worse one because he never pulled no punches. In sparring, in the main, if you get knocked down you get up and you touch gloves and you say, 'You're alright.' Not with Dave Charnley. He put me down and I got up and went to touch gloves and he went bash!"

In the early '70s Bob went to Rhein-main in Germany to work at the USAFE boxing clinic. "They was looking for some coaches to get out there to teach the American forces the British way of fighting. Me and Terry Spinks, and Bruce Wells was also involved, we were out there as instructors to the American Forces in Europe. That was good stuff but Terry you know... he's always been a natural fighter, Terry. Nobody taught him a lot. He just had the natural ability. And patience wasn't his strongest point. The first day we was out there I think we had about 12 people in each of the parties. And we all split up. Anyway we went away, had lunch, come back and now all of a sudden I've got 24 instead of 12! So I said, 'Where did you lot come from?' And one of them said, 'Mr Spinks has told us to come and join your class because he's had to go somewhere urgently.' So anyway, I carried on with the lesson and in the evening I went back to our suite in the hotel and I said, 'Tel, what's all this about? Where did you get to?' He says, and I have to use the language, 'They can't fucking fight.' I said, 'Tel, that's what we're out here to do, to teach them how to fight!'

"I'll never forget during one session on the pads this young American airman called Andy missed and caught me on the chin. Well the pads, they were big black things. And I said to him afterwards, 'Look, the pads are what you hit, the black things. Anything you see that's pink, leave it alone, because that's me!'"

Over the years, Bob has done so much for charity, particularly in his capacity as activities organiser and fundraiser for the Freddie Mills club and Angels with Dirty Faces. These two clubs work in conjunction with each other to help old-aged pensioners and mentally and disabled children and adults. I asked Bob to tell me how he got involved. "About 35 years ago I was working for Lonsdale Sports and the guy that ran the Freddie Mills Club then asked if he could leave a box on the counter, to which I readily agreed. Anyway, he came back six months later and there was hardly anything in the box. So me and Richard Atkins, who was there at the time, said we'd take it down a pub in East Street and have a bit of a do. It was like a one off thing. We raised about thirty-five quid which was quite a bit of money in them days. Anyway, we bought them a radiogram and gave them the balance of the money. After that I went down there a few times and they asked me to get involved with the fundraising side and I've been there ever since. At the time I formed a committee to do things to help the old-aged pensioners. And then later on we formed the 'Angels with Dirty Faces' meaning the kids. We kept doing things for the old-aged pensions and I kept getting letters saying, 'Thank the Angels for this' and 'Thank the Angels for that.' Anyway, we've swung it round now so the committee are the Angels. Once a month we either take them out for a meal and a bit of a sing-song or we fetch them some entertainment in."

One of the pioneering ideas from the Angels is their 'Sorta Boxing Events' which happen at the Kronk Gym in Kentish Town. This involves a disabled person getting in the ring with a boxer. The rule is that the disabled person, usually a youngster but not always, wins – and always by knockout! They have had well over a thousand bouts now and these events are always well attended by the boxing fraternity. Top professionals mix with young amateurs to entertain and encourage their less fortunate opponents. Often the Freddie Mills Club boxer's physical disability is such that they have to be literally carried into the ring. But when that first bell goes, and the boxer comes out of his corner, or hers (Jane Couch once won the coveted award of 'Dive of the Night') the Freddie Mills Club boxer seems to become magically less aware of his or her constraints. This process is truly beautiful to watch. And while the Freddie Mills Club team are proudly strutting their stuff up in the ring, you will always find Bob Paget in the corner shouting instructions and encouragement. The main thing is that everybody has fun and at the same time money is raised from entrance fees and raffles to help keep the whole thing going.

And of life in general for Bob Paget these days, "I'm absolutely potless. I'm living on my pension now. But that does me. I don't owe anybody a penny and I can do just what I like when I like. And that's the way I like it. I mean I used to work for an extremely rich Arab. I was training him. He started playing about so I just come back. And that don't get you nowhere in the boxing world. Some of my mates say, 'Bob, why don't you just take the money?' but you know, your pride won't let you. Even if I thought I needed the money, I couldn't stick to it.

"I've got a little gym up at John Ruskin Street. It's appointment only, you can't just walk in there. Anyway when no one's there I go downstairs in the bar and practice darts. That's how I like to relax. I'm going down the pub to play darts later on today and I really look forward to it. I don't win a game mind you, that's a standing joke down there. And I've got two grandsons and two days a week I have one or the other of them, so they keep me busy enough."

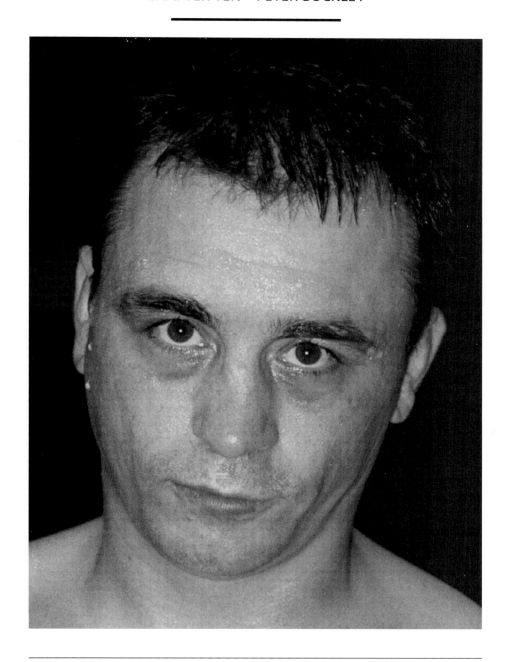

"If there wasn't people like Peter Buckley in boxing, there wouldn't be boxing. Men like Peter are definitely the backbone of boxing." – Spencer Oliver

Boxing has produced it's fair share of superstars over the years, champions and thrillers, fighters who the people love to love. But there is a loyal group of boxers who rarely have their day in the sun. They travel anywhere and everywhere to match wits and strength with anybody and everybody, from up and coming youngsters to champions looking for an 'easy' fight before their next title defence. Often these men travel to their opponents' local area knowing full well that if the fight goes the distance, which it usually does, there will be a 'hometown decision'. They take it on the chin, mostly without complaint. This proud bunch are known as 'journeymen' and a book about boxers could never be complete without one. The journeyman I chose comes from Birmingham. His name is Peter Buckley.

The first time I ever sat and closely watched Peter box in the flesh he lost a points decision to young Welsh prospect Jason Cook. But my eyes remained firmly fixed on Peter Buckley. What struck me about his performance was the clinical way he did his job, the look of complete indifference never leaving his face as he matched Cook's youthful exuberance with the wisdom of an elderly owl. That night I made up my mind that Peter Buckley was now on my hit-list.

I approached him a year later at an Ashford boxing show to request this interview. He was due to perform himself that night and he was sitting in the back row watching the boxing. His fight was scheduled for around midnight. Yet I saw no sign of nerves. No hint of anxiety. He was totally calm. I told him about my book and when I asked him for his help he said, "Yeah. OK. I'll do that."

But first I had other chapters to write and everywhere I went it jumped out at me how popular Peter really is. 'Oh you're interviewing Peter Buckley! He's a lovely boy. What a fantastic idea!' The responses were uniform in their respect for this fighting man of Birmingham. I put it to Peter that he has made so many friends along the way. "Yeah I have. I've got to say that I've never ever disliked any person I've boxed, ever. I've always spoke to them after, had a drink with them or something."

Peter Buckley was born in Birmingham on the 9th March 1969. "I'm the youngest of nine. I'm the baby. I've got five sisters and three brothers. I come from an Irish family but I was born in Acocks Green in Birmingham." Peter likes to see his mother every day. "She's 65 my mum but she works still. She's brilliant my mum is. She's had it hard my mum. You know bringing up nine kids. My dad had a heart attack and died and he was only 48."

Peter stands 5 ft 8 ins and walks around at about ten stone. Over the years his looks have matured from that of the boy next door but despite having close to 200 professional fights he has kept his features in exceptionally good shape. He has short brown hair and slightly hooded, light brown eyes. And the friendly grin is ever present.

On his left arm he has a large, gothic style tattoo. "I had a silly one there when I was younger and I got that to cover it up."

He lives with Tanya, who he has been with since 1986. Their daughter, Sinead, was born in 1991. "My daughter's my life man. I'll take her anywhere and she's into a lot of things. She's into dancing and she's really good. And she's a brilliant singer as well. I mean, she's in all the school plays. She's a performer. She's on the netball team at school and the rounders team. I see a lot of kids around the streets and that and I think, 'That's not going to be my daughter.'"

As a youngster, Peter boxed for Ladywood ABC. "I started amateur boxing when I was 11. I was a good amateur. I used to box with me hands down, a bit flashy. And I used to turn southpaw, and the officials didn't like it. But I used to just carry on. I used to do it round after round, and I used to knock quite a lot of them out. I mean, my knockout rate as an amateur was fucking brilliant. I used to go up to them and say, 'Who you boxing mate?' They'd say 'Peter Buckley.' I'd say, 'Oh that's me. I'm gonna' knock you out.' That's what I used to be like. I used to be arrogant. I won the Midland title. I got to the ABA semi-finals one year, Nigel Wenton beat me. Another year I got the quarter finals. My last amateur fight, I lost to Mark Tibbs in the NABC Finals.

"I packed it in when I was about 15. My dad died when I was 15 you see. I was only young and I went wild. I was always getting locked up. When I was about 17 I got out of jail and I got stabbed then. I was in hospital for a bit. I had a punctured lung. You see I used to get out of prison, go up the gym and train, and then think, 'Oh fuck that' and go back robbin' or whatever I was doing. Then I got out of prison the last time. I was 20, I was. I had just done two-and-a-half years, and I was drinking with Rocky Lawlor (former Midlands Area bantamweight champion). I've got to mention Rocky. A very tough individual around my area, well respected and that. He was still boxing at the time. He said to me, 'h'ya look, you don't want to keep doing this. Come up the gym, Monday with your kit.' And I thought being up a pro gym would be a big deal. I was like, 'Yeah, yeah.' He said, 'Don't talk to me while you're drunk. Come and see me when you're sober alright.' So I went up this gym, it was over in Dudley I think."

Rocky Lawlor introduced Peter to Norman 'Nobby' Nobbs, the man who would help him reshape his life. Nobby is strong character who is well known in the boxing world for his schooling of journeymen and Peter thinks the world of his trainer, mentor and friend. "When you first meet Nobby you don't know how to take him. Because he's got a mad sense of humour and you don't know whether he's being funny or serious. Say if I'm boxing someone, he'll say to them, 'I hope you've done your running,' just to try and throw them a little bit. And sometimes it does affect them. 'Shut up Nobby,' they'll say, and I laugh sometimes. And believe me, he's nobody's fool. Some people think like, 'Nobby, trainer of losers,' but I'll tell you now, there's not a man... He eats, sleeps and drinks boxing. He doesn't drink. He likes a cigar now and again. But I mean, he goes to work round the markets at three o'clock in the morning, Nobby does. He finishes about 12 and he's up the gym then.

And I mean, we don't pay no gym fees, nothing like that. He pays all the gym out of his own pocket, the electric and everything like that.

"When I first went to him he didn't give me no dreams or anything. He said, 'Keep coming. If you want to come it's down to you.' And we just took it from there really. We'd been going down the Dudley gym for about three months, Nobby didn't have his own gym in those days. And I thought, 'alright, do I want this or what?' Because nothing seemed to be happening. Nobby acknowledged me but I was just another kid in the gym. I suppose he saw them come and go all his life. I thought, 'He ain't paying much attention to me here like.' Then one day I sparred this kid called Leicester something, a big black kid from Dudley, I think he was a middleweight. Nobby's gone, 'In the ring,' and I've thought, 'Fucking hell!' I've got in the ring and I'm going bang, jab, jab and he couldn't hit me. And I've got out and Nobby's gone, 'Yeah!' I saw something there.' And the next thing I'm having my medical done and my brain scan and I've got a fight. I thought, 'God this is going too quick for me.' You know I was thinking professional boxing was like Rocky films and all that." And so the young tearaway from Birmingham set sail on his incredible journey through the ranks of professional boxing. Peter's eyes sparkle as he enthusiastically remembers those early days.

His professional career got off to a good start. His first professional fight on the 4th October 1989 against Alan Baldwin was a draw over six rounds and he won six of his first eight. But then the wins began to gradually fade away and points losses became more frequent. However, along the way he won the Midlands Area super-featherweight title (June 1991), which he defended once (February 1992). A year later he challenged for a WBA Penta-Continental title. He relinquished his super-featherweight crown in February 1995 to challenge for the super-bantamweight version which he won. He lost that title in his first defence. Peter might be a journeyman but every now and then he still pulls a win out of the hat and always if his girlfriend and his mum are in the audience.

His record is peppered with an array of British, Commonwealth, European and world champions. Men such as Colin McMillan, Paul Ingle, Barry Jones, Pat Mullings, Johnny Armour, Michael Brodie, Spencer Oliver, Duke McKenzie, Acelino Freitas and Nazeem Hamed. Peter was the first boxer to go the distance with Hamed. All of these top fighters had learning bouts with Peter Buckley. They all fought Peter to get on in their careers. I asked him if it makes him proud when he looks through his record. "It does, yeah."

Peter has had far too many fights to look at his career in date order. That would be a book on its own. So I have taken his impressions of particular fights, fighters and events. It makes for a bit of a chronological roller coaster, but dates don't matter. Peter's words matter. This is how he feels about ...

Duke McKenzie:

Peter boxed Duke McKenzie twice, the first time in January 1991. McKenzie stopped him in five, becoming the first man to halt him in his tracks. "I mean everyone's always saying to me about Nazeem Hamed but I've always said that the best boxer I ever boxed was Duke McKenzie. The first time I got stopped it was by Duke. It was terrible because I had never ever been stopped in a fight, amateur of pro, ever. It ripped me apart really. It didn't really dishearten me as such but it really, really hurt my pride. I pride myself on going the distance. It kills me to get fucking stopped. Some people say, 'Why don't you just stay down?' But I ain't a staying down person, man.

"When I was a kid, man, I was always in fights, always. And I'd fight the biggest kid in the area. And he could kick me to fuck but I'd get back up and I'd be fighting like, do you know what I mean? And in the end, they'd be the one running off. I wouldn't. And I've never backed down from anybody and I never would. I've got five sisters and three brothers man, and you learn how to fight." I asked him if his older brothers used to beat him up. "No, it was my sisters! They used to kill me, my sisters did. Because I was the babbi of the family. Because I was my mum's little babbi. They used to batter me man, but not in a bad way like.

"But like I say Duke McKenzie was the one. People were saying, 'he can't really punch, that Duke McKenzie.' Well he can punch mate! 'Cos his jab was like someone sticking a broom handle in you're face! And he's so sharp and correct. He's such a correct boxer. But he's such a nice bloke as well. I mean he's a gentleman, a real nice geezer."

Peter's last two fights of 1992 were hard ones. In September he fought Duke McKenzie for the second time and this time McKenzie stopped him in three. "When the offer come up to fight him again I had a bad shoulder. But I needed the poke at the time and I thought, 'fuck it man, I'll fight him.' So I went back in with him and after three rounds my shoulder went and I said to Nobby, 'just pull me out.'" Two months later Peter was in again, with Nazeem Hamed...

Nazeem Hamed:

Peter took Hamed the distance over six in November 1992. This was the first time 'The Prince' had been forced to hear the final bell. "I used to see Naz round the circuit before he turned pro. He used to come with Brendan [Ingle]. Anyway he was a flashy little fucker but I liked him I did. I used to think he was a funny little kid because he was like the hard man! And I used to laugh and I used to think, 'oh, fuck off man.' And then when I did come to box him, he'd won his first five all by stoppage. But I weren't fazed by him. Nobby's gone, 'do you want to fight him?' I says, 'yeah, I'll fight him. He's only a little kid. I ain't worried about him.'

"Anyway, I boxed him down at Liverpool and I had to get in first. But I didn't get in the ring. I've sat on the stool and I've turned it around. So I heard him coming in, doing all his dancing. He used to wear a gold jacket then. I don't even know if he vaulted over the ropes because I was facing the other way. I didn't get in the ring 'til he got in. And the fight was easy."

Peter fought Naz for a second time in January 1994 in Cardiff. This time it was stopped in the fourth round. "When the call came to come back and fight him again he'd stopped a few more by then. I've gone, 'yeah, I'll fight him again.' And it should never have been stopped. I was behind me cross arm defence and I threw a shot and I thought me elbow hit him. He threw a jab and it knocked me head back and the ref stopped the fight! And I thought he was going to warn me for me elbow! I went mad! Actually I think that's the only time I've ever gone mad. Because it done me head in, for him to stop me when I hadn't been hurt or nothing. I said to Naz afterwards, 'that should never have been stopped.' He said, 'yeah, but I was beating you.' I says, 'yeah, you was beating me but you was never going to stop me man!'" Incidentally, that was Peter's third stoppage loss in 53 professional fights.

"A lot of people don't like Naz but I've always found him alright. As big a star as he is he always comes over to me and shakes my hand. I've got respect for the geezer. I mean, fair play, he's a multi-millionaire and I wouldn't mind being in his shoes!"

One of the consequences of Peter's fights with Hamed was that he found himself very much in the firing line. "Well everybody I was fighting after Nazeem, they all wanted to better Nazeem you see. Like, if he can stop Buckley in three rounds, they'd do better than Nazeem did. That's what they all thought. But it don't work like that. Every fight's a different fight. But I knew for a fact that after the second Nazeem fight, everyone wanted my scalp. If they could stop me, that would make them better than Nazeem..."

Spencer Oliver:

In May 1995 Peter lost a points decision to Spencer Oliver. When I interviewed Spencer for this book, he told me that he felt his performance against Peter Buckley would be gauged against that of Nazeem Hamed. He said he had been watching Peter's style and working on a chopping right hand punch. The chopping right that Spencer talked of dropped Peter heavily in the third, taking him right off his feet. Peter stayed down for the count of five before retreating behind his cross arm defence. He remained unbowed to the final bell. After it was over he was quick to applaud Spencer. "Because I'd been watching him and I knew he was a good fighter man. I always rated Spencer and if that wouldn't have happened to him, I think he definitely would have gone on to win a world title. And I had to respect him because he put me over. I boxed him down in Potters Bar. And the main event was nothing man. He was the main event Spencer was. I don't even remember who the main event was. So I've got in the ring and he's come out and all 'The Omen' music was going. Anyway we start boxing and in the third round he sent this right hand over the top. How I ever got up from it I don't know. I don't remember the punch at the time but I've watched it since on video. I fell back and my head didn't even hit the floor. I've got up and tore back into him. And we had a good fight. And afterwards even Nobby said to me, 'how the fuck did you get up off that?' I said, 'I don't know man!' But I like Spencer as well. He's a really nice man."

Peter also fought Sergei Devakov, the man Spencer was in against the night he went into a coma. Peter lost on points to the Ukranian at York Hall. "I boxed him as well I did and I thought Spencer would have no problem with him whatsoever. And when that happened me heart skipped a beat man. I mean I boxed Tony Silkstone who committed suicide. I boxed Bradley Stone who died. And Bradley... I boxed Bradley but I'd spoken to him many times and he was such a nice kid man. I was shocked. And I boxed James Murray. I've boxed a lot of people and sometimes I step back and I think, 'God! It ain't as far away. That could have been me!' When it happens, at the time you get a shiver down the spine. Especially when you've shared the ring with them and spoke to them and had a cup of tea with them. It's horrible. That's the bad side of boxing. But we all know the risks and we all get in there."

James Murray:

In April 1994 Peter lost on points over six to James Murray at Glasgow. James dropped Peter onto his bottom in the fifth. Later that year he would go on to become Scottish bantamweight champion. "I underestimated James Murray a bit to tell the truth. Because he boxed a kid from my gym who couldn't crack an egg and this kid went the distance with him, no problem. So I'm boxing him and I've had me hands down and that, and bang! He's hit me with a left and he's caught me square on. My legs were together and he's put me straight down. It was a square on shot. But he was a good little fighter, James Murray."

James Murray died in November 1995. He was boxing at the Moathouse Hotel, Glasgow, challenging Drew Docherty for his British bantamweight title when he collapsed after being counted out in the 12th round. Suddenly a huge fight broke out in the crowd, mindless thugs smashing chairs over each other's heads and all sorts. The chaos they caused hindered the medics getting James out. Later it was discovered that he had a blood clot on the brain. James died in hospital.

Miquel Matthews:

There is a fighter, another journeyman, who features heavily in Peter's record. His name is Miquel Matthews. *Boxing News* once said of this Welsh warhorse, 'The essential ingredients behind his longevity are good health, Volkswagen-like reliability, a bomb-proof chin, skin of a rhino and a heart the size of Glamorgan.' Like Peter, Miquel has notched up more than a hundred fights and these two soldiers of fortune have many opponents in common. They have fought each other – five times! They are also good friends.

They first fought in February 1990. They drew over six at Evesham. "I've gone in there and I wouldn't say it was my first hard fight, but against a geezer who knew the score, do you know what I mean?" They fought for a second time in October 1990. This time Peter won on points over eight at Cleethorpes. Eight days later they fought again. This time Miquel won on points over eight at Wolverhampton. "Oh that was at Park Hall. I hated boxing at that place. I never ever won there. The changing room was about the size of this table and it was just a dingy, horrible little place."

After fitting in a nimble points win over Tony Smith, Peter fought Miquel for the fourth time. This time he won on points over eight at Birmingham. This was their third clash in one month. And these two met for the fifth and final time in October 1999, nine years after their last time, almost to the day. Peter won on points over eight at Birmingham. For someone who has had so many fights, Peter's recollection of his record is good. But when I reminded him of all the fights he has had with Miquel he had to laugh. His memories of his battles with the hardy Welshman are warm ones. "Our last fight, they told me about three days before. I said, 'yeah, go for it.' I think it was about eight two's or something like that. I like boxing Miquel. He's a nice bloke."

Conn McMullen:

The 29th March 1994 was a winning day for Peter Buckley. He won on points over six against Con McMullen at York Hall. This was his first win in 18 fights. "I love boxing at York Hall. I think it's one of the best venues around. They're hard core boxing fans down there and the crowd know their boxing. Even if you lose they appreciate what you've done. I remember boxing Conn McMullen down there and Mickey Duff was sitting there and he was shouting, 'fucking throw some shots. You can win this Peter!' Because I've boxed on loads of Mickey's shows and when he was shouting that I was thinkingL 'yeah! He knows who I am at last.' And it was a good fight as well."

Paul Lloyd:

On the 6th May 1994 Peter suffered his fourth stoppage defeat, to Paul Lloyd in Liverpool. Lloyd had dropped Peter twice before Nobby pulled him out. "I boxed Paul Lloyd and for a few rounds we had a tear up. He's a very good body puncher and he hit me with a shot and it took the wind out of me. But I think that was the fight where I looked the worst ever. Me eyes was out here. Because we cracked heads, plus he hit me there. And I had my driving test two days later. I turned up at this driving test with two big black eyes and I failed the test. So I think I was going through a bit of a bad patch because I thought I'd passed it. But I must have looked like a right hooligan. I weren't telling them I was a boxer. Yeah I think I was going through a bit of a bad patch. But you know you get 'em don't you?"

His first title:

In June 1991 Peter won his first title, the Midlands Area super-featherweight against Brian Robb. "It was like winning the world title to me. It was brilliant because they had belts then. I've still got that belt to this day. All my mates came, I had three coach loads up there. It was in Wolverhampton Civil Hall. Brilliant venue! The music was blaring and I had me new robe. And I've gone in there and I've boxed him and it was a really good fight, a proper ten round punch up."

Peter defended the title only once. Again it was against Brian Robb in February 1992. This time he stopped Robb in the tenth. "It was at Telford Town Hall. All my mates were there but he had a big crowd there. I'm not classed as a banger but I can hit more than people think really. In the second round as I've gone to punch him I felt my arm go. Nobby massaged it and that. And I was losing the fight towards the end. In the tenth round I've thought, 'fuck it!' and I've threw it and I've hit him. I knew he was gone anyway."

His second title:

In October 1994 Peter lost on points over six to Midlands super-bantamweight champion Matthew Harris at Wolverhampton. In February 1995 Peter relinquished his Midlands super-featherweight belt to challenge for Harris' super-bantamweight version at Birmingham. He won it and lost it in his first defence, again to Harris, in October 1995.

"Well the first time I boxed him I'd had a fight in a pub with this geezer and I fucked me hand up. So I virtually boxed him with one hand. And he was nothing. And then they've asked me, 'do you want to fight for the Midlands super-bantamweight title?' I've gone, 'yeah!' So I was running like hell. I really trained for it. Paul Wesley and Robert McCracken fought for the British light-middleweight title that night and me and Paul had been training together.

"Because Harris beat me when I boxed him before I think he underestimated me. But I was boxing with one hand then. This time I just came tearing into him and I think I cut him in the second round. It was a good fight but every exchange I was getting the better of it. I was stronger than him and I was bigger than him as well. I had him all over the place. There was no way that I was not going to win that fight, on that night. I mean, he was unbeaten at the time. And they would have had to drag me out. I was winning that title. My missus was there. My mum was there. All my mates were coming down. And I just knew I was going to win. My missus has come to watch me about four times and every time she's come I've always won. And my mum and my family, I can't lose in front of them man. I'm a winner to them.

"And then, when I lost the title it was on the Richie Woodall bill at Telford. They phoned up the day before and Nobby said to me, 'there's a ten rounder going. You can defend your super-bantamweight title.' I said, 'I won't be able to do the weight.' Because I was nine stone at the time. He's gone, 'Don't worry about the weight.' So I agreed and I boxed him. It was a ten rounder and I lost by half a point. But I thought I won it right. It was like a sparring session. He wouldn't come near me. The last two or three rounds I give it to him a bit. And I thought, being the champion as well... And they give it to him by half-a-point. And I thought, 'Oh fuck it!' But I got real good money for it because I helped them out. Because they needed a ten rounder and I mean I can do ten rounds, no problem. Because after four rounds I get me second wind and I can go! He'd (Harris) already been training because he'd been fighting an eight rounder on the bill anyway. But it done me head in losing to him because I knew I could have beat him. And to lose by half-a-point, I thought that was a bit harsh to tell you the truth." Peter fought Harris for the fourth and final time on the In April 1997. Harris won on points over six.

Ady Lewis:

In May 1995 Peter lost on points over four to tiny Bury bantamweight Ady Lewis. Ady, who makes a cute little buzzing sound whenever he throws a punch, went on to become British and Commonwealth champion at flyweight and bantam. He had eight stoppage wins in a row but Peter was the fly in Ady's ointment that night, becoming the first man to take him the distance. He chuckles at the memory. "I thought, 'He's only a bantamweight. I'll fight him.' And when I got in the ring with him I couldn't believe how small he was. I looked down at him and I thought, 'No man, I can't be fighting you. You look like a little babbi!' It was like fighting a little kid! Until he started throwing them shots. He's a strong little fucker, man! He come flying out with them hooks and I thought, 'OK. You're gonna have to take a few back.' And I hit him with a left hook and he wobbled a bit. But he was a strong little bugger man. And a nice little geezer."

Scott Harrison:

In January 1997 Peter lost on points over four to rugged Glaswegian and future British and Commonwealth featherweight champion Scott Harrison at York Hall. This was the first fight that I noticed *Boxing News* describing Peter as a 'journeyman.' I wondered how he felt about that? "Well I know I'm a journeyman really, so it weren't no shock to me. I ain't gonna' set the world alight. And Scott Harrison is one hell of a fighter man! It don't seem that there's anything that clever about him but every thing he done he done good. I boxed him twice, Scott. And the first time I boxed him, he perforated me eardrum. And I'm boxing him and I couldn't hear a thing. Even though one ear was perforated I couldn't hear nothing out of the both of them. And Roy Francis is refereeing right and the bell's gone for the end of the round and I'm still trying to throw punches. And Roy's give me a bit of a telling off and sent me back to the corner and I couldn't hear fuck all. But I've gone out and I went the distance with him. I woke up the next morning and there was blood on me pillow. So I went to my doctors and he's told me I had a perforated ear drum." For the record, this was Harrison's second pro appearance and Peter's 91st.

Just over a year after their first battle Peter lost on points to Harrison for the second time, again over four rounds and this time at Edmonton. Peter had become so well travelled that the four men who took part in the two main contests, Spencer Oliver, Fabrice Benichou, Michael Brodie and Brian Carr had all boxed Peter at some time. I put this fact to Peter and he tells me, "It didn't register at the time not until you just said it now actually."

Gregorio Medina:

In May 1997 Nobby pulled Peter out after the second round against Mexican southpaw Gregorio Medina at Mansfield. It was the quickest defeat of his career. "That was a bad fight man. I defeated myself that night. I weren't in shape. I took the fight at a day's notice. Got in there and there was nothing there whatsoever that night. I took the fight for the money. It's as simple as that. And the money weren't that good neither!"

Decisions! Decisions!:

"When you're boxing a home fighter and it's a close call you know he'll get the decision. You know you've got to knock him out to win. I boxed Johnny Armour (October 1991) and he did beat me. But I tell you if that had been me? I've saw fighters with a little nick on their eye and it's stopped. And his face was a mess! It looked like it had been cut to ribbons. He beat me like but if he wouldn't have been a home town fighter it would have been stopped. And it probably done him more damage than if they had stopped it.

"I boxed Donnie Hood in Glasgow (May 1992) and I got badly robbed against him. They was all booing right. Afterwards I was in the hotel, it was the Holiday Inn or something like that. I got in the lift, my mate was with me, and he got in the lift with us and his nose was all busted up. My mate's gone, 'Look at the state of him. Who won that fight?' And

Donnie Hood's looked at me as if to say, 'It's nothing to do with me.' But it's nothing to do with the fighter. That's why I would never say anything to a fighter because at the end of the day they're trying to earn a living just like me. And they ain't put their own hands, up the referee's done it. So I ain't got no qualms with any boxer who I've ever boxed against, not one. Because they're just trying to put food on the table, like me."

Hostile Territory:

Many of Peter's fights have been fought in front of partisan crowds. "Oh I'm used to it now. It don't really faze me. At the end of the day you're in there and it's a ring. And you know a ring's a ring. It don't matter if it's here, there or anywhere really. I mean I get called everything sometimes, 'You Brummie bastard!' and things like that.

"I was boxing down Leeds once. I was boxing Steve Conway. I got in the ring and he was showboating and all that so I started doin' it. And they were like, 'You Brummie bastard!' so when we got in a clinch, I got hold of him and started making faces at them, and they're all shouting 'You fucking Brummie bastard!' and Nobby's gone, 'Oi, calm down here!' because there was lots of them. But I didn't care because I was just winding them up, I was. I thought 'Fuck 'em!' I mean, I can't let it faze me. I've saw too many things man!"

Innocents Abroad - Ruben Condori:

"I remember boxing an Argentinean Geezer Ruben Condori in Germany (Augsburg, May 1992). Top of the bill, we was. It was a ten rounder. He was like a little Mexican, he was and Nobby's gone to me, 'The first punch you're gonna' get from him is one to the bollocks and then one around the back of the head.' And straight away the geezer's come out and BANG! And after that it was any little hole and I just kept him off. Ten rounds, over there! Germany was the best place I've been actually. I've been to Denmark and I've been to Vienna but I liked Germany. Because a few of us went over. There was me, Paul Wesley and Horace Fleary. He used to live in Germany so he could speak the lingo. But the funny thing was this Argentinean who I boxed, he was small, I mean really tiny. Anyway, we went into this night club after we boxed and he was there. We looked over and there he was, white suit on, black collars, dancing around. He looked like a mini John Travolta in Saturday Night Fever! We was in bits, man!"

Finest performance:

One of Peter's finest performances was against Harald Geier, who he challenged for the vacant WBA Penta-Continental super-bantamweight title in February 1993. The fight took place in Vienna. Peter lost an extremely close points decision over 12 rounds. "I trained really, really hard. I mean, I was running ten mile runs. I had my track suit on and everything. I had to be eight stone ten and at the time I was about nine stone six. I got the weight off and I was eating right. I was living like a proper professional. And I was the fittest I've even been. I'd run all the way through Sutton Park and I'd get to the last bit at the top of the hill. Nobby'd be there in his car and I'd go to get in and he'd just lock the door and drive off! I'd be like, 'Oh, fucking hell man!' I had to run all the way back. Anyway, he done that about three times and the next time I got to the top of the hill and turned around and said, 'See you back there!' and I've just run back because I was fit as fuck.

"So anyway, It was like a Frank Bruno fight with all flags and everything. And I'm the guy whose gone there to fight him. So after a few rounds I'm thinking, 'You ain't that much mate. You ain't as good as they say you are.' He'd had about 17 fights unbeaten and he'd knocked about 15 out! And he couldn't punch! He was a manufactured fighter. So in the ninth round I've gone 'Bang' and I've hit him with a left hook to the body, a left hook to the head and he's dropped. He was out! So the referee's practically picked him up right, he's took me over to my corner, wiped my boots. Why? I don't know why? Then he took him back to his corner and wiped his boots. He's wiped all the ring, and the crowd were booing and that then. It never said nothing about that in *Boxing News*. Anyway, I've gone steaming back into him and the bell's gone. And after that man, he was just on his toes. I was hitting him with all these shots and because I was cross armed and elusive, he couldn't really hit me. He wouldn't come near me. But it was a real good fight and everyone was coming up to me afterwards, asking for autographs and things like that. It was a proud night for me. And I never, ever got the video of it. It was shown on TV over there and they said they'd get me the video. But I never got it off 'em. And of all the fights I've had, I'd really love to have that one.

"After the fight we were supposed to stay out in Austria for a week, because of the plane tickets and everything. The hotel we were staying in was brilliant, it was like a health club. And the manager couldn't do enough for me. There was a sports shop there and he gave me loads of sports gear. But it was out in the sticks a bit. One day me and Nobby went on this steam train. It took us three hours to get to Vienna. After a few days I was mad to come home. I was missing my daughter like mad. When I left the hotel I had a phone bill of about a hundred and seventy quid. Because I was just mad on the phone all the time."

Fighting dirty:

"It's hard enough in there anyway, without them being dirty. But if you can get away with it, then get away with it I always say. I mean, I've boxed some kids right, and they'll hit you low five times and then it's 'Sorry about that,' and they'll put their glove out. But they keep doing it. And after a little while you get fed up with it and you think, 'OK, you can have one back now. And I'm sorry about that.' It's part of the game. I mean, it ain't tennis."

Ledwaba and Freitas:

In December 1998 Peter fought two hard men, world class South African Lehlohonolo Ledwaba, and two weeks later brilliant Brazilian Acelino Freitas. Freitas was 23 years old at the time and unbeaten in 18 fights. He had stopped everybody he had fought.

"I boxed that Ledwaba down in Bristol. I heard he was former world champion and all that and I got in the ring with him and after three rounds I thinking, 'Come on then man. You've got to be a bit better than this.' Because I was getting good money for it. Anyway, round four's gone by and I've thought, 'He ain't this much, this South African.' And towards the end I was jabbing him and I was doing OK. So it was easy, that fight was.

"Then the next week I boxed that Freitas. I didn't know nothing of him. Anyway, I've gone down there, I've got in the ring, I've looked at him and I've thought, 'Fuckin' Hell! You're big, you are man!' And the first punch he's hit me with, he's put me straight on me arse! And I wouldn't say he's really a puncher 'cos he didn't knock me out. But then he's caught me with a left hook to the body in the second round and he's took the wind right out of me. I went three rounds with him and I've come back to the corner and Nobby's gone, 'Fuck that. I'm pulling you out.' I've gone, 'I'm alright.' He's gone, 'Nah!'"

Champagne time with Brendan Bryce:

In October 1997, Peter won on points over six against Brendan Bryce at Piccadilly. "Well Brendan used to box for our gym actually. He was a Scottish kid. And I knew I'd beat him because I'd sparred with him enough times. And I had him over as well (in the second), so that was OK. He was a game little kid but he knew when I got in the ring that I was going to beat him. After the fight they presented me with a bottle of champagne because it was my 103rd fight."

... And Craig Spacie:

On the 11th May 2000 Peter fought and lost on points over four to Craig Spacie at Newark. Before the fight began a representative from the Board of Control got in the ring to present Peter with a bottle of champagne to mark his 150th contest. There was one problem. It was actually his 149th! "The thing is sometimes, right, I've boxed twice in the same week. And I've looked in *Boxing News* and they've only reported on one fight. So I think they've missed some fights. But I've got a bottle of champagne anyway." By the time the Board realised their mistake Peter had secured a firm grip on the bottle!

... And Jimmy Phelan:

His next fight, his true 150th, was on the 25th May 2000. He drew over six against local man Jimmy Phelan in Hull. "Me 150th fight then, down in Hull, Sky came down and they done a thing on me, they followed me around all day. And I had a draw with Jimmy Phelan. I had him over in the second and everything right. And I did win the fight but Mickey Vann give it a draw, so I weren't too pissed off." After the fight, Peter was presented with another bottle of champagne. I asked if he likes champagne! "I do now yeah! But I don't buy it that much."

Landmark fights:

I asked Peter if he celebrates when he reaches landmarks in his career. "Nah. What it means to me now is that I've bypassed the record of current British boxers having the most fights and that's an achievement in itself. When I had my 100th fight right, I didn't think, 'Oh, I've had my 100th. Now I'm packing it in.' I was just thinking I'd go on and have more and more. But anyway, I would like to have 200 fights, just to say I've had 200. I don't know if I'll get there, I just take it one fight at a time now."

The latest call:

"I was in the house one night, watching Coronation Street, and a kid that I know was supposed to have boxed but he didn't turn up. So Nobby's come, bibbed the horn, I've looked out the window and he's gone to me, 'Grab your kit. We're going to London.' I've grabbed me kit and I'm in the car, I didn't know where or who I was fighting or whatever. Went down there, boxed, I think it was Marlon Ward and I thought I'd won. But they give it to him! And I thought, 'Hang on! I'm doing youse a favour here by coming out of me house late at night to come down to London with fuckin' two minutes notice. But I got paid so I can't really moan."

The cool customer:

"I've seen boxers in the training rooms right, I mean I was probably like it when I first started. It's like, 'You're on now, you're on now.' I see some kids in the changing room and they're so tense and they're sitting there for five hours. But I'm out watching the boxing or just relaxing myself really, do you know what I mean. They let it get to 'em too much."

The moment of truth:

"When I step in there I'm going out to give them a performance. And try not to get hurt. That's the utmost, not to get hurt. If I come out of that ring without a mark on me, to me that's mission accomplished. I don't like walking around with black eyes and things like that. I don't want my daughter to see me with a black eye. My objective is to earn as much money as I can without getting hurt. That's how I see it. If I know it's going to be hard, as long as I've done my running I haven't got a worry in my mind. But if I've took a fight at short notice and it's a hard fight, and I haven't done my running, that's when I... I don't really worry. I never get butterflies. I'm never scared. I'm never, ever scared to fight. But that's what I think, as long as I don't get hurt. It's like people tell me I've got a good chin. Well I might have got a good chin, but I don't take too many shots on the chin if I can help it. And if I come out with black eyes, well that's no good to me."

How long?

Despite Peter's solid defence and wily tactics, a fight at the end of the day is still a fight. He knows that he cannot go on for ever. "I've been training some fighters on and off for a few years. I've took people here and there, over to Ireland and places like that. And I like it. People think that because I've lost a lot of fights... But when I take someone in, nothing gives me a bigger thrill than seeing them win. I took Gary Flear to fight over in Belfast against a kid who'd already beat him. So he's come back after the first round and I've gone to him, 'Gaz you can beat this kid.' And I told him what I would have done. And he won! And I remember I took this kid called Warren Stephens. He had won one fight out of 15 and he was on the Bruno bill at the NEC. And I've took him in and he's only won like. I was just really chuffed for him like, because he lost most of his fights but he had plenty of bottle. He ain't fighting no more. This was a few years back. I feel good when they win. Especially when they follow my instructions. Because I can read fights quite easily. It's nice when they do what I tell 'em."

Biggest influences:

"My girlfriend and my daughter and my mum, and Nobby. My missus, she was with me when I had nothing. Nothing at all man. She had a good job, she was manager of a company. And all the way she's backed me 100 percent. She's my backbone man. Her and my daughter, and my mum. I wish my dad was still here. He'd be proud as punch man, I know he would. And my mum loves Nobby for what he's done for me. Because she knows where I would have gone."

Conclusive words:

"People say to me, 'You must be loaded.' Well I ain't loaded, right. I wouldn't still be boxing if I was loaded. I get by. I don't work full time or anything. But if a bit of driving or something comes up I do it. But I just love fighting and the money's a bonus at the end of the day.

"When I first started it all come a bit quick. And when I won the Midlands super-featherweight title there was talk about a British title fight. It never come off but I was having quite a good little run at the time, I think. And having said that, if I had fought for the British title and lost, I probably wouldn't have had as many fights as I've had now. Because if you lose that, with a lot of kids, there's nowhere to go. It's like you can only go down from there.

"There have been times when I've had little bad spells, especially when I've had real bad decisions, and I've thought, 'fuck it man. I ain't got it no more. I can't do it.' Do you know what I mean? We all go through it. I mean, world champions go through it. In every walk of life, not just boxing. I think it's getting too hard. And then, I'll have two weeks off and, you know, I can't just sit around doing nothing. I love being round the gym. And I know for a fact that if I hadn't have got into the boxing, I'd probably be an armed robber or something. I would have done something and I'd probably be spending a lot of time in prison now.

"When people say, 'you lost, you lost.' I don't give a fuck about losing. I've still got my face and I'm still out there. And my daughter's got me, and my missus' got me. As far as I'm concerned that's all I care about. We go on nice holidays every year. I've got a decent car and a nice home. My missus don't want for nothing. My babbi don't want for nothing. To me that's my achievement. I don't have to go out robbin' and have the police knocking on my door. To me, I'm a winner in my own right. I'm in love with boxing. I love fighting. I get in the ring and I'm a somebody, do you know what I mean. And I'm respected for it, and it's nice."

"We send them out fit and well and ask them to do their best. The name of the game is not getting hurt and earning a few quid. Anything else is a bonus." – Nobby Nobbs

In boxing, as in all sports, there must be winners and losers. The concept of the journeyman has been accepted in the boxing world since the sport originated. The journeyman is the fighter that goes in as 'an opponent' against a fighter who is 'a prospect.' You cannot have a prospect without an opponent. For a fighter to win, another fighter has to lose.

One man who has no illusions about the opponents' place in the grand scheme of things is Norman 'Nobby' Nobbs. This six foot, three inch stalwart of the Midlands boxing scene runs diligently his gym in Birmingham's city centre. Nobby's stable includes some of Britain's most durable and established journeymen, along with many kids off the street. The first question I asked Nobby was if he had ever boxed himself and I'm going to let him loose briefly now with his repertoire. Take it away Nobby!

"I was a colourful fighter, I was black and blue all over. My cornerman was the only cornerman to use a red towel, so it never showed the blood. It cost me fuck-all in transport, because I always went home in an ambulance. They used to call me Battling Rembrandt, I spent that much time on the canvas. I used to have three cutsmen, one for me bum, one for me knees and one for me eyes. In me last fight there were seventy-five thousand people, at Villa Park when I had a bottle over me head when they played Manchester United." As ever the deadpan expression never leaves Nobby's face and I clapped my hands and told him he was very good, but had he ever boxed? "No, I found out I was crap. I went to a boxing club and I just ended up training the others. It was the Golden Gloves in Birmingham. That was when I was in my early twenties. I was a doorman for 20 years. And I worked on the market." I asked if he had ever done anything else? "I could have been a doctor, but I never had the patients. And I could have been a millionaire, but I never had the money." I tell Nobby that I have the same problem, and we move swiftly along to his career as one of the top fight figures in the Midlands.

Nobby Nobbs is talked of as a genius in the art of defence, and I put this to him. "I teach kids to look after themselves. The name of the game is to earn as much as you can without getting hurt. It's like me when I was a doorman. If I got beat up, I got twenty quid. If I didn't get beat up, I got twenty quid. So what do you do? You don't get beat up. That's it! It's the same with my fighters. It's a TV sport see. Winners in the red corner, losers in the blue corner. And invariably, mine come out of the blue corner. Because all the top amateurs and the English internationals, they go with the Frank Warrens and the Barry Hearns, so I get the kids off the streets really. Any kid that wants to come to my gym and train, they can do. And then we can teach 'em the right way to survive. Because a kid who's easily hit ain't gonna last very long, and he's not gonna earn no money.

"The secret of a good gym is to always have a couple of good fighters. If you've got a couple of good fighters in the gym, all the others will learn off them. And I've had some good fighters over the years. I mean Peter (Buckley) was a good fighter as a junior. And then he got into a bit of trouble and he had a few years off. And then Rocky Lawlor, who was a fighter of mine, introduced me to Peter. And ever since Peter's been with me." (Rocky was Midlands bantamweight champion and fought in a final eliminator for the British title.)

"For about a month I didn't really notice Peter because he didn't really show me anything. And I took him to a gym in Dudley and he sparred with a half decent pro and he jabbed his head off. And I thought, 'he's alright.' And since then he's been two times Midland champion, he's fought for an Intercontinental title and he's fought the best. I've had loads of fighters who have fought the best and Peter's one of them. And I'm proud of what Peter's achieved. Of course I am. He's a credit to the game. We've never had a contract. I never have no contracts with mine. To me, Peter's a champion, even though he's not one on paper. To me all my fighters are champions."

Nobby is a great man for making wisecracks from the corner. For instance, if his fighter is just warming up in the third of a four rounder, he's been known to cheerfully ask the referee if they could possibly make it a six rounder. One time the lights went off during one of his fighters' performances at Dagenham. When the hall was re-illuminated, Nobby told the referee that it was no use, he was 'still ugly!' The referee simply smiled. Often he'll call out to the other corner, 'I hope your boy's done his running!' or some similar remark. And I remember one time, at the Elephant and Castle, 'a prospect' went over on an obvious slip. Nobby started counting loudly, 'A-One-a!, A-Two-a!' Referee Larry O'Connell immediately issued the warning, 'Oi! I'm the referee OK!' O'Connell had a big grin on his face at the time, because everybody knows Nobby.

"Oh yeah, that's to relax them. You've got to be good at reading situations. We understand what we're doing. I mean, you get some trainers, they come to these big shows and they honestly think their kids are gonna' win. Them are dangerous. And when the kid comes back, often on the wrong end of a points decision, the trainer's shouting at them, saying they should have done more running. And the kid could have run to Glasgow and back and he still wouldn't have won the fight. You've got to have the talent and heart plus some sort of chin. You can't put in what God's left out.

"I mean Peter's a tough guy, so's Paul Wesley and Brian Coleman. But they're what you call in the trade 'cuties.' They don't stand for no five card trick. They know how to slip and slide. And when they go in to box a three minute round, they only really box for a half of that time. The rest of the time they're just fannying. That's what my kids do. For a six round fight they only really box for three rounds. You can do it once you've learned how to do it, and I teach them how to do it.

"And hardly any of mine get stopped. During the course of a year you can count on one hand the number of mine that get stopped. I'd never put a fighter in just to get stopped. You'd only be running a meat factory if you did that. They stand half a chance and I see how it goes. If things are looking a bit sticky, I pull them out and they live to fight another day. You've got to be able to live with yourself after, haven't you?"

Over the years the average number of fights a boxer has during his career has dropped dramatically, but not at Nobby's place. "Not mine! Mine have all had 50 plus. It's like racehorses. If you've got a racehorse and it don't race, you shoot the fucker. I don't want to shoot none of my fighters. It's no use having horses that don't race. It's no use having boxers that don't box. You can live in the twilight zone and have a kid who has two fights a year, and wins them, and live in a false world. Or you can attack the game in a realistic way and see how good your kids really are. And if they ain't gonna' be champions, earn 'em some money. At least then they get something out of it.

"I always ask if they want to fight somebody, and if they do, that's OK. Then it's my job to make sure they don't get hurt. You have to use the system. We're like prostitutes. Anybody can fuck us as long as they pay, end of story. It's a harsh way of looking at it, but that's it. So if you lose, OK, but in one way you win. All my lads earn their money legally. They don't rob, they don't knock old ladies on the head. So good luck to 'em, whether they win or lose. I respect them and I help them as much as I can, and that's about it really. But we use the game. You know, it's like with football. You can't all play for Manchester United. Somebody's got to play for Bolton and Preston. Half a loaf's better than none ain't' it? Don't let the system beat you. It's like life. Don't let life beat you. If you don't play you can't win. At least ours are winning. It might not be on paper, but they're winning. They're winning in life, aren't they?"

"He wants looking after sometimes. You'd have to nail him to the floor to beat him, know what I mean? Alan could go on to be one of the greatest fighters we've ever had. The boy's something special." – Doug Bidwell

ABA champion and Olympic bronze medalist. Twice British middleweight champion and owner of a Lonsdale belt. Twice European middleweight champion and finally, undisputed middleweight champion of the world. Alan Minter was indeed, 'something special.'

I arranged to meet him for this interview at the Covent Garden restaurant where I had met his friend Billy Walker. Waiting in the nearby square, I was watching a most exquisite mime artist. Made up like a porcelain statue, she cut a striking figure. Suddenly I sensed somebody was watching me and there, smiling across the crowd, was Alan Minter. I walked over and we stood quietly for a few moments before he said, "Just down there you've got the Opera House. There's a really beautiful dome inside but years ago it started coming apart. I had a plastering company and we got the contract for it. We went in there and put it right." I replied, "Oh? And which bits did you do then, the cupboards?" The reason for my cheek will become obvious as this story unfolds. The reaction was a sharp look that said, "Oh, I see somebody's been doing her research then, Madam!"

Riding shotgun for the occasion was Alan's close friend of many years, Tommy Mulholland. I was lucky enough to befriend Tommy, who has been a great man for boxing, a few months earlier at an Angels with Dirty Faces charity golf match. Tommy is totally blind but he sees everything.

Minter's eyes are clear, piercing blue. Sometimes ice. Every now and then, they light up as he flashes the disarming grin which must have got him out of a fair bit of trouble over the years. But when I asked him about his career he was not looking for escape routes. For some reason his brutal honesty, particularly about what he saw as his own shortcomings, took me by surprise. I was asking this man to pick out the finest details from a whole mesh of memories. Before he answered certain questions he became thoughtful to the point of almost being distant. But then the blues eyes flashed into focus and the stories flowed.

Alan Sidney Minter was born in Penge on the 17th August 1951. He spent the first two weeks of his life in an incubator. "Yes I was dying. I had my last rights read to me and everything. They got the vicar in and they said, 'he won't survive. He won't come through.'" A few days old and Alan Minter was already a fighter.

His father, a Londoner called Sidney and his mother, a Fraülein called Annalisa Freda Hilda Albereght, met while Sid was doing National Service in Germany. "My parents have been with me from day one. I remember when I've gone home after boxing with black eyes, banged up and oh, my Mum's cried her eyes out. But she never once said to me, 'you don't want to do that.' She never said nothing. She's 74 and still right as rain, they both are. He goes plastering once a week, he's seventy-odd. He's a respected man, a lovely man." Alan has a younger brother, Mickey, also a tasty fighter in his day, once challenged for the Southern Area light-middleweight title.

Alan Minter fought as a southpaw, the only southpaw in this book. I asked him how it all started? "I was at the Sarah Robinson school. I was always in trouble, spent most of my time being put outside the class room. And I couldn't do football, rugby, nothing. And one day my PE Master, bless him, Mr Hansom, asked me to get a boxing team together to represent the school, which wouldn't happen now because boxing's banned in schools. Anyway, we all got beat. And that's when I joined Crawley ABC and I lost seven fights in a row. I boxed on a Tuesday, so I'd never go to school on the Wednesday. Because the kids would say, 'you got beat.' So I never let that happen because I never went to school. And one day I'm in school on a Wednesday, in assembly, and the whole school's sitting there. And the headmaster's come on the stage and he's gone, 'well, well! He's in school for the first Wednesday in many, many months. He must have won his first fight. Alan Minter stand up.' And I got up and the whole school applauded and cheered. It was unbelievable. It had never happened to me before, but it happened then. And that was it. That was what made me carry on. And I've always said it's sad for children who are doing something, and they don't get the pat on the back. And Mr Hansom, he's written to me since. Not recently but when I achieved what I achieved. I sometimes wonder if he's still alive."

Alan left school when he was 14 to start work in his father's plastering business. But unfortunately plastering really wasn't really his bag and he rapidly found himself relegated to the cramped world of cupboards. Hence the reason for my earlier impertinence. "For years I was known as 'The Shoe Cupboard Kid.' I was in the cupboards for years! But see a lot of plasterers right, when they do cupboards they aren't bothered but my cupboards were spot on!"

It was during this time that a major force was to enter his life, a man he would grow to respect and trust. His name was Doug Bidwell. "When I joined Crawley Boxing Club Doug was the competition secretary, and as I progressed as an amateur he become my trainer. So I suppose I was about 13 or 14 when he got involved with me and we stayed together all through my boxing career, amateur and pro." Firmly under Bidwell's wing Alan's boxing skills blossomed and in February 1970 he was chosen for the England Olympic training squad. This involved spending a weekend every month at the Crystal Palace Olympic training centre at the mercy of national coach David James. "David James was very much like a headmaster. You know, we were young, we were boisterous, we were at Crystal Palace with all the other boxers and we didn't really want to listen to what he was saying. But the thing with him, although he had never had a glove on in his life, what he said was spot on! Everything he told you to do was a hundred percent right. As we progressed, boxing for England, in the corner you listened to him. He was like Doug Bidwell in the sense that if Doug told you to do something, you'd do it and it worked. There is the trust. There is the belief in the guy. And David James was exactly the same. Mind you, I'm not saying Doug Bidwell never boxed because he did."

One of the pranks that used to drive David James to distraction was the night-time escape committee, headed by Alan Minter, John Conteh and Larry Paul. Every Saturday night they would diligently plan their emancipation past what they believed to be a sleeping David James and out to the Crystal Palace Hotel. One evening they discovered they were not as clever as they thought and James caught them red-handed. They simply revised their strategy and headed for the fire escape. "Yeah, we used to sneak out and have a drink. It was nice. We trained hard, honestly. See, it was an honour to be picked to represent your country and to go to Crystal Palace and train with all the England squad. All together. They got us on a Friday and a Saturday and by the time we left Sunday lunch time we couldn't walk! We'd gone through so much. And The Crystal Palace Hotel. A few pints of light and bitter. It was beautiful."

Early in 1970 Alan was picked to box for England. He travelled to Dublin, his first time in an aeroplane. His first fight there was against Willie Cullen. The blue eyes sparkle. "We arrived in Belfast and our hotel was surrounded by tanks and barbed wire but there was no trouble out there, no trouble at all. The people were so nice. See, when they show you on the news, they must show you different parts of Belfast. They show you the worst. They are so nice, the people, beautiful! I had two fights out there. Both hard men. Both boxed for their country before. Experienced. And I beat them both. It was a big honour. First Willie Cullen in Dublin and then John Rogers in Belfast." And after his first English international our hero wasted no time in sinking a well earned pint of Guinness.

After the Irish trip and a few more amateur fights including one very close points win over Kevin Finnegan, a man he would go on to box three times as a professional, Alan was chosen to box for England at the Multi-Nations tournament in Holland. Shortly before he was due to leave he was billed locally at Crawley's Starlight Ballroom but his opponent pulled out at the last minute so he did an exhibition with Jan Magdziarz. Alan would also fight Magdziarz three times as a pro. But the 'exhibition' got a little too real for Doug Bidwell who, sensing impending eye damage and a cancelled trip to Holland, jumped in and pulled his charge out. "Oh yeah! Right! That was supposed to be an exhibition. But he tried it on. And I tried it on. He come out and went 'Bang!' He's hit me with the right hand and it's turned into a battle. And it got out of hand so they stopped it. But I think I was marked though, I don't think I was cut."

In May 1970 Alan fought Peter Lloyd of Wales at Utrecht in the first leg of the Multi-Nations and it was on this night that he was christened 'Boom-Boom'. "Yeah, boom-boom! That's when it happened. See, I used to make this grunting noise when I threw a punch. And the referee kept warning me, 'don't make that noise.' 'Sorry.' 'Box on.' Kept making the noise again. 'You're making that noise.' 'Sorry.' So the referee stopped me and said, 'if you keep making that noise I'll disqualify you.' And I said: alright, I won't make that noise.' But it was a habit. And even if I didn't throw a punch the noise was still coming out." Referee Bril ended up smiling and Alan beat Peter Lloyd on points.

Next came Rotterdam for the semi-finals against former European bronze medalist and Mexico City Olympian Ion Covacci of Romania. Before the fight Alan was introduced for the first time as Alan 'Boom-Boom' Minter. "Whenever I was boxing after the warnings fight, as I was coming from the dressing room to the ring and I would climb into the ring all the crowd would shout 'Boom-Boom!' It was lovely." Covacci, known as 'The Iron Man', proved to be a hard night's work but Alan defeated him on points. He lost the final against Wittold Stachurski of Poland and returned home with a Multi-Nations silver medal. "And after all the warnings and everything, I got the 'Best Boxer' of the whole tournament. My dad's still got the plate on his bedroom wall. And I've got the bowl indoors."

His next trip overseas to represent England was to America. He fought at Columbus University and won all three of his fights inside the distance. Afterwards he went to watch Johnny Nash playing at Ohio State Fair. It poured down with rain but Johnny kept on going anyway. Alan loved it.

Next on the England trail was Hungary for the European Under Twenty One championships. On the first day of the competition Alan lost to Russian Viateschev Lemeschev, who went on to win the championship, an Olympic gold and a world amateur title. Shortly after that Alan fought American Marvin Johnson at the Anglo American Sporting Club at the Hilton, Park Lane. Alan won the majority decision and Mickey Duff, Jarvis Astaire and Harry Levene were all on their feet as the crowd rose in a standing ovation. Marvin Johnson went on to become three time world light-heavyweight champion.

Alan boxed 30 times for England in total, winning 25. But the blue eyes were firmly focused on the 1972 Munich Olympics. "Well it's funny. You know, I've got to the Olympics and I'm still working for my dad's plastering company, and I'm still in the cupboards! So my dad's come round to the site to tell me that I've had a letter to say I've just been picked for the Olympics. And he couldn't find me because he didn't know what fuckin' cupboard I was in! [raucous laughter]. When he did manage to find me the whole site closed down. Everyone got booze in and we had a party because I had just been picked to represent my country."

Alan made history by being selected at two different weights, light-middle and middle. "It's never been done before, or never been done since. I boxed at light-middle in the Games. I was ABA champion, in 1971 and in the 1972, which was Olympic year, I boxed in the quarter-finals against a guy from Croydon called Frankie Lucas. He stopped me on a cut in the second round and went on to become the ABA champion. In that era if you were ABA champion you would go to represent your country in the Olympics. He was more or less going to be picked. And lo and behold they've asked me to box him on our own show at the Greyhound in Croydon. So anyway, in the second round I've knocked him spark out and I clinched the position to represent my country in the Olympic Games. They should never have let him fight me really.

"We went out to Munich and I had my 21st birthday out there. All the trainers and everything, we all went out for the night and it was brilliant. They don't serve pints, they serve litres of this German brew and it was powerful. Anyway, when we got back to the Olympic

Village we couldn't get back in. All the doors and gates were locked, the security was phenomenal. There was helicopters, guys with machine guns, we couldn't get near. There had been a massacre. All the Israelis were killed." That night 11 Israeli athletes were taken hostage in an Arab guerrilla attack. The terrorists had infiltrated the Village and were demanding the release of two hundred Arabs held in Israeli prisons and a safe passage to Egypt. The rescue attempt by German marksmen at Fürstenfeldbruck Airbase went badly wrong and nine of the hostages were killed, along with one of the Arabs.

The boxing began on the 26th August 1972 and Alan had his first fight three days later against Reggie Ford of Ghana. Alan stopped him in the second. "My first fight of the Olympics. I've got a picture of him at home with both his feet off the ground." Alan's next opponent was Valery Tregubov a Russian southpaw who was twice European champion and nine years older. "Tregubov was the only one I was worried about. I had respect for his reputation. He was a good fighter and he was powerful. He would walk through anyone. And I couldn't sleep at nights, I don't know why. I knew they'd drew me against him and I was worried. Anyway, I nicked it on points. And from that day forth, in the Olympics, it was very difficult to get motivated. Because he was the most dangerous man there in my weight class, and I beat him. And I couldn't get no butterflies or nerves boxing anyone else. I couldn't get motivated at all." Next came the quarter-finals against Algerian Loucif Hanmani. Australian referee Arthur Arbarhart gave Alan three cautions and a public warning for grunting, but aside from that he got the verdict. He was now assured of a bronze medal.

His opponent in the semis was blonde southpaw Dieter Kottysch from Hamburg in Germany. This would be Alan's last fight as an Olympian, and as an amateur. "He never won it, he never won the fight. And the crowd knew he was beaten. I've seen the film since and I can't get over how tiny I was, I was like a little boy. And I'm standing there and they announced the majority decision to him and he jumped up in the air, and I just couldn't believe it. And the crowd booed and jeered. They presented him with the gold medal and then they presented the silver and then it was the bronze medal to Alan Minter, and again, the crowd erupted because they knew! And I was only skinny.

"I had no intention of turning pro. I could have got picked for the Olympics again but that was another four years off and four years is a long time. So I thought, 'alright, I'll give it a go,' and that was it. I turned pro with Doug." During his professional years, apart from Doug Bidwell, Alan would have Doug's son Keith in his corner along with Jimmy Revie and Bobby Neill (both former British featherweight champions.) Also on the Minter team was John Hillier, one of Alan's original trainers at Crawley ABC, and Danny Holland as cuts man. For the record Holland was also cuts man for Henry Cooper.

On the 31st October 1972 Alan Minter walked down the gangway of the Albert Hall for the first time as a professional boxer. His opponent was Antiguan born Maurice Thomas of Bradford. "I was with him the other day. I'm speaking at this venue and I'm in the room before I go in and they've gone, 'Alan, this is Maurice Thomas.' And I've gone, 'Jesus Christ! Maurice! How are you?' And you know, he runs all the doors in Birmingham.

Anyway he's gone, 'Alan, I've never told anyone that I ever boxed you. Nobody knows.' So when I finished speaking I said, 'before I sit down, I would just like to make a tribute to somebody I didn't realise I would ever see again. This is the guy I fought in my first professional fight, my very first one, and everyone in this room knows him so well. Gentlemen, can we have a round of applause please for the one and only Maurice Thomas.' And he looked at me and he stood up. And everyone was applauding and saying, 'I never knew he fought Alan Minter!' And afterwards all these people were going up to him and asking for his autograph. And I've even gone up to him and said, 'Maurice, can I have your autograph?' He said, 'I'd love to Alan!' He wrote, 'To Alan Minter, best wishes from Maurice Thomas.' And I thought that was nice." The night they fought, Thomas had over 30 professional fights behind him and Alan stopped him in six.

Fourteen days after that Alan stopped John Lowe in three. Three weeks later he stopped Australian champion Anton Schnedl in seven, and then Ronnie Hough of Liverpool in five. This was his fourth fight inside of six weeks. "In those days I often boxed twice a month. But I was happy to do that because while I was boxing I was in good condition all the time." He rounded off 1972 in style when, on Christmas Day, he became engaged to Lorraine Bidwell, Doug's daughter. This union produced two children. First Kerry, who presented Alan with his first grandchild, a beautiful baby girl called Elise nearly two years ago. Then came Ross, a charming young man who is currently cutting a dash on the professional boxing scene. Alan has another son from a subsequent marriage. His name is George and he boxes for Newmarket ABC. George and Ross sometimes train together but George's first love is golf.

On the 8th January 1973 Alan knocked out Mike McCluskie of Maesteg in five in Manchester. A week later he went the distance for the first time against Pat Dwyer at the Albert Hall. "He was a good fighter, Pat Dwyer. He was tricky. You see, they'd had all more experience than me. They're all there to test you." Alan won on points over eight rounds. Before January was over he stopped Pat Brogan in seven at York Hall but not before getting cut for the first time – in the first round. He got through it and became the first man to halt Brogan. "I didn't even know I was the first man to stop him. Look, he's there to be beaten, like I'm there to be beaten. I'm not bothered if I stop him or if I beat him on points, as long as I've won. And that's probably why I'm never a guest at his promotions!"

The following month Alan stopped American Gabe Bowens in seven at the Albert Hall. Three weeks after that he beat a tough Liverpudlian who had been in with both Emile Griffith and Ruben Carter. His name was Harry Scott and Alan won on points at Wembley. Before March had past Alan notched up another points win over Irishman Frank Young at the Albert Hall.

On the 9th May 1973 Alan stepped through the ropes to do battle with King George Aidoo, who was born in Ghana but based in New Jersey, a tough mix. Alan stopped him in five. "I fought him at York Hall and if you saw the man, it was frightening. At the weigh-in, he took his clothes off to jump on the scales and you've never seen a body like it in your life.

And when he was in the corner they took his dressing gown off, and now he's smothered in Vaseline and the lights are hitting his body. I was nervous anyway." Alan floored Aidoo in the second and the Ghanaian pulled him down with him. They were both up at five. Alan floored him again in the fourth and this time Aidoo was up at two. In the fifth and final round, Alan landed with a massive left that laid Aidoo out on the canvas. He was up at seven but totally bewildered. Referee Sid Nathan stopped the fight.

Four weeks after that Alan Minter tasted professional defeat for the first time. He was stopped in eight by Scottish veteran Don McMillan at the Albert Hall. McMillan was down three times during the fight and Alan was ahead on points but his eye damage was too grim for Harry Gibbs to allow the fight to continue and as they say that's boxing. "That was a bad cut. It was at least two inches long. Clash of heads. But I wasn't worried at the time because I should have been cut. You get a clash of heads like that and someone's going to be cut. And the cuts that have happened to me, they've been brought on by myself. Frustration. Instead of boxing when I should have boxed, having a fight. They used to say, 'walk in there, hit Alan Minter, stand back and wait for him.'" After a three month break Alan stepped back in for a points win over Octavio Romero at Wembley. Three weeks later he stopped American Ernie Burnes in five at the Albert Hall.

On the 30th October 1973 Alan had his first of three professional fights with Jan Magdziarz, the Southampton-based Pole from the 'exhibition' of three-and-a-half-years before. That night they were at the Albert Hall, a far cry from Crawley's Starlight Ballroom and a lot of water had flowed under the bridge but Magdziarz was to prove no less of a threat now that the vests were off. In the third round Alan's eye was cut up so badly that Harry Gibbs stopped the fight. Six weeks later he fought Magdziarz again, at the Albert Hall. This time referee Benny Caplan pulled Alan out in the sixth, again because of eye damage.

In March 1974 Alan scored a points win over eight against Tony Byrne at the Albert Hall but the following May cut eyes were again to be the cause of a third round stoppage loss, this time against Rickey Ortiz at Wembley. Then, his injuries having healed, Alan fought Jan Magdziarz for the third and final time, on the 29th October 1974 at the Albert Hall. Harry Gibbs disqualified both boxers half way through the fourth round. The reason? Neither had landed more than twice since the first bell.

Prior to this fight Alan been stopped four times in his last seven fights, all on cuts, twice by Magdziarz. "I was frightened I'd get cut again. It was an eliminator for the middleweight championship of this country and we was both disqualified, both slung out of the ring. I'll tell you what he had, that right hand, it was so fast and straight he couldn't miss me with it. I shouldn't have fought him. Every fighter has a bogeyman, and he was mine. I didn't need to fight him. He was coming forward and I went back. I came forward and he went back. And neither of us threw a punch. The crowd were going berserk." The audience whistled and booed, stamped their feet and threw meat pies, one of which bounced off Magdziarz's back. Harry Gibbs, who later said that he had never before had to resort to such action, received a round of applause when he stopped it. The boxers were both later fined £300 by the Board.

A month later events took a turn for the better when Alan travelled to Munich to fight Shako Mamba of Zaire. For this, his first trip to Germany since the Olympics, the crowd gave him the best reception ever and Alan won on points over eight. In January 1975 he continued his winning ways against Henry Cooper. No, 'Our 'Enry' had not been on a serious diet. This Henry Cooper was a tall, slim, bearded Scotsman. Alan knocked him out in the first round. The following month he beat Tony Allen on points and six weeks later he outpointed old drinking partner Larry Paul. In May 1975 he returned to Germany, this time Hamburg, where he knocked out Peter Wulf in six.

On the 4th November 1975 Alan had the first of three epic battles with Kevin Finnegan, the Battersea boy who had an equally enthusiastic following of fans as Alan. The prize was the vacant British middleweight title and this fierce 15-rounder was fought at Wembley. The previous year Finnegan had won the British and European titles. He had also held his first exhibition of his own paintings at Mason's Yard Gallery in London's west end. He was three years older than Alan and the clash between these two popular pugilists was eagerly anticipated. "I never used to stay away in those days before a fight, and me and my wife went to London and I wasn't disciplined. I was in Harrods drinking milkshakes. I wasn't even thinking about me weight. On the morning of the fight we went to the 'Beckett and I was six pounds over the middleweight limit. Doug Bidwell done his nut. I had an hour-and-a-half to get six pounds off. I worked and worked, skipped and skipped and I had three plastics on me and the sweat was pouring out. And I'm laying there, I'm crouching down. I jumped on the scales, dried off and I was bang on the 11 stone, six limit. And that night I still boxed 15 rounds to become the middleweight champion of Great Britain. And I felt alright."

It was a ferocious and hard battle. Both had everything to fight for. Earlier that year Finnegan had lost his European title to Gratien Tonna and he was trying to fight his way back by taking the British title. Should he win, Kevin would make history by becoming reigning British champion at the same time as his brother Chris who held the light-heavyweight title. No two brothers had ever held British titles simultaneously before. I asked Alan if he was intimidated by the fight in any way? "Yeah. I never thought I was unbeatable. All I wanted to do was do my best. If they were capable enough, if they were good enough to beat me, that would be it. And they were good enough, all of them. I beat Kevin Finnegan by the smallest possible margin of half-a-point." There were no knockdowns but both were jolted. Minter was marked beneath both eyes and Finnegan's nose was bleeding. Finnegan got in some great body shots but Alan was not flinching. Alan seemed to come into his own in the last two rounds and Finnegan seemed to fall apart. Referee Sid Nathan scored it to Alan by half-a-point. Afterwards Alan received a telegram from his old Olympic foe. It read, 'well done. No man deserves a title more. Dieter Kottysch.' Alan confirmed this but he did not seem overly impressed.

After a January eight round stoppage over Trevor Francis at the Albert Hall, Alan made his first defence of the British title. On the 27th April 1976, he defended against Billy Knight at the Albert Hall. Knight, three weeks older than Alan, was born in St Kitts and lived in Walworth. He was three time ABA light-heavyweight champion and Commonwealth Games gold medalist. "My best mate of all was Billy Knight. He and I were room mates for years and years. I went to his wedding. He come to mine. And it was beautiful! He was a lovely man. They said to me, 'how can you fight a friend? How can you defend your title against your mate?'" But friendship was thrown through the ropes that night and Alan stopped Billy in two. "In those days champions and former champions were introduced into the ring. One night before I fought him, they introduced us both. I walked down the isle, shaking everyone's hand. And Billy's walked down the isle shaking everyone's hand. He's got in the ring and I've gone, 'alright Bill?' and he's gone, 'fuck off.' And he stood beside me and I thought about what he had just done, in front of everyone and I thought, 'that's the finest thing you could have ever done to me. Now you've got a problem.'

"He was a good all-round fighter, Bill. A typical class fighter. He had fast hands, accurate punches. Doug says, 'whatever you do, don't let him get into a pattern. If Billy Knight gets into a pattern, you've got a problem. As he start's settling down, you've got to break his style. Break it." Alan floored Knight twice, backed him into a corner and tore into him, teeth gritted. Referee Sid Nathan stopped it right on the bell to end the second round and a jubilant Alan hugged everybody he could get hold of, including Sid Nathan. Today, Alan seems surprised that it was stopped. "I thought he could have gone on when he got up. But the referee had a look at him and stopped it. And there was no complaint from him. He went down and got up but he was OK wasn't he? Or was he? I don't know. Only the referee knows." Knight needed six stitches in a cut over his right eyebrow and his trainer Frank Duffett confirmed that he was going to pull him out at the end of the second anyway. For the record, this was the quickest finish to a British title fight in nearly 13 years, since Mick Leahy stopped George Aldridge in one at Nottingham in May 1963.

A month later Alan returned to Germany to stop Frank Reiche in seven. "I was in Munich when Ali boxed Richard Dunne. And I boxed Frank Reiche, the powerfullest... He had already beat Finnegan. In the whole of my career that was the best I ever boxed. And after my fight I'm at Muhammad Ali's dressing room door and I wouldn't knock on it. And Bob Arum come round and says, 'do you want to go in and see him?' And I said, 'oh, I'd love to.' And we went in and he was laying there on the couch. And I had two black eyes and he said, 'hey, you been fightin' man?' I said, 'yeah.' He said, 'how d'you get on?' I said, 'I won, thank you.' And that was it. I mean, I was only about 23."

On the 14th September 1976 Alan made his second defence of the British title. The challenger was Kevin Finnegan. Alan won this, their second clash, on points over 15 at the Albert Hall and as in their first, the distance between them was paper thin. Both boxers were out before the first bell and Roland Dakin had to wave them back to their corners. As battle commenced Alan seemed more in charge during the early rounds. In the ninth Finnegan caught him with a right to the jaw and seconds later another right sent him back to the ropes and Finnegan laid in. The crowd was deafening as Alan fought back on pure instinct. They got tangled up and both fell to the canvas, Alan on top. They fought on and Finnegan knocked Alan's gum shield out and Alan punched back. In the last round Finnegan knocked

Alan's gum shield out again. "Did you see the second one, when he had me. I was bashed up in the 11th round and the last. At the end of the 13th the corner told me, 'you've got one round to go. This is the last round. Go and win it big. If you don't win this one we're going nowhere.' When the round was over I went over to the referee to have me hand put up and he says, 'there's one more round to go.' I went out for the 15th and I couldn't do it. I was drained. I thought it was the end of the fight and now I've got one more round to go. There was nothing there." When it was over Finnegan offered his hand to Dakin who smiled gently, shook his head and moved across to lift Alan's arm. It was so close but Alan had done it again and won his won his Lonsdale belt outright. After the fight a hostile crowd gathered around the ring, angry at Dakin's decision. Crumpled programmes and coins were thrown in the ring. Again, Alan had won against Finnegan by half-a-point. And this time it was Finnegan who came on strong at the end and Alan who seemed to fall apart.

After the fight promoter Mike Barrett said, "It was one of the greatest fights I've seen. Minter was magnificent and Finnegan was superb. I thought neither deserved to lose. They must meet again and I'd love to promote the fight." Minter said, "That was Kevin Finnegan at his very best. He fought even better than the last time. Sometimes I felt I was fighting for my life. I knew it was close." Finnegan said, "I was the guv'nor and he knows it. I thought I won the first fight. I know I won this one."

Before the year was over Alan stopped Tony Licata in six and Sugar Ray Seales in five but despite his blazing form, just before Christmas, he was stripped of his British title by the Board of Control. "Well, it was ridiculous. But I had to give up the British title to fight for the European. And then Kevin Finnegan won the British title. I mean, today it would never happen. You wouldn't have to do it."

The opportunity came to fight for the European title on the 4th February 1977 against Italian Germano Valsecchi. The venue was the Nuovo Pallazzo dello Sport, Milan. This was Valsecchi's second defence of his title, which he had won from Angelo Jacopucci the previous year. "I was the first Englishman to beat an Italian for the European title in over 50 years. We went over there and we had a lot of people with us from different parts of London. And I stopped him in five rounds. And I won the European title." There was no way Alan Minter was returning home without the European title that night. He proved to be far too strong for the Italian, nearly stopping him in the second and the third. But somehow, Valsecchi managed to remain on his feet and spurred on by the 10,000 strong crowd, he landed with a solid right at the end of the fourth that made Alan's legs buckle. The crowd went bonkers but Alan came out for the fifth as fresh as a daisy. Shortly after forcing Valsecci to take two standing eight counts, Alan clubbed him to the floor with a hefty left. Silver-haired referee Herbert Tomser counted Valsecchi out ten seconds before the end of the round. Alan's ecstatic supporters mobbed him as he left the ring. "So I won the European. Who did I fight next after that?

"Ronnie 'Mazel' Harris! The most feared American middleweight ever! He won a gold medal at the Olympics and he'd been a pro for about eight years. No one wanted to fight him. He was too dangerous. Anyway, I've took the fight. I saw it on film the other day and I didn't remember 'til I watched it that I was stopped sitting down in me own corner." At the end of the eighth Alan's lip was split in two. The referee went to his corner and stopped the fight, but had he visited Harris first it might have been a different story. The American had double vision and his jaw was broken in two places. "But like I said, I saw the fight on film recently and I thought I was getting beat."

In July 1977 Alan traded leather with Emile Griffith. The 39-year-old American had been a pro for 19 years and had boxed 115 times. He was still respected, still dangerous. Alan won on points over ten. "I boxed Emile Griffith at Monte Carlo." The blue eyes glow with pride. "He knew everything. Six time champion of the world. Three times welterweight, once at light-middle and twice at middle. After the fight I told him, 'Emile, I'm proud to have fought you.' He said, 'Oh? Maybe we can do it again some time.'"

In September 1997 Alan defended his European title against Gratien Tonna in Milan. He had been looking good when, in the sixth round, Tonna opened up a two inch long cut on his forehead. Alan was stopped in eight. "Yeah, but it wasn't that bad was it? It was only because the blood was running into me eyes."

After the disappointment of losing the European title, Alan went back after the British title at the Empire Pool, Wembley on the 8th November 1977. Once more Kevin Finnegan was in the opposite corner. Once again Alan won it by half-a-point. Once again it was close, but not as close as the others. "The third one? No, it wasn't so close. It was more of a comfortable win. It was still by half-a-point though. But it was much easier for me." This would be the last battle between these two proud British battlers. In his autobiography *Minter* Alan describes Kevin as, "The cleverest fighter I ever met... One of the toughest and classiest fighters ever to lace up a glove."

In February 1978 Alan had his first professional fight in America. He stopped Sandy Torres in five at Las Vegas on the night that Muhammad Ali beat Leon Spinks to regain his world heavyweight title. "Sandy Torres! At Vegas! Vegas was beautiful! Beautiful!"

But there were bleak times ahead for Alan and boxing. One of it's most solid and loyal exponents was about to pay the ultimate price for his bravery. His name was Angelo Jacopucci and he died after fighting Alan for the European title in Italy on the 19th July 1978. The title was vacant, a title that both had held and both had lost. As they stepped through the ropes at the Municipal Stadium in Bellaria, Jacopucci had lost only three of 37 professional fights but despite these impressive credentials he was not well respected by the Italians. They said he was the worst fighter Italy had ever produced. They called him a coward. But that night Angelo Jacopucci fought like a tiger. In the final round of a fight that left Alan bruised, cut and bashed up, three right hooks sent Jacopucci backwards and a final massive left put him down. As Angelo lay against the ropes he was not unconscious but on the count of four he shook his right hand in what looked like a gesture of surrender. Although Angelo Jacopucci did not win the European title that night, he did finally win the respect and admiration that he had craved throughout his career. But for the proud and brave Italian this gallant performance was his last. Shockingly, he collapsed in the early hours of the following morning. He died two days later after unsuccessful brain surgery.

The blue eyes are dulled by sadness now. "Anyway, he died after I boxed him. See, the Italian press were saying that he was the worst fighter they had ever produced. They gee'd him up and he gee'd himself up to prove 'em wrong. And he give me a tough fight, I was marked up and everything. And afterwards we went out for a meal and he said 'Minter, you good fighter.' I said, 'Thank you. I'm honoured to have fought ya!' So he sat down at the table and he was alright. I woke up the next morning and they told me he was in a coma. He died two days later." I asked Alan how Angelo's death affected him, not just as a boxer but as a man? "I don't know. What symptoms would you show? I don't know. If you had a guy hurt? But he was never hurt. I hit him and he went and that was it. It happened."

Less than four months later Alan stepped back through the ropes to defend his European title against Gratien Tonna and avenge his previous loss in six rounds at Wembley. "I thought it would be hard to get back in but before, when I boxed Tonna in Italy he came in with a massive entourage, showing his power, and he's gone to me, 'Minter. I kill you! I kill you!' I've gone, 'hold up a minute.' And he had me worried because I didn't know he'd go to the extreme of saying that. So now I'm fighting him in London." The blue eyes are blazing ice. "He's come to my country, my weigh-in, my people and he's intimidated me in his country, in Italy, even though he was a Frenchman. Anyway, before we had our re-match he's come up to me at the weigh-in and he's gone, 'Minter, how are you?' I've gone, 'fuck you! You've got a problem tonight.' He's gone, 'Minter. We friends.' Anyway, they've pulled us apart. And I've stopped him. He's turned his back and thrown his arms in the air. He swallowed. He turned his back. He was a bully. And I'll tell you, fight a fire with fire and bully a bully."

Later that month Alan relinquished his British title to concentrate on securing a world title fight. But first there was other business to attend to. A February points win over Rudy Robles was followed by a May ninth round stoppage of Renato Garcia who later declared, 'I felt like General Custer saying, 'where are all those bloody Indians coming from?' In June 1979 he stopped Monty Betham in two and in October he outpointed Doug Demmings and finally after all the hard work the opportunity came to fight the undisputed middleweight champion of the world.

His name was Vito Antuofermo. This rugged and aggressive Italian had lived in Brooklyn since he was 16 years old. He had been there and done it and it showed in his face. Hugh McIlvanney, in *The Observer*, described them as 'Mary Poppins versus the Wolf Man.' Four months earlier Alan had travelled to Las Vegas to watch Antuofermo and Marvin Hagler draw in the very same ring as he would get his chance. "I seen the fight and it was a good draw. And I wished Hagler would have got the nod, because I would rather have fought Hagler than Antuofermo. That's how silly I am. I mean, if that would have been the case I would never had won the title I don't think. I don't know."

Two days before the big night a dark shadow descended over the event. At 11.15 a.m. local time on Friday, March 14th, Polish Airways Flight 007 from New York crashed as it approached Warsaw Airport. There were no survivors and the entire USA amateur boxing team, 22 strong, 14 boxers, eight officials were killed.

Two days later, on the 16th March 1980, Alan Minter stepped through the ropes at Caesars Palace to fight Vito Antuofermo for his world title. Before the fight began, ten tolls of the bell cut through the electric silence in tribute to the American boxing team. And then the crowd went wild. "We got to Caesars Palace for the most important fight of my entire life. There was a big contingent of English supporters come over, loads of them. So anyway, Antuofermo's come into the ring and there's now 15 rounds of boxing." Antuofermo was brave and hard but Alan fought a brilliant tactical fight to take the Italian's title.

"At the end the crowd all jumped in the ring, 'cos in those days the crowd could get in the ring. And as they dispersed the bell went, ding ding ding and it happened, the one thing I dread, a split decision! 'Ladies and Gentlemen, we now have a split decision.' Anyway, the judge from Germany scores it 134 Minter 133 Antuofermo, so I'm one up. The second judge scores it 134 Antuofermo 133 Minter, so now we're level. And the third judge, all the way from England, Roland Dakin scores it 130 for Antuofermo 136 Minter, and I thought, 'That'll fuckin' do me!' The crowd went berserk. It was unbelievable."

After the decision was announced Alan dropped to his knees and cried with relief.

Among the delirious ringsiders were former world middleweight champion Terry Downes, who had screamed at Alan throughout the fight, and former world heavyweight champion Joe Louis who declared, "That Minter's one helluva good fighter!" And Frank Sinatra, who went to the Minter dressing room afterwards, sang 'My Way' and honoured the new champion by giving him his suite. "And when we got upstairs there was no beds, there was no television, there was no nothing. It was an empty room, he give me. And I phoned downstairs and I said, 'There's no bed in the room!' They said, 'Press the button.' Boom! And everything happened. Beautiful. A television screen come out of the wall. And it was nice.

"And the next day Larry Holmes was working out in the gym. And all the English people were there to watch him train. The gym was packed and before he started he got in the ring and he says, 'I'd just like to say to all you English people here today, thanks for coming to watch me work out, but I'm proud to say you have the new undisputed middleweight champion of the world. And you tell Alan Minter, don't wee in the street, don't spit in the main road, do everything a world champion should do.' And with that, I've walked in and he said, 'Alan, congratulations.' And it was marvellous!"

The citizens of Crawley turned out in force to welcome their champion home. "Gatwick airport! The crowds and the bands and the music. Ah Christ! It was packed. It was something that I never expected, ever. The next day, I don't know how they kept it a secret, they picked me up, my management and my family and they drove me through Crawley to the council depot and there was a stage coach with four grey mares and all my family got on it. I felt totally embarrassed. And as they took the stage coach out, I'm sitting on top, there's a few hundred lads going, 'Well done Alan.' And I thought, 'Well I'm not going to sit on this stage coach much longer, there's no one's come to see me!' And a few more people turned up, 'Well done Alan.' 'Thank you.' 'Oh fuck! I'll get off in a minute.' And as we get into Langley Green where I was brought up there was all people. You couldn't see a bit of grass or pavement or road. The roar! And as we've gone through Langley Green they were 12 deep on the pavement. They was in the road going up the hill towards the M23. Thousands! Cars were stopping. Going down into the High Street, 15 deep in the road. In to Queens Square, the finale. People. Thousands and thousands of people. I've got photographs of people who were there and I can get my magnifying glass and go, 'Yeah, that's so-an-so!' It was unbelievable.

"Winning the world title was the greatest moment of my life. 'Ladies and Gentlemen, The new undisputed middleweight champion of the world.' But saying that, when I think back, as a child watching telly, I remember watching a pro having that Lonsdale belt wrapped around his waist and thinking, 'That must be the greatest thing that could ever happen to me.' So if I'm honest, when I look back at everything that I've done, I couldn't say that one thing tops the other because everything was an achievement. British, European and world, it was just a lovely moment in time."

On the 28th June 1980 Alan defended the world crown in a re-match with Antuofermo, this time at Wembley. Vito was cut in the first round and things spiralled downwards for him from that moment. He retired in eight. "I watched it the other day and from the first round, second, third, fourth, fifth... They would never, ever have let it go on today. It should have been stopped earlier. The seventh round come, they called the doctor and he's let the fight go on. So the eighth round come and his corner men pulled him out." Antuofermo's craggy face was a mess by the end, this brave warrior having gone well beyond the call of duty. But the staunchest of challenges could never overcome a world champion who was on top of his game. A world champion who wanted to rest a while.

"See, what you've got to remember is that when a champion wins his title he can bask in the glory of being champion. He can choose who he wants to defend against and make a lot of money. After I won the first fight with Antuofermo I got a letter from the WBC and WBA saying I had 60 days to defend against the number one contender Vito Antuofermo. So I beat him at Wembley. Then I had another 60 days to defend against the number one contender or be stripped of the title. And who was the number one contender? Marvin Hagler."

So on the 27th September 1980 Alan Minter fought Marvin Hagler, the shaven-headed southpaw from Brockton. The ruthless, menacing switch-hitting American who had beaten 49 of his 53 professional opponents, 40 inside the distance. Ten months earlier he had drawn with Vito Antuofermo to be denied the world title and he was said to be furious. He let it be known that he regarded himself as the uncrowned world champion. Did this get Alan's goat? "No. No. He's got to beat me first."

At the weigh-in, Hagler was forced to strip naked to make the weight. Alan weighed in wearing Union Jack underpants. The air at Wembley Arena was thick with tension that night, fuelled by the rumours that during the build-up to the fight Alan had uttered the words "I'll never lose the title to a black man." This quote has been repeated so many times over the years, and yet Alan's best friend Billy Knight was black so I found it hard to believe Alan was racist. I asked him if he actually said those words? "Yeah! I said it. I was told to say it." I asked, by whom? "It doesn't matter. But I was told to say it. Because I wouldn't have had the knowledge to say that. You see, Marvin Hagler was slagging me off. So I said that and all of a sudden everybody's jumped up and they're on the phone. It's the way the press built it up. That's the problem."

Before the fight Vito Antuofermo was introduced from the ringside and as that proud and brave man stood to take a bow he was cruelly booed by thousands in the crowd. Hagler's walk down the gangway was serenaded by 'Go home, you bum, go home.' The US national anthem was drowned out by furious boos. The British anthem was sung with such intensity that Harry Mullan wrote in *Boxing News* that it was more "a hymn of hate than an expression of pure patriotism."

Battle commenced and Hagler cut Alan's left cheek in the first 30 seconds with his razor sharp right jab. In the second, Alan shook Hagler briefly with a right hook and called him in "Come on!" As Hagler responded Alan caught him with a right to the chin that buckled his knees. But aside from that moment, Hagler's punch perfect performance, along with Minter's reactionary lack of defence told it's own story. By the third Alan's face was in ribbons and half way through the round referee Carlos Berrocal stopped the fight.

What happened next would go down in boxing folklore for ever more. Hagler, now the new middleweight champion of the world, dropped to his knees and as he did so the first missile flew over the ropes. Seconds later a spiteful cascade of plastic bottles and glasses descended upon the canvas. The second Hagler's corner men realised what was happening those loyal chaps leapt on their man to form a heroic human shield. Hagler was rushed from the ring under police escort and still the bottles kept raining down, forcing everybody at ringside into a desperate dive for cover.

After it was over, Hagler seemed quite calm in his dressing room. He praised the policemen who had rescued him and the referee who had stopped it. He said he thought that Alan could not see too well because of the injuries. I asked Alan if Hagler was right about that? "I could see. I was getting hurt though. I wasn't too happy they stopped it but I think they probably did me a favour because he couldn't miss a shot. I was getting hurt. When I think about it now I should have gone and let them strip me of the title. I'm not saying if I had been given a rest I would have beaten him. I wouldn't have done, I don't think. But I fancied my chances. If he couldn't beat Antuofermo, and I beat Antuofermo comfortably, then how could he beat me? It doesn't work like that but that was my plan. He couldn't beat me. But he couldn't miss me. I mean, I was cut in the first round, the second and the third. I couldn't avoid the man. I don't think that at any time in my life, or in my career, no matter what I decided my tactics would be, there was no way that Alan Minter would ever have beaten Marvin Hagler, and that's a fact. I didn't really want the fight, but then again, if I had have won it, I would have wanted it."

In March 1981, six months after the loss to Hagler, Alan was back with a points win over Ernie Singletary at Wembley. The following June he lost on a highly questionable points verdict to Mustafa Hamsho at Caesars Palace. "I was working in Birmingham and I was out getting drunk, and I got a phone call saying I'm fighting an eliminator for the championship of the world against Mustafa Hamsho. Undefeated! And I took the shot. Anyway, three weeks I was training, and I had to go to Caesars Palace to fight him. I was tired. I wasn't right. I was walking around at 12, 13 stone and three weeks I had to get that off. And in Vegas it's a dry heat and you can't sweat, you can't lose any weight. And I'm dead at the weight. But I won it, and they give it to him."

Six months later Alan Minter was to fight his last fight. On the 15th September 1981 he stepped through the ropes for the last time to fight 23-year-old Tony Sibson for the European middleweight title at Wembley. "And after Hamsho I've got to fight Sibson for a title that I've won twice. Why do I want to fight for the European title to fight again for the world title which is governed by Marvin Hagler? I'm getting old now and I'm fighting for titles which I've had, and won, and vacated! At 30 years of age?" Sibson crushed Alan in three, putting him down twice in the final moments before referee James Brimmell stopped it without taking up the count.

"Tony Sibson never knocked me out. The referee stopped the fight when I was on the floor. See, when you're boxing you train for a fight whether it's ten, 12 or 15 rounds. I would never look to see what round it was. I've trained for 15 rounds and that's what I'm there for. Now in Wembley Stadium they had a big, blackboard that tells you what round it is. And I'm sitting on my stool, I don't know how many rounds have gone past, and I've turned round and I've looked at the black board and it said, 'Round Three'. And I've still got 12 rounds to go. I was gutted. Demoralised. I had enough. I was bored. I was fed up with it. I didn't want to do it. And that was it, full stop."

I can see distinct similarities between Alan Minter and Billy Walker. Maybe they were both victims of their own success in a way? Both dropped straight in at the deep end? "Yeah. We wasn't nursed. It was a different thing altogether in those days. It was a different era, different people about. And we used to sell out Wembley on a phone call. And I always felt the same for all my fights, amateur or professional. 'Please God. I've trained right. I've lived alright. I've done nothing wrong.' You just hope you don't get cut. You just hope that the hard work you've all done in the gym don't get thrown out the window by being silly on your part. My problem was if I got caught I used to try and get me own back too quickly and there could be a clash of heads. So I used to pray that no injury would occur, and that I won."

These days, at 50 years-old, Alan still looks in great shape. "When I go running on me own I feel like nothing's changed. When I run with Ross, I'm out of it. And I've had that kid turn round to me and say, 'Dad, we should have stayed at home, shouldn't we?' You don't think you've slowed down, that it's still there. It's not until you're running with an athlete, someone that's much younger than you, somebody who's active, that you realise what a dope you are!

"And you know something now, I've only got to walk in the Albert Hall or Wembley, even now and I get dreadful butterflies. It's the smell. You walk down the steps to where the dressing rooms are and you can smell the same smell that was there when I was boxing. And even driving to Wembley, the way I used to go when I was boxing, it's the same thing. And it's like now, when the air's getting cold and it's wintry, autumnal. That's the start of the boxing season." The blue eyes shine brightly.

"If you study Johnny's record there are no easy touches. Every opponent was well known by name and reputation. A few years ago he was inducted into the Scottish Hall of Fame to join his idol Benny Lynch. A just reward for two boxers who did their country proud." – Ron Olver

It's funny how, sometimes, you can walk through a door and without realising it at the time, you are stepping into a totally different world, somewhere you have never been before. That is exactly what happened to me as a direct result of my first meeting with Johnny McManus. It started when I got talking to one of his sons, Michael, in the pub on a Saturday afternoon. Mike and I have been using the same watering holes for many years. He said to me, "I don't know if you would be interested but..." And he started to tell me a bit about his father. I replied, "Interested? Of course I'm interested. When can I meet this man?"

The following Saturday afternoon, Michael took me to his parents' home to make the introductions before departing subtly. Then Johnny's wife Dorothy disappeared into the kitchen to prepare a tray of tea and biscuits while he and I settled down in their cosy front room for a lovely chat about times past, and the years when Johnny had a highly respectable boxing career, culminating in him becoming Scottish lightweight champion in 1944.

"I was born in Canada in 1920. When I was six years old my parents took me to live in a town called Twechar, that's near Glasgow. I started seriously training to box when I was about eight years old. My father Edward used to train me. I started boxing at school."

Benny Lynch:

When Johnny was a 15-year-old amateur he was asked to do a sparring session with Benny Lynch, the fabulous flyweight from the Gorbals who went on to become world champion in 1937 by beating American Small Montana at Wembley. "I was doing well in the amateurs and Benny was looking for good sparring partners. The first time I ever met him I was only about 14 and I just got introduced to him and he said, 'Oh aye, I've heard of you.' He was a bit abrupt at first. But then we became good friends. Benny was a good lad.

"When I was 17, in 1937, I turned professional. I started at bantamweight and I went up to lightweight, just before the war started. As a professional I became Benny's chief sparring partner. He used me for all his major fights. Benny and I were both managed by George Dingley, so whenever Benny was boxing I got on the bill too. He was a great manager George Dingley. He had a great big American car and he could drive us to London in under eight hours.

"Benny Lynch was the fastest little thing I ever set eyes on. I've seen Benny box in Glasgow Green, in the boxing booth. He would take anyone on. And he used to do well at it too. I've seen him come out with 38 shillings for an afternoon's work. Lynch loved it. He liked to fight. He was such a little fella but God could he punch. He was one of the greatest boxers I've ever seen. And I mean boxing, I don't mean fighting. Parrying. He could stand there and just dodge them, just moving his body, it was terrific. He was left handed you see, although he boxed orthodox, and he had a wonderful left uppercut. And when he hit you, he could hit. For a little bloke, he had a tremendous punch. And he used to go in hard when you were sparring, but you got paid for it. It was tough. He couldn't afford to hold back, because if you start doing that you'll do it at the wrong time. I think he was the greatest little boxer I ever set eyes on. There's no doubt about it. Wonderful. It's just a pity he couldn't manage his life the way he managed his fights.

"Aye, he was a boy alright. But when he was sober and you got him in the training he was great. Every time we had a fight lined up we used to go away to the training camps, up in the hills. We worked hard. It was a wonderful experience for me. And I was new to the game then. I learned everything from him. But it was a disaster when he got drunk. He used to disappear and he'd have a fight coming up and we'd all go out to look for him. Once we found him lying under a hedge in his pyjamas, nearly frozen. And then, two weeks later he fought ten rounds. That was the constitution of the man.

"He was so popular. He would go in the pub and it would be, 'Benny, come and have a drink.' And that would be it. I used to tell him, 'Benny, you know if you go in here you'll spend pounds and pounds. They'll buy you one drink and then you'll be buying them all night.' He used to say, 'Oh, that doesn't matter.' Mind you, we had some fun together. I used to go into pubs with him but I didn't drink and he never tried to get me to drink, and I respected him for that. When he was sober he was full of life, always laughing and joking.

"When World War II broke out I was enlisted into the Army and later I was sent to India. I served in the Army Physical Training Corps. You had something to do and you just got on and did it, that was all. Once you got used to it, it wasn't too bad. And I wasn't the only one. Put it this way, it was an experience and it made a man of me, but I don't want it again. I later went to Burma and I was on the staff at the PT School for a long time. It wasn't bad really. There was plenty of training, we kept ourselves fit. You had to rough it, that was all. There was lots of poverty among the local people, very harsh poverty. That was hard to stomach.

"After I came out of the army I got the opportunity to take a job as a youth and community worker. I packed up boxing and started working with the youth in 1947. I went to see Benny, I said, 'Look, I've got a job and I'm moving to England. I'm not going to see you so much now. But I'll see you when I can.' Before I went into the army Benny had everything. A lovely wife and kids, a nice house. By the time I came home again he had lost it all. He had lost everything. His home was gone. His wife had left him. Everything. Through drink. That was the last time I ever saw him. Two months later he died."

Benny had become a desperate alcoholic. His death came at the tragically young age of 33. Johnny's eyes clouded over as he remembered. "The night he died, he had been at a large dance hall and they found him in the street, in the gutter. They got him to hospital but he died that night. Thirty-three years of age. I was so sad when he died. What a waste eh? Oh dear."

Johnny McManus:

Johnny's official professional record comprised of about 60 fights over his ten year career, but including exhibitions and army fights and all the amateur stuff, he stepped through the ropes over 300 times. His moment of glory came when he became Scottish lightweight champion on the 13th June 1944. He beat the current champion Joe Kerr by a fourth round stoppage in Glasgow. "But for me, the highlights of my career were when I fought the top men, like Johnny King, the British Empire bantamweight champion. And Jimmy Warnock. Unfortunately King beat me twice. But I beat Warnock and he had just beaten Benny Lynch. And there was Len Hampston, and I beat him and he had beaten Lynch too."

Family life:

And aside from his boxing, Johnny and Dorothy McManus have made their own outstanding contribution to the human race in the form of their extraordinary family. Their first son, Edward was born in 1943. Then twins Michael and Gerald came along in 1948. Terry was born in 1950 and in 1952 a special delivery arrived in the form of triplets, Mary, Anne and Rita. Dorothy is such a petite lady but she has this inner strength. When she came in with the tea tray she told me, "When the girls came along they were the first set of triplets to be born in Hartlepool for about 70 years. It was so rare on those days. Especially as we already had the twin boys. One of the newspapers came to interview us. They asked the boys if they were happy with their little sisters. Gerald replied, 'Well they're very nice, but I wish one of them had been a puppy!'

"When I met Johnny I'd never met a boxer before. And my mam thought he would hit me! I had a very quiet upbringing you see. We were just three girls. I never went to any of his fights. But mam went once. She went to watch him box in Glasgow. But I don't agree with it really, all that punching." Johnny told me, "I've been very fortunate. I've got a good wife. It helps a lot if your other half comes and goes with you. It's a great thing to have the right partner."

Johnny the youth worker:

"I started in 1947 as a youth worker at Hartlepool Boys Welfare Club. It involved laying on programmes of activities like billiards, gymnastics, drama and things like that. In those days the age recognised by the Ministry of Education was 14 to 25. We also had a junior club from 11 to 14. It was mainly for the youngsters because when they grew up they didn't want to come in then. We catered for them five nights a week, Monday to Friday. Usually on Saturday we had a football afternoon. And we had a big gym there and there was boxing. It kept the boys off the streets and out of trouble. And they learned something. They came from all sorts of backgrounds but they were mostly working class boys. In those days they were looking for some pleasure in life that you could give them. These days kids are different. I don't know if I could handle the kids of today. I was there for ten years and in 1957 I moved to Sussex where I was the area youth officer. Stayed there for about three years and then I moved over to Kingston upon Thames where I became the youth officer for the borough. That's it. I believe in giving back instead of taking all the time, there's too much of that goes on. It's very encouraging when you get involved in something like that and you realise there's something in it."

Johnny on boxing:

Johnny feels that every boy should learn to box today. He thinks it's a wonderful sport for building character and to the would-be abolitionists Johnny has this message. "Boxing is not fighting. It's a totally different thing altogether. It's a beautiful thing to watch. A bloke dancing about on his feet, it looks graceful. And he throws a straight left and he blocks a punch to throw an uppercut. The grace in the movement, when they are parrying punches and blocking punches and ducking out of the way and it looks so good. To somebody who doesn't understand it, it's just a fight. But it's more than that, so much more than that. It's different altogether from fighting. I say to people, any fool can fight. You don't have to be taught to fight. But you have to be taught to box. But it's hard telling people that. Some people you'll never get through to because they'll only see what they want to see. You see these boxers, if they're fully fit punches don't hurt them the way they would hurt a normal person. You're arms are able to catch punches. You learn in the gym. You put in the practice but people don't see that. They can't see it. At least they don't want to see it.

"It's like honing a plane. You hone a plane to get it sharp. And a boxer's the same. He trains. He's fit. His brain is working fast. His eyes are fast. His limbs are fast. His body's tough. He's trained for it. You could punch a boxer on his tough skin and there's no mark. It's only when you get punched in the eye, the head and the face, that's different. But it doesn't do half the damage that you think it would. But you can't tell people that when they start shouting about boxing. They have it in their minds that it's wrong and that's it."

The London Ex-Boxers Association (LEBA):

A few hours after my arrival at the McManus home, Dorothy re-appeared and said gently, "I'm sorry my dear but I think he's had enough now." Shame on me! I had become so enamoured with our conversation that it had totally escaped me how tired my new friend had become. But before I left, Johnny said, "I'll tell you what I'm going to do. Next Sunday I'm going to take you to the London Ex-Boxer's Association." I said, "OK Johnny. That will be lovely." As I walked down the road I thought, 'That's nice.'

The following Sunday morning, Johnny introduced me to LEBA. We arrived at Argyle Square in Kings Cross, walked up a tiny alleyway, through an indifferently black painted door in to the St Pancras Social Club and up the stairs to the room where they all congregate on the first Sunday morning of every month. Hundreds of boxers, most of them in their 60s, 70s and 80s. Some of them in their 90s. All chatting, all dressed in their Sunday best. As Johnny took me through the room several of them turned to me and smiled warmly, "Hello dear." And to Johnny, "You've done alright there mate!" Johnny sat me down with a charming Canadian gentleman called Solly Cantor, who in years past had been a contender for the world lightweight throne, and Ron Olver of *Boxing News*. I told them I was writing a book about boxing and before they could answer, Johnny jumped in, "She means it too. She's keen." Johnny's word means a lot to the members of

LEBA. It was only when we arrived there that I discovered that for many years he has been a vice-president of the organisation.

Eleven o'clock arrived and the meeting began. Chairman Mickey O'Sullivan took the centre of the small stage. Mickey is a born comedian and he sparkled, as he always does. As he entertained everybody with his lively banter, he readily engaged in a few highly spirited verbal tussles with members from the floor along the way, as he always does. At this point I took a sneaky look around the room. There was a bar down the other end with a picture of the Queen above it, when she was about 25 years old. There was one of those giant mirror balls hanging from the ceiling. And the decor was that old fashioned fluffy flock wallpaper. The whole thing reminded me of something out of the '70s. An hour flew by and as the meeting drew to a close, the bar opened and drink was taken. I came away from there knowing that I had been somewhere special.

The following month I asked Johnny if I could go back again. He said, "Of course my dear. I'm just glad you enjoyed it." I went back again the following month and the month after that Ron Olver said to me, "I'll tell you what I'm going to do. I'm going to propose you as a member." I glowed with pride because I had, by now, fallen in love with LEBA and everything it stands for. Since that time I have rarely missed a monthly meeting. The thing with LEBA is that although a strong element of chaos never fails to abound, at the same time so much is achieved. Not only do they look after their own, but they also maintain strong links with other Ex-Boxers Associations all over the country, many of whom visit the London version on a regular basis for a good old fashioned knees-up. LEBA also does a lot of work for charities and a month does not go by when these fabulous stalwarts of the pugilistic world do not help somebody somewhere.

There is no class system at LEBA. Old booth fighters and world champions proudly rub powerful shoulders, and it's not just for the golden oldies. It was at LEBA that I first met Colin Dunne and Alan Minter. Spencer Oliver is also a member. And during my time there I get so many hugs and kisses that I have to re-apply my lipstick several times! The LEBA motto is, 'It's nice to belong' and that is a sure thing. It's brilliant and I would not miss it for the world.

And so you see, that first Saturday afternoon I spent in the McManus home, I thought I was simply going for a bit of banter with an old fighter with a few good stories to tell. And when I asked him if I could write about him in this book he initially put up a bit of a fight. "No Mel. Don't waste your time on me. There's far more interesting boxers that you could be writing about." And the following week Johnny McManus opened the gateway for me to walk into the London Ex Boxers Association. And I found myself in a different world, somewhere I had never been before. And for that I will always remain in his debt.

"I threw everything at him but he made me miss so much, at times I thought I was in the ring on my own." – Jimmy Anderson

I know that none of the boxers in this book will put up a fight when they see I have given the last word to the late, great Howard Winstone. In my eyes, 'The Welsh Wizard' was one of the finest boxers, in the purest sense of the word, Britain has ever produced. Not only was he a fabulous boxer, he knew how to fight when the need arose. Most importantly, he knew exactly when to box and when to fight. Howard became world featherweight champion in January 1968 against Mitsunori Seki of Japan. But he will always be remembered for his three epic battles with Vincente Saldivar. Although he never beat the outstanding Mexican warrior, Saldivar paid his Welsh rival the ultimate tribute when, after their third bout, he grabbed the ring microphone and announced his retirement, declaring that he could not fight this Welshman any more.

Howard's style of fighting was neat, sure and instinctive. His precise economy of movement foxed so many of his opponents with the slightest twist or turn. His footwork was so elegant that he often appeared to glide gracefully around the ring. His left hand was reputed by many to be the best in the business. His right hand could bang a bit too, despite a distinct handicap which he always defied. He was as hard as nails and yet, just a tiny bit vulnerable. The crowd could empathise with him because Howard Winstone was just like them. He was human. And because of that they loved him unconditionally.

I travelled to Merthyr Tydfil in September 2000 to meet the man himself and, even though I am Welsh born and bred, I soon became hopelessly lost. I found myself driving up the steepest of hills in first gear when I saw a man and woman getting into a car. I pulled over to ask if they knew where Howard lived. The lady smiled fondly, pointed across the road and said, "Look over there love. Can't you see the boxing gloves on the door?" And sure enough, there were the stained glass gloves, red of course, staring me right in the face. Above the gloves was the aptly chosen name, 'Lonsdale House.'

As we settled down in Howard's front room, a veritable photographic gallery of his boxing life and the friends he made along the way, I found him a man of few, softly spoken, words. He sat in his armchair and I sat on the fireside rug at his feet, not unlike a disciple. For the most part, Howard was happy for me to tell his story, but occasionally he lent his own magic touch.

In his heyday Howard was a snappy dresser who favoured well-cut suits. It was a style that wore well on his neat featherweight frame. He was always in perfect physical condition, and his mop of thick dark hair and his sparkling smile were his trademarks. He was characteristically modest when I pointed out that lots of his fans were women. "I can't help that now, can I?"

He was born in Merthyr Tydfil on the 15th April 1939, one of four children. He remained in his home town until the end with his wife, Bronwen. This was the second marriage for both of them and between them they produced six children. I asked Howard how many grandchildren he had and he shouted to his wife for assistance, "Bronwen! How many grandchildren have we got?" Bronwen emerged from the kitchen, "Thirteen, and two great-grandchildren, and another great-grandchild on the way."

As a small boy Howard was a bit of a tearaway and one day his father, and namesake, brought home a pair of boxing gloves. Howard senior also erected a punch bag on the garden tree and from then on sparring sessions in the kitchen were a regular occurrence. When young Howard was ten years old he started learning to box at the Drill Hall, Georgetown. Eventually, he moved to Dowlais Boxing Club.

Howard's hero, Eddie Thomas, who became his manager and trainer, won his ABA title for Dowlais ABC in 1946 when Howard was seven. Eddie was also taught by the same trainer as Howard, a man named Ephraim Hamer. Howard was 12 years old and selling newspapers on the street corner the first time he met local idol Eddie, then the British, Empire and European welterweight champion. Eddie took a newspaper, gave Howard two shillings and told him to keep the change. For days afterwards Howard chattered excitedly about his encounter with Eddie Thomas to anybody who would listen.

Howard's blood was a mixture of Welsh, English and Irish. "My father's family were English. My granny Winstone was from Newbridge, and my granny Davies was from Swansea. My other grandfather come from Cork." During my research for this chapter I read in a few different articles that Howard also had Jewish blood. "Nah! That was my manager, Eddie Thomas' idea. There were some good Jewish fighters around at the time and Thomas thought it would be a good idea to tell them I was Jewish as well."

Even in his early years Howard was a natural talent. In 1950, he won the Welsh schoolboy championship. He won the Welsh schools again the next two years and in 1954 he won the British schoolboy title. He left school at the age of 15 and his second job was at Lines Toy Factory. On the 19th May 1956, when Howard was 17, he had a dreadful accident. At work one day his right hand got trapped in a power press. The machine ripped the tops from three fingers on his right hand. When he had recovered from the shock and the pain, Howard began to tread the long road to recovery. During this time he met Benita, his first wife. They had a whirlwind romance and were soon married with a family. First came Wayne and then Roy. Although he would never again be able to form a fist with his right hand, the following year Howard returned to the gym to box at bantamweight. "I was out for a bit with my fingers. Then in late '57 I started back with Eddie Thomas." Thomas was a major force in Welsh boxing. He and Howard understood each other and Howard would go on to stay with him until the end of his boxing career. "We had a good relationship. We had a bit of fun you know? You could have a laugh with him. You might not see him for half an hour. Or he might come in and go again. But he always had a couple of the others there, timing us and things like that."

1958 was a tremendous year for young Howard Winstone. He won the ABA's at bantamweight and a gold medal at the Empire Games, which were held at the Sophia Gardens, Cardiff. He was the only Welsh gold medalist there and the crowd raised the roof with their special rendition of their national anthem, 'Land of My Fathers' while Howard stood motionless with tears in his eyes. He stepped down from the dais and declared he was turning professional.

However, shortly after the Empire Games he was called up for National Service. He reported for duty at the Maindy Barracks in Cardiff on the 18th September 1958. "I didn't go out of the country. I shouldn't have gone really, because of my fingers. But because I won a gold medal they had to call me up didn't they? Fifty-seven days later they sent me home again" Howard returned to Merthyr where he began preparation for the professional ranks. Eddie's training regime included chopping up logs and running up the unforgiving Brecon Beacons come rain, shine or snow. There were endless hours of gym work and sparring with all sorts, from bantams to cruisers. Among his sparring partners were Dai Gardiner and Colin Lake and, later on, Ken Buchanan, who trained alongside Howard under Eddie Thomas. Howard and Buchanan became close friends as well as gym mates. Also, Howard was quick to remind me about his regular sparring mate Billy Thomas. "He's from Caerphilly he is. He was a regular sparring partner. But I used to spar with all of them from Cardiff. You name them, I've boxed with them all." Another character in this book who sparred with Howard was Jack Lee who told me, "I was only a young kid at the time, about 19. But I was a southpaw and they wanted a southpaw for him so I went to Merthyr to spar with him. It was supposed to be for a week but I was only in there a couple of days. And how many times do you think I hit him? Not once!"

When the night arrived for Howard to make his professional debut it was on the Willie Pastrano versus Joe Erskine bill at Wembley on the 24th February 1959. Howard outpointed Billy Graydon of Stoke Newington in six. "I was glad to get it over with. I was very nervous. And the crowd there at the time, for Pastrano and Erskine! It was packed when we went in. We were the first fight on the bill. I was glad that I won it. I didn't want to lose my first fight. I went back and changed and came out to see the big fight."

In two months Howard notched up points wins over Peter Sexton, Tommy Williams and Jackie Bowers. Then in June 1959 he beat rugged Londoner Jake O'Neale through the thunder and lightning of a summer storm at Porthcawl. Howard continued his points wins over Glaswegian, Ollie Wyllie in July 1959 and the following month Londoner Hugh O'Neill.

Then came the first of three fights with Billy Calvert of Sheffield. The moment I mentioned 'The Sheffield Cowboy's name Howard's face broke into a wide grin and he jumped up from his armchair to show me Billy's photo on the wall, "That's him!" Incidentally, Billy, who was six years older than Howard, was christened with his Western style nickname by Ron Olver, of *Boxing News*, because he was bowlegged. Their first fight was held on 1st September 1959 at Aberdare and Howard stopped Billy in seven. "He was a good little fighter, Billy. He was short. He had bandy legs." I asked if they became friends. "Yes, after." And after his first win by stoppage Howard felt, "Alright, It was an early night."

I had the pleasure of meeting Billy Calvert at the August 2001 meeting of the London Ex Boxers Association. He is such a livewire, a charming little man who sparkles. Everybody, and I mean everybody, wanted his time at that meeting but Billy made sure that he set aside some time for me and we sat together for 20 minutes while he reminisced about Howard Winstone. "Our first fight were a short notice fight. I didn't get to know about it until the Saturday, and the fight was on the Monday. But we took it, naturally. We set off at five o'clock in the morning on the train and we finally got to Aberdare at one o'clock for the weigh-in. Then we went to the pictures and had a meal. I don't remember what we saw at the pictures because I wasn't interested to be honest. I remember I had a little mouse under me eye, I got it playing football. And Howard caught it in the seventh round. It blew up like a balloon and the referee did the right thing and stopped it. Johnny Cooke from Liverpool was on before me and after I fought Howard I went back to the dressing room, a little hut in the field, because we fought in a football field. I've gone in me bag to get me trousers and Johnny Cooke had taken them. So I didn't only lose the fight, I lost me trousers! So the landlord, where we had the weigh-in, he was a short chap but he was wide. Anyway, he lent me some trousers and I had to fasten them to my braces. And Johnny Cooke sent someone afterwards to give me my trousers back. He didn't mean to take them, it were an accident you know." More from Billy later on.

Two weeks after Calvert, Howard hit the floor for the first time as a professional. The perpetrator, Joe Taylor, who had come in as a late substitute, caused a sensation that night in Ebbw Vale, decking Howard twice in the first round. "It was terrible. I didn't know what hit me to be honest with you. Because he was a good puncher, that fella. And I was giving a couple of pounds away." Howard returned the compliment big style by flooring Taylor five times and stopping him in the fourth.

In December 1959 Howard had his second fight with Billy Calvert. This time they went the distance and Howard won on points. The crowd were so impressed by these two stunning young athletes that afterwards they showed their appreciation with nobbins (coins thrown into the ring by an appreciative audience). Billy told me, "That one were at the National Sporting Club in London. There weren't a lot in it and Howard got the decision." The 'nobbins' amounted to £68 "Howard, he said 'Bill, I don't want anything of that' and he give me all the £68. I said, 'No Howard, we'll share it.' He said, 'No. You're on a smaller purse than me and that's it. You can have that.'"

The year was made complete for our hero when he was crowned Welsh Sportsman of the Year. When we met, Howard still had the little cup they gave him on his mantelpiece. He kicked off 1960 with a seventh round stoppage win over Belfast boxer, George O'Neill, in Cardiff. The same month he beat Robbie Wilson on points in the National Sporting Club, London. A week later he stopped Colin Salcombe in six at Birmingham.

On the 24th February 1960 he fought Terry Rees in Cardiff. Rees, who hailed from the Rhondda, was Welsh featherweight champion but his title was not at stake that night. "It should have been because we were the same weight, under nine stone, see. I don't know why it wasn't for the title. I couldn't tell you." Howard floored Rees four times and the fight was stopped in the eighth round. Rees was a tough, rugged fighter and I asked if he made things difficult at all which brought a mischievous twinkle to Howard's eyes, "No, he was alright. I wish I could have had more fights like him to be honest!"

Howard was amused when I told him that Terry, a publican until his retirement in 2001, got me drunk one time. "He's always laughing isn't he? He took us to his pub about two years ago. 'Give us a lift home from London,' he said. He took us about three hours out of our way! He's crazy! But seriously though, I always liked Terry. He's a nice man."

A month later Howard had a lusty fight with Gordon Blakey at Cardiff. The Sophia Gardens was packed to the rafters and they fought like tigers. In the eighth round Blakey's manager, Benny Jacobs pulled his fighter out because of an eye injury. "He's a hell of a boy. I see him now. I see most of the boys." Howard did not emerge from this battle unscathed. Blakey gave him a cauliflower ear for his trouble, which Howard kindly allowed me to examine up close. "Sore it was. It takes a couple of weeks before it stops hurting. It's like iron now."

On the 9th May Howard stopped cockney George Carroll in four at the Swansea Vetch Field. Ten days later he was back in against Jamaican Con Mount Bassie. Bassie was based in Birmingham and Howard went there to fight him and won on points. Six weeks later he returned to Birmingham, this time to stop Australian Noel Hazard in three. "I never met Noel Hazard before or after I fought him but one of my pals was over in Australia a couple of years ago and he bumped into him. He said that Hazard was asking after me. Funny isn't it?"

Next up, on the 27th July 1960, was Phil Jones of Cardiff, a hot prospect who beat Howard as an amateur. The rain poured down that night in Porthcawl's Coney Beach. Before Howard stepped in with Jones, European heavyweight champion Dick Richardson, who was top of the bill against big American Mike Dejohn, was disqualified in the eighth round for alleged misuse of the head. When referee Eugene Henderson, an Edinburgh man with a strong voice, waved an authoritative finger at Richardson and sent him back to his corner the disgusted crowd erupted and soaking newspapers, beer-cans, chairs and other debris, including an umbrella, were hurled into the ring. The authorities were relieved when the audience settled down to watch Howard save the day with a brilliant boxing display. He beat Jones on points over ten and he readily admits he felt he had a score to settle from their amateur days. "Oh aye. And then we became good pals after that. He died about four years ago. He was a nice fella, Phil." Jones' photograph was included in Howard's living room gallery.

The following month Howard stopped cagey Italian Sergio Milan in six at Aberdare. When Milan stepped through the ropes he looked by far the older man, his balding hair adding years to his appearance. Howard chuckled, "He wasn't that old but he was baldy on top, which made him look older." Howard's next two fights were against hard case Belgian champion Jean Renard the next month. He won the first by stoppage in the last minute and it was rated the fight of the night. He won the second on points. "It was such a good fight the first time that they wanted it again."

Although he was now starting to travel further afield, up until this point most of Howard's fights had been in Wales. "I liked fighting in Wales. All my pals could come and see me then." His last fight of 1960 was a November points win over Nigerian Roy Jacobs at the Market Hall, Carmarthen. Jacobs put up such a fabulous fight that referee Billy Jones made a point of congratulating him after delivering the verdict to Howard.

Howard's first fight of 1961 was a hard one, in January, against British Empire champion Floyd Robertson of Ghana. Robertson was the stronger of the two and nearly upset the apple cart in the final seconds of the fight. Howard managed to stay on his feet and his hand was raised at the end.

On the 2nd May 1961, 11 days after Howard's 22nd birthday, he had his most important fight to date. He challenged Londoner Terry Spinks for his British featherweight title. Howard had been in 24 fights in just over two years. Along the way he had captured the hearts of boxing fans all over the country. "I was like a gypsy. I wasn't working so I wanted the money didn't I? There was no work around here. It's picking up a bit now but I don't think it's all that clever." The big fight took place at Wembley. Olympic gold medalist Spinks was the most popular of British champions. The public was smitten with his baby face and cockney personality. Howard, on the other hand, was the darling of Wales, proud and brave. This oncoming battle was eagerly awaited by millions. Promoter Harry Levene cleverly capitalised on the fact that both fighters had won gold medals and billed the fight as the 'Battle of the Golden Boys.' He even had golden hand bills printed. Howard had one of these framed in pride of place in his living room.

Howard ripped the title away from Terry Spinks that night. The Londoner was fast handed but Howard left him standing at the first bell. Eddie Thomas had told his boy to hold back, anxious to see what Spinks had up his sleeve. But by the end of the sixth Spinks had become desperate, forcing the fight and slugging away, fighting to save his reputation. Howard seemed only to happy to oblige him, riding the waves of aggression the way dolphins do when they swim before the QE2. Howard turned to Eddie at the end of the sixth and asked, "Can I let go now." Eddie replied, "Don't bother. Spinks is gone." It was only Spinks' sheer courage that kept him on his feet. By the ninth round he had taken a nasty beating, and yet he came back to show exactly what he was made of, making it his best round of the fight. But the writing was on the wall in mile high letters for the brave little cockney. The tenth round was to be his last. Howard caught him with six straight lefts to the face with no retaliation. Terry returned to his corner at the bell and said, "I've had enough." Referee Ike Powell stopped the fight. At the time of the stoppage, Howard was unmarked and he was the new British featherweight champion. "Winning the British title was marvellous. Because the British title then was the British title. Today nobody seems bothered. But in those days it was a big deal to be British champion." It was certainly a big deal for the hundreds of delirious Welshmen who tried to clamber into the ring to get close to their hero. Howard chuckled fondly at the memory, "You could tell them but they wouldn't listen!"

Looking back at this fantastic night of 40 years ago, I asked Howard if he ever had any doubts about going in with Spinks. He shook his head, "Nup." I asked if he ever had any doubts about going in with anybody. "Nup." But when Howard remembered the brutal events in the ring that night a sad look clouded his eyes. The fighter's wisdom, the painful knowledge that so often somebody has to suffer so dearly in order for someone else to win.

The new British featherweight champion returned to his home town and a royal reception. He was driven through the town in an open-topped car with a police escort. When he arrived at the Town Hall the Mayor, Alderman C E Webb, an ex-miner and a big boxing fan, was waiting to greet him. Also waiting were his two sons, Roy and Wayne, each wearing a tiny pair of red boxing gloves. "When I come through the town there was thousands there, thousands! And I didn't think there would be anyone there like." Howard became the first Welshman to become British featherweight champion for 46 years, since Llew Edwards beat Owen Moran in May 1915.

After the Spinks fight, Howard took a well earned rest and spent some time with his pregnant wife. But before his twin daughters were born he squeezed in a points win over Ghanaian Ayree Jackson. "That was a terrible fight. I had never seen anybody fighting like him. He just crawled all over you. He was the worst I've ever seen. I told Eddie, 'It won't be a good fight. This fella's on top of you all the time.' You couldn't hit him man, he just kept crawling all over you and he would take anything you give him."

Eleven days later Howard fought his first American, big hitting Gene Fossmire at Cardiff. Howard was cut quite badly in the sixth but he came back to win on points and bashed up the American into the bargain. "I didn't used to cut badly, just little nicks you know. Some people used to have big cuts but I just used to get little nicks." Two weeks after the Fossmire fight, Howard's twin daughters Fay and Benita were born. Fay was named after Jack Solomons' wife. "He was alright Jack was. I had more to do with him than Harry Levene. Jack was a showman really. He was a nice fella. When Eddie was going up to see him in his office, I'd always go up." Howard's last fight of 1961 was a points win against unbeaten Ollie Maki at Nottingham. The year was topped when the Boxing Writers' Club voted Howard 'Best Young Boxer of the Year.'

He began 1962 in fine style by getting up from the canvas in the sixth to beat Brazilian champion Oripes Dos Santos on points at the Royal Albert Hall. Then, in April, came his first defence of his British title. His opponent was Irish-born Derry Treanor of Glasgow and they fought at Wembley. Treanor became a naturalised British citizen so that he could box for the British title. "He came flying out of his corner at the start of every round but he didn't come out for the 15th. And he was a hard man, him."

A month later Howard defended his title against Harry Carroll of Cardiff. The Maindy Stadium was packed with 10,000 supporters. Carroll's courage was never in question but his manager, Benny Jacob decided enough was enough and pulled him out at the end of the sixth. Howard was now the proud owner of one Lonsdale belt, and he was still only 23.

Three more fights came in the next six weeks. First, on the 2nd August, he beat Ghanaian Dennis Adjei on points at the Sophia Gardens, Cardiff. Seventeen days later he beat George Bowes of Heseldon on points over ten at Newtown. Two weeks after that he stopped brave 19-year-old cockney Billy 'Kid' Davies at Wembley Pool in the seventh.

After 34 fights and 34 wins Howard experienced the bitter taste of defeat for the first time in his professional career on the 5th November 1962. In the other corner was 25-year-old American Leroy Jeffery. It was bonfire night and there were fireworks in the Leeds ring that night. Jeffery, an exceptional amateur, had won many of his professional fights by stoppage. In the second round he put Howard down but referee Jack Lord allowed it to go on and Jeffery went for it hell for leather, desperate to return home with Howard's scalp on his belt. Howard, blood flowing from a cut on his right cheek bone, walked into another of Jeffery's bombs and he went down again in his own corner. Eddie Thomas was frantically screaming, "Stay down" but Howard was too proud for that. As soon as he was on his feet, Jeffery pounced and Jack Lord decided enough was enough and stopped the fight. Howard sat in his dressing room afterwards, a dejected figure. "Oh, it was terrible. The loser's dressing room is a lonely place. These days, when they ask me about that fight I tell them that I forgot to duck!" Leroy Jeffery was beaten three weeks later by Billy Calvert and I am not sure he boxed again.

Howard did not allow himself to dwell in the land of loss for too long. A month later he was back in against Freddie Dobson of Manchester. If the hostile crowd at Manchester's Free Trade Hall had any effect on Howard he did not show it. Referee Jim Mahoney had to step in and rescue the home boy in the third round. Dobson's face was a mess and he was helpless. Seventeen days later Howard stopped American Teddy Rand in three at the National Sporting Club.

He began 1963 with a January match against Scotsman Johnny Morrissey. The fight took place at Kelvin Hall, Glasgow and the audience got behind their man. Morrissey was very brave, he got up from the floor three times before referee Wally Thom stopped the fight in round 11. "The Glaswegian crowd were very hostile and loud but it didn't worry me because I went up there on my own about two months before to see the fella I was going to fight. I saw the reaction of the crowd. So it didn't worry me going up there. Thomas said to me, 'Look at this crowd!' I said, 'It doesn't worry me man, I saw them a couple of months ago.' I knew what I was walking in to."

Howard and Eddie decided it was time to go for the European title. Three continental fighters paved the way, the last would be for the title. First was former European champion Gracieux Lamperti of France. This one took place in Cardiff in April 1963. Lamperti was past his best and Howard won every round before referee Joe Morgan stepped in halfway through the eighth. A couple of weeks later came Juan Cardenas of Barcelona. He was a tough guy who had won his last 12. Howard fought him in London and won every round.

Then finally, in July 1963, Howard got his chance for the European title against champion Italian Alberto Serti. Promoter Jack Solomons managed to get this one in

Cardiff. Howard stopped Serti in the 14th round. Despite the handsome Italian's courage and determination, referee Georges Gondre could have stopped it as early as the ninth because Serti was being knocked all around the ring. "He could have stopped it earlier, yes." Howard Winstone was now European champion. Ten thousand supporters got to their feet and filled the open air stadium with their sweet Welsh singing and applause. Millions of tears of joy were shed that summer night in Cardiff.

Howard's story cannot be complete without the re-emergence of Mr 'Cowboy' himself, Billy Calvert. Having beaten Leroy Jeffery, Howard's only conqueror, Calvert was entitled to the first crack at Howard's European crown. So on the 20th August 1963, Billy stepped through the ropes to face Howard for the third and final time. As always, these two great fighters brought the house down. Howard the boxer against Calvert more the fighter. And Billy can always rest assured that he was the first man to take Howard Winstone the full 15 rounds. And there were times when Howard looked really worried in there. Howard's only comment on that point was, "Well, he was short see." Billy told me, "I fought him for his European and British titles. It went the distance again, 15 rounds. It were another close one. See Howard was a boxer and I was a boxer-fighter really. He had got the reach and the height so I had to get in, you know. And I waited for Howard to lead and then I went and did what I had to do."

A month later Howard was back in action against Miguel Kimbo. This was a non-title ten rounder which Howard won on points at Corwen. Money was coming into the Winstone family regularly now, but Howard was always aware of the need to secure his family's future. On the 9th December, he rounded off the year with a defence of his British and European titles against John O'Brien from Glasgow. This one was at the National Sporting Club in London. "He was a hard man, again." That night, Howard outboxed the Scotsman from the first bell to the last. He also won his second Lonsdale belt outright.

In January 1964 Howard travelled to London to fight powerful American Don Johnson, rated fourth in the world. Johnson looked the far bigger man and all the press reports suggest that Howard outboxed him all the way. However, the American was the aggressor and perhaps this is why referee Jack Hart raised Johnson's hand at the end. Hart's decision was so questionable that he was brought before the British Boxing Board of Control to explain himself. "If you get beat, you get beat. But not like that. When they raised his hand I thought, 'What's happening by here?' But I never felt like packing it in. I just felt like fighting him again."

Two months later Howard fought Rafiu King, from Nigeria, at Wembley. King predicted he would knock Howard out in the fourth. "He put me down with a left hook in the second round. He could punch, him." King waded in after the eight count and was warned by referee Harry Gibbs for hitting low. Howard put his boxing skills in action and won the decision over ten rounds.

In May 1964 Harry Levene matched Howard with Italian champion Lino Mastellaro for his next European title defence. The fight took place at Wembley. Howard stumbled on his way up the steps to the ring but did not put a foot wrong afterwards. He was on great form that night and he stopped Mastellaro halfway through the eighth round. After referee Bernard Mascot jumped in to rescue Mastellaro, the Italian, whose eye was badly swollen, was taken to hospital where it was discovered he had two broken ribs. Howard quietly acknowledged that enough was enough and again, that look of sadness passed through his eyes. Six weeks later, Howard stopped Phil Lundgren of Bermondsey in seven at the National Sporting Club, London. "He was always well dressed. He still is today."

Now the time had come for Howard and Eddie to set their sights on the world featherweight title. Meanwhile, across the Atlantic, world featherweight champion, Sugar Ramos was losing his title to a 21-year-old Mexican southpaw named Vincente Samuel Saldivar Garcia. Vincente Saldivar, one of nine children, was brought up poor and hungry. Like many of his peers he turned to boxing at a young age. In 1959 he won the national Golden Gloves title and the Mexican Federal District championship. From there he went to the Rome Olympics but his mind was distracted by the death of a close friend and he did not get past his first bout. He returned to Mexico and after a lot of soul searching he decided to turn professional and become world champion. Just over four years later he achieved his dream. It was Vincente Saldivar that Howard would now have to face to take the world title.

But there were other fish to fry before facing Saldivar. Next on the hook, in September 1964, was Jose Bisbal. Howard travelled to Manchester to out-point him in ten. Next came world rated Baby Luis of Cuba who had floored Saldivar twice the previous year. Saldivar went on to stop the Cuban in the eighth. Howard went the ten round distance with Luis and won it well. Afterwards Angelo Dundee, who was in Louis' corner declared, "Winstone is the most brilliant boxer I have seen in my lifetime." Thirteen days later Howard beat Algerian champion Boualem Belouard over ten rounds at the Nottingham Ice Rink. After the fight Belouard raised Howard's hand in tribute.

In January 1965 Howard went to Rome to defend his European title against Frenchman Yves Desmarets. This was the first time that Howard had boxed outside Britain and from the crowd's point of view it was truly a baptism of fire. A big crowd of Howard's supporters went along to cheer on their champion but the majority of the crowd were behind Desmarets. Howard won it well on points over 15. Every picture tells a story and afterwards Desmarets' face was a mess whereas Howard looked untouched. The crowd were so much for Desmarets that when referee Nello Martinelli announced the decision there was quite a long pause before a mixture of various types of fruit were thrown into the ring. In *Boxing News,* Ron Olver made the interesting observation that the referee's hesitation in announcing the decision gave the crowd time to gather their missiles 'So that bombing could commence on schedule.' As Howard remembered the crowd reaction he told me, "Fifteen thousand of them! In Rome, to watch a Welshman fight a Frenchman! Can you imagine if I had been fighting an Italian?"

Two months later Howard settled the score with Don Johnson, winning a rematch on points over ten rounds in Carmarthen. Next on his hit list was Mexican Lalo Guerrero.

Howard out boxed Guerrero in June 1965 and referee Harry Gibbs stopped it at the end of the fifth. They said Guerrero's style was similar to Saldivar's. "By then it was all about fighting Saldivar. Harry Levene and Mickey Duff were trying hard to put the fight together. They wanted it in London."

On the 22nd June 1965 Howard stepped in with tough Cuban Jose Legra. Legra was highly rated and this was meant to be a warm-up for Saldivar. The fight took place at the Winter Gardens in Blackpool. One of Howard's sparring partners for this one was Colin Lake. As is often the case in boxing, communication was poor. Subsequently, 'Lakey' turned up at his hotel a week early. When Eddie and Howard arrived at the hotel, they were greeted with a grin. "Hi. You'll never guess what I've gone and done. I've turned up a week early haven't I?" Eddie was not amused, "I know that, I've just seen the bloody bill!" Howard is very fond of Lakey. "Aye, he's a good boy, Colin." He shouted out to Bronwen in the kitchen, "Bronwen! She knows Lakey." Bronwen came into the living room with a smile, "We call him the tipster!"

Howard's fight with Legra was a hard one. The Cuban also had his sights set on fighting Saldivar for the world title. The action was fast and furious for the full ten round distance. Howard won but Legra made him work for it. "I wasn't supposed to fight Jose Legra. I'd just boxed somewhere and Eddie used to say 'have a few weeks off and have a couple of glasses of beer.' I didn't realise it at the time but I was putting the weight on. I think I might have had water trouble then because I used to put the weight on quick. Then Eddie sent my mate to see me to tell me not to drink no more. He said I was fighting next Friday. I asked who I was fighting. My mate said, 'Thomas reckons nobody of note.' I said, 'Well who is he?' He said, 'Oh, some Spanish kid. Some kid called Jose Legra.' And funnily enough, that weekend *Boxing News* had done a big article about Legra. Jose Legra had won 50 odd fights on the trot! Eddie said, 'Aye, but who's he fought? He haven't fought nobody.' And I'll tell you now, I wasn't fit for it. I beat him, but I wasn't fit for it. It wasn't a hard, hard fight. He was fast and clever and all the nonsense. He cut my eyelid in the second round but I beat him anyway. If I had had time to train properly I think I would have beat him easier."

And so, finally, the scene was set for Howard's first fight with Vincente Saldivar, and the whole world was taking notice. The Mexican had a fearsome reputation. They said he never stopped. They said he was as dangerous in the 15 as he was in the first. Howard refused to be bothered by all the talk, "Oh I felt great. I felt great for all of my fights." Although Saldivar was two inches shorter than Howard, he seemed to have it all in the right places. His record was almost perfect at the time, 26 fights and 25 wins. The loss was to Baby Luis on disqualification, which he later avenged. Saldivar came over to London and set up training camp in the Boxing Board of Control gym at Chalk Farm, North London. He looked great in training and was an expert at cutting down the ring. The bookies went to work and Terry Downes made Saldivar the slight favourite. I asked Howard if this got his goat. "No, not really. Do you ever see Terry around in London? I liked him. You can't tell with Downsey what he's going to say. Crazy! And he's flashy isn't he?"

On the 7th September 1965 Howard Winstone and Vincente Saldivar had their first battle at London's Earls Court Arena. And what a battle it was. Out of the audience of 18,000, 12,000 were Welsh. It was a good clean fight and referee Bill Williams had an easy job, his most energetic moment coming when he had to get between the boxers at the end of the 12th round because the noise of the crowd drowned out the bell. In the 13th, Howard went out and stood toe to toe with the Mexican and almost stopped him in his tracks. But, true to form, in the 14th Saldivar came out as fresh as a daisy. He caught Howard with a massive punch right under the heart. Howard would not, and did not go down. The last round took place before a massive backdrop of noise from the Welsh supporters who stamped their feet and roared as their man made a real fight of it. The crowd sang as they awaited the decision and then referee Bill Williams raised Saldivar's hand. After the fight Howard said, "I have no complaints about the decision. He was the toughest man I ever met. I found his southpaw stance awkward to get to grips with and I never really got into my stride." Saldivar said, "Winstone gave me a terrific fight and the crowd was the most sporting I have ever come across." The following day Howard returned to Merthyr and received a glorious welcome.

A month later he was back in the gym looking for another fight. After a wait of three months he got his wish, against Midlands Area champion Brian Cartwright of Birmingham at the Cafe Royal, London. The referee for this one was again Bill Williams and he stopped the fight in the ninth to save Cartwright.

1966 arrived and in March Howard defended his European crown against Andrea Silanos. Again Howard travelled to his opponent's back yard. The fight took place in the Terdi Theatre in Sassari, Sardinia, and Silanos was the local hero with 27 wins out of 28 fights. "He was a tough fight. He won the earlier rounds and he cut me in the sixth with his head." Instead of going on the back foot, Howard came back with all guns blazing. He proceeded to bash up Andrea badly and as the Sardinian got up from the floor in the 14th it was a testimony to his courage that he came back out for the final round. "I floored him again then and the referee stopped the fight in the last minute. After fighting him, I broke a bone in my foot in training and I had to take six months out."

As soon as he was fit, Howard defended his European title against Jean de Keers of Belgium on the 6th September 1966. "That one came at very short notice. And for the first time I can remember I had problems making the weight. I had to skip it off and get in the sauna." The fight began with de Keers on the attack and by the end of the first Howard was bleeding. He was convinced de Keers had butted him and in reply he gave the Belgian such a savage beating that referee Domenico Carapellese had to drag Howard off in the third.

In October 1967 Don Johnson came back for a third fight and score settler. They fought in Manchester at the Free Trade Hall. Referee Jack Lord disappointed just about everybody in the place by disqualifying Johnson in the fourth for low blows. Next up was Welsh champion Lennie 'The Lion' Williams of Tonyrefail. Both boxers had massive followings. Local interest brimmed over and naturally the fight was staged locally, in the newly opened Afan Lido in Port Talbot. The date was 7th December 1966. Howard's British and European featherweight titles were at stake. Although Lennie had courage befitting his nickname, he had insufficient skill to cope with Howard Winstone on his most brilliant form. Referee Bill Williams cried, "Enough!" and stopped it in the eighth. As Williams led Lennie back to his corner he whispered into his ear, "A good try lad." Both Lennie and his manager Benny Jacobs protested. Lennie was in tears. In January 1967 Howard fought handsome Chinese-American Richie Sue at the Albert Hall. Richie managed to pull a few tricks out of the bag and at times, he proved to be a handful but Howard won it overwhelmingly on points over ten.

It was on the 15th June 1967 that Howard had battle number two with Vincente Saldivar. Before the fight Howard received a telegram from Jimmy Wilde – 'The ghost with a hammer in his hand' – to wish him good luck. "Yeah, I didn't know him well but I'd met him a few times." The venue this time was Ninian Park, Cardiff. Howard entered the ring with a new,cropped hair style. He seemed to radiate sheer determination, an image he sustained throughout the fight. This fight was even better than the first. But Howard took a bad beating in the 14th when he was trapped in a neutral corner. He went down but managed to pull himself back up to survive the round. Howard kept on the move in the 15th and by and large everybody felt he had done enough to win, more than enough. The crowd were singing at their heartiest, hugging each other, crying tears of pride, convinced that they were about to see their hero crowned world champion. And then referee Wally Thom shocked the audience and the fighters alike by raising Saldivar's hand, scoring it to the Mexican by half a point. There is a famous photograph of Saldivar raising Howard's hand after the fight. If you cover the faces and look at the eyes, Saldivar looks sad. The Mexican knew how fortunate he had been to keep his title that night. Howard's eyes were simply a picture of resignation. As if to prove this point, Saldivar said, "There should be two world champions, me and Winstone... What a left hand, you don't see it until it hits you and it hit me a hundred times tonight." Snowy Buckingham, Saldivar's assistant trainer, declared, "When Vincente failed to stop Winstone in the 14th, we thought we had lost the fight." Howard went home to Merthyr and was greeted with a hero's welcome.

Then his life began to fall apart at the seams. He began to suffer regularly from weight problems. He was getting older and this happens – I can certainly testify to that! Meanwhile, rumours were rife that his wife was having an affair. Howard could not have picked a worse time or place to face Vincente Saldivar for a third and final time. "We boxed in Mexico. I liked the Mexicans. They were nice people." Three weeks before the fight, Howard travelled to Mexico with Eddie Thomas and sparring partner, Billy Thomas. When they arrived they were sent 80 miles up into the mountains to a training camp where conditions were diabolical and the weather was worse. After wasting the first week, they returned to Mexico City where Benita and Howard's mum arrived. The first thing Howard and Benita did was have a huge row in their hotel room.

On the 14th October 1967 50,000 fans clambered into the Aztec Stadium which had been built for the Olympics to be held the following year. Howard boxed well for the first four rounds but in the fifth Saldivar came into his own, catching Howard on the ropes and banging away. After that things started to even up. Saldivar tried his best to finish it in the tenth and Howard cut him under his left eye for his trouble. In the 11th it was mainly Howard. Then in the 12th, Howard got caught with a massive right hook in the face. Saldivar followed up on this success like a man possessed and Howard sank to the canvas. He got up and tried to carry on but Eddie Thomas had seen enough and threw in the towel. "I went mad with Eddie when he stopped it but I calmed down after." Seconds after the fight was stopped, Saldivar grabbed hold of the ring microphone and announced his retirement, declaring that he could not fight this Welshman again. For the record, Saldivar did return to the ring. He went on to beat Jose Legra in a WBC title eliminator and in May 1970 he took the world featherweight crown from Johnny Famechon. He lost his title seven months later to Kuniaka Shibata of Japan in the 11th round. In 1973 he attempted one last comeback and was knocked out in four rounds in a world featherweight challenge against Eder Jofre of Brazil.

Howard genuinely liked Saldivar. He even had his own way of understanding his arch rival. "The others couldn't understand him, but I could. Don't ask me why but I could. He could tell me what he was saying. We was in a do somewhere, I can't remember where, and they was asking Saldivar some questions and one of the boys in the crowd said, 'I'll tell you who will understand what he is saying. Winstone.' So they asked me if I could interpret him and I told them everything he was saying. I couldn't really understand him but he made me understand. Do you know what I mean? Saldivar was a nice fella."

Howard returned to Merthyr and Benita moved to Paddington, leaving Howard with their four young children. Fortunately, Howard's mother was on hand to take care of the young ones. Howard had been forced to forfeit his European title to take the Saldivar fight. Christmas was on the doorstep and he knew that he must start again. These were bad times but there was light at the end of the tunnel. With Saldivar's retirement, Howard was now number one in line to fight for the vacant world title, or at least a version of it. With Saldivar out of the picture, the Californian Commission recognised Raul Rojas as the new champion and the WBA followed suit three months later. The WBC, however, eventually bowed to Britain and the European Boxing Union and nominated Howard to fight Mitsunori Seki of Japan, their other number one contender. Seki had lost two to Saldivar and one to Sugar Ramos so with three world title challenges each, he and Howard were all set to get it on. Howard entered into training for the fight amid clamouring media trying to get an angle on his domestic troubles. Eddie Thomas moved him from the Afan Lido to the less public Carmarthen Rugby Club gym where he could train in peace.

The fight was scheduled for 23rd January 1968. The Albert Hall was completely sold out and many of the crowd were Welsh. "Seki was a good fighter. He was another bloody southpaw, just like Saldivar! He caught me in the first. I came back in the second and a couple of rounds later he marked me up, over the eye. I cut him in the fifth." By the end of the seventh round both boxers were battered and bruised. The action in the eighth was ferocious and referee Roland Dakin stepped in in the ninth, to examine Seki's damaged eye. The cut was in an awful place, between the eye socket and eyebrow. Dakin called the fight off and the crowd were elated. Howard Winstone was finally world featherweight champion and he jumped into the air in celebration. It took ten minutes to clear the ring of Howard's amorous supporters. To make things perfect, Saldivar had travelled to London especially to present Howard with the world title globe. Mitsunori Seki remains involved in boxing to this day. He is the manager and promoter of the Yokohama Hikari Boxing Club and has produced two world champions, Takanori Hatakeyama and Yutaka Niida. He also works hard cultivating youngsters in his gym in Yokohama.

That night the Welsh fans invaded the West End to celebrate in fine style but after a short party Howard jumped on the train home. At nine o'clock the next morning he was in the Cardiff divorce court. After granting Howard his decree nisi on grounds of adultery, the judge, Sir Owen Temple Morris QC, called him to the bench to shake his hand and congratulate him on winning the world title.

Meanwhile, 20 miles away up in the valley, a celebration was brewing like no other. Merthyr Town Hall was under siege as a crowd of more than 6,000 packed into and around the square. They were up lamposts and hanging from windows. They were everywhere. When the champion arrived at the Town Hall, he had to go in the back way and when he came out onto the balcony with Fay and Benita in his arms the police had to hold the ecstatic crowd back.

Now that he was world champion, Howard was in much demand. He was invited to dinners, charity functions, and awards and accolades were heaped upon him. British Boxer of the Year, *Boxing News* Fighter of the Year, Welsh Sports Personality of the Year. But there was not a lot of money coming in and Howard had four children to take care of. So, mainly for financial reasons, he took a fight against British junior lightweight champion Jimmy Anderson on the 9th April 1968. This was a catchweight contest and many wondered at Howard's wisdom for taking it. "He decked me in the first round with a massive right hand on the jaw." The crowd were almost as stunned as Howard but he got up and survived the round. He went on to take the rest of the fight winning it on points by a mile. Shortly after this fight Howard received the MBE in the Queen's Birthday Honours List.

Howard had his final fight on the 24th July 1968. It was at Coney Beach Arena in Porthcawl and his world title was on the line. It was during the annual miners two week holiday so there were thousands of pitmen there. The fight was against previous victim but now European champion Jose Legra. Howard entered the ring to the singing and applause of his fans but storm clouds were looming on the horizon. He was floored twice in the first round. Referee Harry Gibbs looked closely at his damaged left eye at the end of the round but let the fight continue. Howard managed to hold Legra off for a few more rounds but in the fifth Gibbs took another good look. "The eye was closed so tightly. Eddie couldn't do anything with it. He couldn't cut it because it was swollen from the top down. I couldn't see out of it and Legra was catching me." Howard pleaded with the referee not to stop the fight and Gibbs let it go for two more minutes. The crowd were now so subdued that the boxers' boots could be heard quite clearly squeaking on the canvas. Then Gibbs did the right thing and stopped it. So Howard's only defence of his world title ended in defeat. Afterwards Eddie Thomas made his charge sing all the way home in the car to stop him dwelling on his loss.

Eddie knew that Howard's best fighting years were well behind him and strongly advised his man to retire. So with a professional record of 67 fights and 61 wins, Howard retired with dignity and all his faculties. In April 1969 Howard was made a Freeman of Merthyr.

But now what? He had no business, no trade, nothing to fall back on. What would he do next? First he and brother, Glyn opened up a kiosk cafe in Merthyr. Then he went into the pub game and the hangers on played their part in Howard's change of lifestyle. He discovered alcohol and parties. After his spartan years in the ring, if was like stepping out of one world and into another completely different one. And after a few drinks there were always those fools who wanted to challenge him to a fight.

During his career Howard's fans were so loyal to him, they followed him everywhere. "Oh, it was marvellous. And even today, I still talk to a lot of people. When I'm walking through the town with my son, he says, 'Oh, it's talk to Howard day today.' It's great. They was marvellous days." A year after his retirement Howard met Bronwen Williams. A year after that they were married, on the 23rd January 1971. Bronwen told me, "Howard had four children by his first marriage, I reared them. I had one boy, and then we had one between us. That's Howard junior." Howard remained involved with boxing, and in 1996 he became President of the Welsh Ex-Boxers Association.

Eddie Thomas continued to keep boxing alive in Wales, often putting his money where his mouth was when other promoters refused to take the risk. Among his success stories were Ken Buchanan and Colin Jones. He became an independent councillor and in 1994 Mayor of Merthyr. He died at the age of 71 in June 1997 after an eight year battle with cancer. He always remained adamant that Howard Winstone was the greatest boxer Wales ever produced.

Vincente Saldivar invited Howard to Mexico as his guest for the 1968 Olympics and during his visit Vincente admitted that he knew that Howard won their second fight, even though he was not given the decision. "I stayed with him for three weeks. It was marvellous. I had a great time." Saldivar died from a heart attack at the age of 42 in July 1985 . When the Mexican was inaugurated postumously into the Boxing Hall of Fame, Canastota, in 1999, Howard made sure he was there to witness the induction of an old rival who became his friend.

Last words from Billy Calvert. "I had a lot of respect for Howard. He was a great lad. He was a beautiful man. I wish I could have disliked him, and then I might of licked him! [raucous laughter] But seriously, he respected me a lot and I did with him. And it's nice that."

Among Howard's closest friends was prominent sports journalist John Lloyd who told me, "As far as the people of Merthyr are concerned MBE stands for Merthyr's Best Export. But to me, the 'M' stands for Modesty more than anything."

And so my meeting with 'Merthyr's Best Export' drew to a close. Two hours came and went like a slip on a banana skin and when the time came for me to leave, I hugged him and kissed him goodbye and thanked him, "It has been an honour to meet you." Mr Modesty himself, he simply replied, "Thank you." He came out onto the doorstep to watch me walk to my car with the warning in his voice but a twinkle in his eye, "Be careful of these roads now. We're fast up here in Merthyr, not like you lot in London!" I came away from the Welsh Wizard with a big smile on my face and a certain feeling that I had been touched by some of his magic.

Three weeks later, on Saturday morning 30th September 2000, I received a phone call from John Lloyd. John's voice was choked with emotion as he told me the news. Howard Winstone had died in his sleep earlier that day. He had been suffering for years from water retention problems and now his final battle was lost at Merthyr's Prince Charles Hospital, a stone's throw from the old Penydarren Gym where he had trained as a boy. His devoted wife Bronwen and all their children were at Howard's bedside when the moment came.

Howard's funeral was held at St Tydfil's Parish Church, Merthyr, on Saturday, 7th October at 11am. Several of my London friends headed to Wales to attend and I would have liked to have gone with them. However, we at the Foley ABC had two boys on at Broadstairs and I knew that Howard would have preferred me to be with them, where I could do some good and where I was needed. Many people from the boxing world turned up to pay their respects including Steve Robinson, Robbie Regan, Alan Minter and Terry Downes. The church was so packed that Terry was forced to stand outside in the rain with his stick. Ken Buchanan travelled down from Scotland, his first visit to Merthyr for 31 years, to the place where he and Howard trained together under Eddie Thomas' watchful eye. Ken's tartan scarf was draped among the white lilies on Howard's coffin as it was carried into the church. As Lord Jack Brooks of Tremorfa spoke movingly of his old friend, his voice was relayed by speakers to the hundreds of people who had lined the streets. His words fell upon the respectfully hushed crowds. Afterwards, Lord Brooks told *Wales Today,* "If he's looking down now, and I'm sure he will be, he'll look at the crowd and he'll say to himself, 'That's the best crowd we've had since my last fight.'"

Rest in peace champ. Howard Winstone MBE.

ACKNOWLEDGMENTS

I would like to thank, in order of appearance: Reg Gutteridge OBE, Jimmy Tibbs, Steve Robinson, Dai Gardiner, Mickey and Tracey Cantwell, James Cook, Colin Dunne, Colin Lake, Billy Walker, Spencer Oliver, John Oliver, Jim Oliver, Jack Lee, Jess Harding, Crawford Ashley, Bob Paget, Peter Buckley, Nobby Nobbs, Alan Minter, Johnny and Dorothy McManus, Howard Winstone MBE and Billy Calvert.

I want to pay my deepest respects to the memories of Bradley Stone, Dudley McKenzie, James J. Braddock, George Francis, Jimmy Dunne, Joe Erskine, Sonny Liston, Harry Levene, Tony Silkstone, James Murray, Doug Bidwell, Angelo Jacopucci, Joe Louis, Harry Mullan, Benny Lynch, Eddie Thomas, Phil Jones, Jack Solomons, Vincente Saldivar and Howard Winstone MBE.

I would also like to thank, in no particular order: Max Schmeling, Jim and Val Dawson, Harold Alderman, Ralph Oates, Gene and Tony White, Chris Amos, Golly, Jan and Freddie Mack, Rosemary Ellmore, Bob Lonkhurst, Barry Hugman, Ron Olver, Bronwen Winstone, John Lloyd, Steve Holdsworth, George Zeleny, Mickey Duff, Jack Fox, Nigel James, Tommy Mulholland, John Davidson, Michael Ayers, Audrey Howard, Carmen, Hayley Wilkinson, Tony Breen, Sammy McCarthy, Matt Brown, Frank Bruno, Jimmy Flint, Mark Kaylor, Ron Peck, Jimmy Anderson, Don Ewing, Patricia Walker, Mandy Byrne, Martin O'Leary, Michael McManus, the British Boxing Board of Control, the National Newspaper Library, Claude Abrams, Daniel Herbert and everyone at the *Boxing News*, photographer Les Clark and my publisher Randall Northam of SportsBooks Limited.